Early Modern Drama and the Eastern European Elsewhere

Representations of Liminal Locality in Shakespeare and his Contemporaries

Monica Matei-Chesnoiu

Madison • Teaneck
Fairleigh Dickinson University Press

Associated University Presses
2010 Eastpark Boulevard
Cranbury, NJ 08512

The paper used in this publication meets the requirements of the American National Standard for Permanence of Paper for Printed Library Materials Z39.48-1984.

Library of Congress Cataloging-in-Publication Data

Matei-Chesnoiu, Monica, 1954–
Early modern drama and the Eastern European elsewhere : representations of liminal locality in Shakespeare and his contemporaries / Monica Matei-Chesnoiu.
p. cm.
Includes bibliographical references and index.
ISBN 978-0-8386-4195-8 (alk. paper)
1. English literature—Early modern, 1500–1700—History and criticism. 2. English drama—Early modern and Elizabethan, 1500–1600—History and criticism. 3. Europe, Eastern—In literature. 4. East Europeans in literature. 5. Other (Philosophy) in literature. 6. Ethnicity in literature. 7. Geography in literature. 8. Space in literature. 9. Liminality in literature. I. Title.
PR428.E88M37 2009
820.9′35847—dc22 2008034365

PRINTED IN THE UNITED STATES OF AMERICA

Contents

Acknowledgments

MY GRATEFUL THANKS ARE DUE TO THE MANY SCHOLARS, PAST AND present, whose published works I have quoted in this study. In addition to works cited, I am indebted to the following Shakespeare scholars: James L. Harner (Samuel Rhea Gammon Professor of Liberal Arts, Editor, *World Shakespeare Bibliography*), Professor Frances Barasch, whom I greatly respect and appreciate, Professor Stanley Wells (*The Shakespeare Centre*), Dr. Susan Brock (Capital Centre, University of Warwick), and Professor Arthur F. Kinney (Director, Renaissance Center, University of Massachusetts). I am greatly indebted to the editors at Fairleigh Dickinson University Press for the care with which they read the manuscript in its various stages and their stylistic suggestions.

I wish to acknowledge the help of librarians, archivists, and other staff of the following institutions: the *Shakespeare Institute Library*, the *Shakespeare Centre Library*, and the *Munich Shakespeare Library* (especially Dr. Ingeborg Boltz). The *Romanian Academy Library* has granted me the permission to reproduce copyright material.

Above all, I must thank those who have given me generous expert advice: Harry Keyishian (Fairleigh Dickinson University), Ton Hoenselaars (Utrecht University), and Balz Engler (Basel University). For particular interest-sharing and friendly support I am grateful to Werner Brönnimann (Basel University), Douglas A. Brooks (Texas A&M University), John and Ellen Mahon (Iona College), Mariangela Tempera (University of Ferrara), Andreas Höfele (University of Munich), Krystyna Kujawinska (University of Lodz), and Angel Luis Pujante (University of Murcia). I thank all the Shakespeare colleagues and friends who helped me with this and other projects. My apologies to those I have omitted, and to my Romanian colleagues, whom I consulted for their expertise in Latin, archeology, or ancient texts and history.

I thank my late parents for being at the source of all this, and my daughter, Joanna, for just being there. The remaining mistakes must lie where I did not ask for the further help I needed.

Early Modern Drama and the Eastern European Elsewhere

Introduction: On the Margins of History and Geography

THIS STUDY EXPLORES THE INTERCULTURAL EXCHANGE IN EARLY MODERN Europe and the impact of geography and travel on the framing of a specific British spatial imagination in relation to Eastern Europe. In mapping out a preliminary Shakespearean "geographic imagination," in John Gillies's coinage,[1] it is important to reconsider the configuration of what may be conventionally called Eastern European space as seen in English literary, historical, geographic, and travel accounts of the late sixteenth and early seventeenth centuries. These texts rewrite European traditions about a multifaceted antiquity and a conflicting early modern present, with consequences for developing notions of racial and cultural difference. An understanding of these texts might help clarify the issue of the Eastern European others: Who are they? What do they tell us, either about the Western hermeneutic construction of "Europe," or about their examination of the margins of the Continent, seen as exterior to the civilized center? Are "Western" and "Eastern" Europe part of the same system of geographic and cultural coordinates? Where would the politics of marginalization originate and where does it lead, in the context of early modern discourses of race and foreignness? Is the otherness of Western Europeans' view of the East as "exotic," or "alien," a fact of nature, convention, or conjecture? What do the Eastern European others have in common in point of social and cultural status? What discursive heritage—contemporary or traditional, ethnographic or political—do they share? What, if any, is the connection between the Western imagination about ancient and Renaissance Eastern Europeans, and between the classical exotic narratives and the information stipulated by the new geography?

The informational obscurity of early modern texts about Eastern European or faraway spaces should not be too puzzling, considering that the history of travel, exploration, and discovery is mainly an achievement of men of action and unlearned people—not of scholars. Men of letters thought they could distinguish fact from fantasy but seemed to walk backward to the future, trying to give the airy nothing a local habitation and a name. They favored the constructs of the imagination and graciously combined fact and fiction, without any pretense at total accuracy. Therefore, a distinction should be made between informative and literary accounts of foreign spaces. This kind of imaginative approach, however, when viewed on the tangible setting of the stage, may have been responsible in the end for more satisfactory knowledge than the merely abstract satisfaction of an elusive scientific truth. Whenever the geographical limits of cognition were reached, when the borders of the maps became blurred, there began a specific rhetoric of romance very similar to the imaginative activity. In ancient writers, even the most responsible geographical treatises seem to shift to the vague articulation of romance as limits of knowledge are reached. Wherever located, the relative margin of geographical certainty was a point commonly charged with inexplicable significance and even with precarious hazard. There was the tendency to create an inverted map of an exemplary universe, where the less known territory was generically labeled as "elsewhere," and attributed hazardous connotations. In this particular symbolic design, space becomes discourse and layers of fictionalized assumptions gradually efface real places and people's features.

This study is about a specific cultural mediation of Eastern European geographic space (real, mapped, or imagined): that of early modern texts, in their cartographic, historical, travel narrative, and literary/dramatic constituents. The interdisciplinary methodology, combining history of ideas, literature, and geography, is associated to a comparative approach that brings into focus two areas of cultural consideration, positioned east and west. In the study "Shakespeare's Geography of the World," Krystyna Kujawinska divides the plays into four groups, according to the setting. The last subdivision refers to the plays set in "Shakespeare's Outer World,"[2] a marginal area of Europe in which Kujawinska includes Vienna, her native Poland, and Bohemia. Extending the geographic range to a larger area, the focus of this study is on Shakespeare's and his contemporaries' assimilation of the Eastern European space, particularly in the context of classical and early modern hermeneutics. Three kinds of questions are raised here. First, what are the relationships between early modern accounts and "cartographizations of space,"[3] the literary discourses in relation to them, and the real spaces they describe? Since mapping constituted one of the major cultural achievements of early modern Europe, how did these particular texts relate to the tangible area they describe? Second, how do Elizabethan and Jacobean drama in general and Shakespeare in particular mediate these geographic and ethnographic discourses? Was there an action of intervention, propagation, and transformation of the itemized and standardized icons provided by the age's geographic images at the level of a particular country? If atlases and chorographies were a site for the accumulation of traditional symbols and metaphors, were these particularly relevant for the Western world's appreciation of ethnic, social, and political relations in Eastern Europe at a given time?

In a book first published in 1932 and significantly entitled *The Making of Europe,* Christopher Dawson defines the constituent qualities that made up Europe, while also setting it apart, as viewed from an avowedly Catholic perspective. Dawson challenges the thesis that the Christian religion sapped the Roman Empire of its vigor and highlights the role of monasteries in maintaining classical studies; in general, in this view, the church is a benefit to humanity. A dominant theme is the peculiar mix of elements contributing to what Dawson regards as European civilization and the creative tensions inherent in such interaction. Concerning what the Greeks called "the barbarians," Dawson sought to vindicate this term and defined it as being "by no means the same thing as savagery"; for him it essentially denoted societies resting on the principle of kinship rather than that of citizenship or of the absolute authority of the state."[4] For that reason, when analyzing the metamorphoses that populations formerly under Rome's sway experienced, it is essential to keep this aspect in mind, because it may account for the essential social, political, and ultimately cultural diversity between what we now call Western and Eastern Europe, or, more recently, "Old" and "New" Europe. The geographic area forming my concept of Eastern Europe is much more comprehensive in this acceptance, including territories rather than countries, and states of mind rather than exact national characteristics. This definition of Eastern Europe as a site of cultural exchange, therefore, is almost as loose as attempts to ascribe definite borders to the countries belonging to the Shakespearean imagination. The process of assimilation of the space concept "Eastern Europe" as a land of elsewhere is similar to that involved in attributing Bohemia a seacoast.

Since most early modern writers were preoccupied with problems of perception and belief, it is interesting for a foreign eye, well acquainted with the Renaissance cultural landmarks, to view national spaces and cultural dimensions through a different perspective. Critical and cultural pluralism is the main issue here, and by looking at Shakespeare and his contemporaries describing the general area where we live, it is easier to learn more about what we think others think we are. These readings look outside a narrowly delimited literary canon of texts, to certain areas of geographic and travel writings that may have been ignored. The lenses of the critical telescoping perspectives go backward in time, to the discourses the Renaissance produced for a certain audience, and eastward in space, to the geographic area containing the Carpathians, the Balkans, the farther end of the Danube, and the western coast of the Black Sea. The third exploratory dimension goes downward, to the fluid zones of symbolic reflections, which require a semiotic code. In considering the hermeneutics of some Elizabethan translations of ancient writers, who speak about what they see as remote and curiously mysterious places, we find out that these texts were influential objects of belief for early modern writers. Moreover, in a Renaissance world still reveling in the medieval descriptions of marvels and wonders, almost no one needed a real seven-headed Hydra, only the idea of a world in which such creatures were possible. Thus, the texts of the imagination and the visual and conceptual images about certain realities come together in many literary productions negotiating distant spaces in the early modern period.

Geography was traditionally thought of as the eye of history, and the visual combination of time and space dimensions in Renaissance narratives about the known territories of the less known parts of Eastern Europe generated texts that provided a complex and more accurate perspective on the places under scrutiny. Literature, however, maintained the cognitive ambivalence characteristic of ancient and medieval geographic texts, where wonderful happenings and beings could still walk through real life. Elizabethan drama, particularly the Shakespearean "poetic" geography,[5] was an operative user and generator of national or cultural stereotypes and fictional mystification among the early modern audiences' perceptions of foreign spaces. This study follows the theoretical notions and hypotheses advanced by ancient or early modern geographers, adventurers, or travel writers about Eastern European space. It continues with the visualization of this geographic area produced by cartographers and chorographers and enriched by the Shakespearean allusions. In addition, examples of references to Eastern European locations from the drama produced by Shakespeare's contemporaries show that these preconceptions of marginality and peculiarity appear in many plays by Elizabethan and Jacobean dramatists. Therefore, this monograph is an attempt at understanding the cultural diversity of a particular space, but it is also an endeavor to recuperate what knowledge we may have, or have had, about who we are. Thus, we all think through Shakespeare about those issues that affect us most. This special discernment may derive from the diverse descriptions that other people, in various periods, thought to leave us, but also from how Shakespeare and his contemporaries integrated them in the fabric of their culture.

The initial chapter of this study deals with ancient writers' discussions of the Black Sea area, including Caius Julius Solinus, Pomponius Mela, Plutarch, Pliny, and Herodotus. Their texts in Elizabethan translations discuss space and locality, customs and travel, revealing how the ancients saw these places or only heard about them. The comments on the Shakespearean theatrical interpretation of the classical world suggest that, when it comes to allusions to this Eastern European region, Shakespeare was not different from his contemporaries in assuming attributes of abnormality and barbarity about these places. What he knew from and about the ancients, however, became tangible dramatic performance, and this particularly impersonal mode of address may have certain privileges. By showing his audiences the materiality of certain locations, he might have shattered some of their preconceptions about center and margins through the ambivalence of dramatic presentation. Manipulating allusions to these spaces drawing on the classics, Shakespeare reinforces and subverts his contemporaries' cultural assumptions and expectations. He uses the descriptive dynamic method of ancient narratives, which move from west to east around the Mediterranean basin. In addition, he combines the active theatrical method of comparison (derived from Plutarch) with the technique adopted in the classical narratives of wonder. By involving the audiences in an imaginary journey, he manipulates the order of the play's action to follow the progression of a fictional geographic narrative. Thus, the average London citizen, as well as the more informed cultural aristocracy, would go to the Globe to see how their personal fictions about distant places confronted these dramatic interpretations.

The period this book covers is mainly 1585–1616, but some incursions in earlier or later works are inevitable because of the fluidity of the cultural paradigm. Therefore, chapter 3, "Early Modern Chorographies of Eastern European Regions," is an incursion in geographical and travel narratives on the area of Eastern Europe, but the time frame is somewhat larger, going well into the seventeenth century, when these types of discourse gain in consistency. While the classical *topoi* were located somewhere between geography and fiction when referring to these unexplored areas of Europe, Elizabethan and Jacobean discourses took over these ideas and were governed by the repertoire of the ancient discourse of barbarism, which posits irreducible differences between Western Europeans and others. The next two chapters examine the way in which early modern drama took over these images about Eastern Europe. Since in early modern drama the passage of information is rapid and frequently disruptive, the playwright's goal is to present as much knowledge as possible. With the aim of creating a framework wherein the audience is given a sense of control over experience, early modern writers took over the preconceptions on these alien and savage places generated in other texts, mainly of classical origin, incorporated in the geographical narratives of their contemporaries. The image of incomprehensible and different customs in Eastern European locations came to life on the stage, where it was given a new corporeal dimension.

Elizabethan or Jacobean geographers, translators, philosophers, natural historians, and practical travelers have written about events and places as seen through their filtering glass of knowledge. The chapter entitled "Romances and Theatrical Geography" examines how the atypical configuration of Shakespeare's romances matches partially the contemporary system of geographic signification. The romantic narratives of recovery and loss, which make the plot stuff of the romances, render these plays more adaptable to a specific geographical translation. By borrowing the structural patterns of the ancient wonder narratives, the plots in the tragicomedies incite the audiences' curiosity and invite them to travel to distant lands they have never seen before. Despite the ready availability of extensive information about eastern Mediterranean and Eastern European spaces, the Jacobeans were not aware that their data were most often improper or insufficient. By going to the theater, they believed that, though bound in a nutshell, they could still think themselves kings of infinite space. Through the condensation of geographical space in the romances, and the illusion of a fluid itinerary, Shakespeare manages to suggest a theatrical geography that plays on the common exclusionary presumptions about alien spaces but raises significant issues of cultural integration and tolerance.

Elizabethan and Jacobean drama offered a mirror of the early modern world through its evocation of concrete, physical reality in an immediate presence suggested by the language and the body of the actor. The centrality of the body on stage makes it possible to incorporate any representation of a definite geographical space or period in history into various social, political, and cultural meanings, which signify differently according to the modern directors' intentions and the prerequisites of modern theater. Because of the puzzling ambiguity and materiality of the theatrical discourse, many nations, including the Eastern European countries, have used Shakespeare in the same kaleidoscopic ways as he had used his sources. Shakespeare's English audiences tended to perceive the Eastern European space occupied by Romania and other countries as distant and foreign lands, yielding connotations of liminality and barbarity. Antithetically, Romanian twentieth-century audiences and directors accepted Shakespeare's theatrical canon as the accredited locus of Western European civility, a cultural barometer of a nation's enlightenment. As S. Schoenbaum points out, "Because Shakespeare is, of all, the artist about whom curiosity is most intense, it is not surprising that many in search of revelations would delve into his works and find what is not there."[6] As had their predecessors, Romanian translators, twentieth-century directors, writers, and critics took over abundantly and exploited extensively what the transmitters of traditions and the makers of myth have made of Shakespeare. Thus, the national culture of an Eastern European land, which Shakespeare and his contemporaries rather neglected and disregarded, became one of the European cultures that most enthusiastically adopted and capitalized on the Shakespeare myth.

1

Ancient Fables of Eccentric Lands: Histories and Roman Plays

THE SERPIERI SCHOOL OF INTERTEXTUAL ANALYSIS[1] EXPLORES THE SHAKEspearean operations of making theater from narratives, or history plays and tragedies from chronicles. Serpieri uses intertextuality as a critical instrument to move from telling to showing. As Louise George Clubb points out, "Intertextuality is an interpretive key to any culture, especially one like the Western European tradition."[2] In examining the accumulation of migratory motifs and references to Eastern European lands from the classical texts into the Elizabethan and Jacobean theater culture, the aim of this chapter is to elucidate a process. How did Shakespeare use the classical references and myth related to distant and alien places in the Black Sea area to compare, but mainly to contrast, these territories with his contemporaries' assumptions about them? In addition, it is interesting to look at how Shakespeare made (tragic) drama out of classical historical texts, or from the geographical narratives of wonder abounding in ancient writers when they referred to distant places. Shakespeare used allusions embedded in these Greek and Latin texts, most of which were in English translations, as potent generators of contrasting perspectives, in the process of assimilation and theatrical transformation of the data deriving from classical writers. Shakespeare's geographical and cultural integration of Eastern European spaces as borrowed from the classics in his plays is a digested and atopical product, in the same way as the appropriations of the Shakespearean canon have been for Eastern European countries in later times. Thus, Shakespeare has been used in modern times exactly in the same way as he used his classical sources.

Shakespeare's command of the classics[3] has been for a long time the subject of intense debate. A primary question was whether his connection to classical texts was direct or oblique. Did Shakespeare read the original stories he appropriated, or did he rely mainly on translations? This question is no longer a problem, and current scholarship has answered it cogently.[4] According to Russ McDonald, "Not only was Shakespeare able to read Latin literature in the original, but he also seems to have liked it and to have decided that theater audiences would too."[5] Robert S. Miola examines how Shakespeare transformed his sources and the traditions they embody. In the last chapter of his *Shakespeare's Reading,* entitled "Shakespeare as Reader," Miola proposes several reading/borrowing habits. Among the points that Miola makes are that Shakespeare reads competitively, seeking to outdo his sources; he reads eclectically; and he emphasizes contrast in locality.[6] This practice of shifting locales sets the foreign spaces he alludes to in permanent contrast to his contemporary Elizabethan and Jacobean England. On the other hand, however, Shakespeare's audiences were reputedly varied, so no one is certain what they inferred from the plays they saw, or what they preferred to see. Similarly, no one is sure about the extent to which the theatrical community intersected with the more conventional literary circles in Shakespeare's time. Therefore, information about Shakespeare's access to certain classical texts published in his lifetime is uncertain. However, the plays' text and performance potential pull for different kinds of reaction from the audiences, and most probably secure them.

In the "Dedicatory Epistle" to *A World of Wonders,* a compilation of various ancient texts and of passages from Herodotus, Henry Stephen announces to his readers that they will learn about "the rusticitie of former times, and the fashions of forrain countries."[7] Discussing the virtues and vices of people in ancient times, the author speaks of Poets, who delight in their own fictions, as if they were the truth. Such tales, when reported and augmented by others, became the stock material for more stories, handed down for generations. Stephen complains about the credulity of those who believe these tales, concluding in a skeptical tone that people's credulity is irreversible. He notices "how men in olde time by entertaining of fables, and suffering them to lodge and harbour in their minds, have beene brought to beleeve many fond fooleries, which have been conveyed from hand to hand, and delivered by tradition from father to sonne."[8] Reciting a number of such "poeticall fictions," Stephen argues that historiographers, such as Herodotus, cannot take great liberties with their accounts, so their writings should be more believable. Being purged of strange and foolish assumptions, the texts of the Greek historiographer and geographer are expected to be conforming to the truth. As did many before him, Stephen observes the role of the narrative as a prime mover of fictions about peoples and places. He admits to the importance of recurrent recitals of classical origin in the fashioning of a range of sometimes complementary, sometimes contradictory assumptions about the distant places outside the English shores and about their inhabitants.

In tracing the history of classical ideas in the early modern period, Isabel Rivers writes that the intellectual assumptions, the literary conventions, and the terminology that the Renaissance poets shared with their contemporaries in point of classical and Christian traditions were very eclectic. According to Rivers, these "came not only from first-hand reading of the texts . . . but also from popular handbooks and encyclopedias which digested these traditions for them."[9] An example of such compilation is the 1570 translation of Demosthenes by Thomas Wylson. Although generally sound in scholarship, this translation was never reprinted and is now, as it may have been when it was first published, of interest mainly for Wylson's preliminary discourses, which appear to have been intended to arouse English patriotism against the Spanish threat. In the introductory address to the reader, Wylson deplores the current state of Greece under Ottoman rule, comparing this country's past glory with its present decadence: "The Greecelande esteemeth all other Countries and people as Barbarians, whereas now they themselves are the most barbarous people living. . . . And yet albeit these men did minister examples of understanding and knowledge: the Romaines for all that gave ever more plentiful matter of vertue and good living, as who shoulde saye, the Grecians rather excelled in witte, than in worthinesse, and coulde speake better than they woulde doe, according to that saying: *Athenienses sciunt quod facere debent, sed facere nolunt.* The Athenians knowe what ought to doe, but that they will not doe."[10]

Wylson's critical commentary on the lack of enterprising spirit and practicality on the part of the Athenians, once famous for their intrepidity and wisdom, indicates the purpose of his book. He intends to parallel ancient events with Elizabethan times, so that his contemporaries might draw the right conclusions about the world they lived in. Each reader is invited to "compare the time past with the time present, and even when he heareth Athens, or the Athenians, to remember England and the Englishmen, thet we maye learne by the doings of our elders how we may deale in our owne affayres, and so through wisedome by our neighbours example avoyede all harme that else unawares might happen unto us" (sig. Bjj). Preventing present inconveniences by learning from errors of the past may not have been such an effective form of advancement for all Elizabethans. However, at least this compilation from Demosthenes, as did many others in the early modern period, informed them on the title page that Thracia was the ancient name of a country that, in their time, was called Romania. It is difficult to prove that Wylson's didactic considerations had some effect on Elizabethan readers or on later Shakespearean audiences, yet Wylson's compilation has one point in common with Shakespeare's theater. In using the allusions to distant places to reinforce connotations of marginality and roughness, as his contemporaries would expect, Shakespeare has constantly in mind his contemporary England and his compatriots. However, these expectations are relocated in the dramatic exchange, where nothing is but what is not.

Ancient writers constructed their description of spaces they had not seen according to the classical genre of *periplus,* an elaborate form of writing in which the account can be a visualization of the regions under scrutiny, a graphic and global representation of the world on a small scale. Another method was a composite of ethnography and history, a description of peoples and their history and myths. Claude Nicolet elucidates several facts about the geographical knowledge of the ancient world and considers that each of these two original methods of representing the globe has developed along with the extension of voyages of discovery. Whether they were maritime or exploratory, military or political, such voyages contributed to the construction of "global knowledge,"[11] a form of theoretical inquiry that would later emerge into modern geographical science. As early as the fifth century BC, Herodotus had simply entitled his work "Inquiry," or Ιστορία,[12] and he gave data about the land, the customs, and the region's climate, as they were reported by travelers, merchants, and the inhabitants of the place. The Pythagoreans formulated the hypothesis of a spherical terrestrial globe, by means perhaps more philosophical than empirical. It was not until Plato and Aristotle, however, that this idea of a round globe could take root. The veritable father of ancient scientific geography was Eratosthenes of Cyrene, the fourth director of the Library of Alexandria, a third-century BC mathematician, philosopher, astronomer, and grammarian. He was perhaps the first to entitle one of his works

"Geography," and he developed a map with new measurements of the Earth.

The ways of communication in the ancient world, the rivers and seas, were the landmarks of all geographical representations because they were the grand routes of commerce and provided access to remote areas of the Earth. Since the accessibility of these naval routes was only relative, classical writers seldom based their accounts on direct information of the faraway Eastern European regions. Herodotus, for example, quotes his sources in a general way, making a distinction between the travelers' reports and the legends about distant regions, and justifying the scarcity of facts through the remoteness and inaccessibility of the inland territories. Most ancient writers had to rely on other people's reports about these lands, which restricted their firsthand knowledge to the Mediterranean basin. This fact gives the ancient historical and geographic narratives a questionable note of extravagance and makes them subject to certain exaggerations. In these texts, the readers can make no clear distinction between the informative accounts, based on visits, and the fantastic stories about the regions north of the Danube and the Black Sea. Most classical texts about these territories are based on reports from travelers, and even those are relative and incomplete. Exceptions are Ovid's references to the western Black Sea area in his books of poems *Tristia* and *Ex Ponto.* However, since this evidence exists in works of poetic fiction, not objective historical texts, it is difficult to see it as infallible. It is acceptable, therefore, to consider these ancient texts about Eastern European regions as cultural constructs, dubious representations of real people and places, which the Elizabethans and Jacobeans took over indiscriminately, as part of their classical education.

In the introduction to the monograph of the first-century CE Roman geographer Pomponius Mela, the translator F. E. Romer notices an important distinction regarding the method of Mela's account. While Greek geographic writers regularly began their descriptions of the Mediterranean littoral at the Strait of Gibraltar, continuing in a clockwise direction with the European coast all around the *mare nostrum,* Mela began his narrative counterclockwise around the Mediterranean, through Africa first, then Asia, and Europe last. Romer explains this deviation from the norm as a form of suggesting that the order of the narrative may incorporate and become the order of the world. The text becomes what it describes, and the readers are pursuing a journey of their own. The reader is the traveler, and the mixed geographic and narrative order of the text becomes the reader's/traveler's order. Although travel was relatively common in those days, ancient writers could not have expected their readers to make the journey they described. According to Romer, "Mela has made explicit what was known intuitively all along, not only that the narrative order is the order of the journey, but that this journey depends on the power of speech."[13] Ever since the ancient geographic accounts, we are confronted with the fiction and/or convention of the narrative as journey and of the reader as tourist. The descriptive "realistic" text becomes a more or less inciting tale, as well as a source of information for motivated would-be travelers, or contented stay-at-homes.

The Roman Empire provides an illustrious model of geographer-narrator, who assimilated fact and fiction and created a concoction of stories very much like a palimpsest, in which stories from varied sources were rearranged and refurbished to produce an eccentric historical-geographical narrative. Caius Julius Solinus, surnamed Polyhistor, or "Teller of Varied Tales," provided the standard source of geographic myth for more than a thousand years in the Western world. Solinus can have no claim at originality, since nine-tenths of his *Collectanea rerum memorabilium* (Gallery of Wonderful Things), first published about AD 230–40, was taken straight out of Pliny the Elder's *Natural History,* though Solinus does not even mention his name. The rest is drawn from a variety of sources, none of which is of outstanding quality. The emphasis throughout the book is on the marvelous, the unusual, and the unbelievable. He reported about people who sacrificed to Apollo by dancing barefoot on burning coals, pythons that grew long and fat by feeding on the udders of milk cows, and lynxes whose urine congealed to the hardness of precious stones, having magnetic powers of the color of amber. In Solinus's teratological compendium, human monstrosities existed in remote parts of the world.

Despite the conspicuous fictionalization of reality and the obvious exaggerations, Solinus's word was taken as unchallenged truth by great minds for more than a thousand years. St. Augustine drew on him, and so did Isidore of Seville, when he wrote his encyclopedic *Etimologiae* in the seventh century. Solinus's statements are reflected in the world maps of the Schoolmen of the late Middle Ages, and in the Hereford and Ebstorf maps of the thirteenth century. The book was still of enough interest to warrant reprinting both in the original Latin and in translations into the languages spoken in sixteenth-century Europe. Arthur Golding[14] made the only English translation of Solinus's *Collectanea,*[15] along with the more famous *Commentaries* of Caesar, the *Metamorphoses* of Ovid, and an English version of the works of Pomponius Mela. George Kish, the author of the modern introduction to the facsimile reproduction of the 1587 edition of Solinus, certifies the popularity of this weaver of fabulous tales among the Elizabethans. According to Kish, "Doubtless Golding translated *Collectanea,* though thirteen hundred years old, because the book most likely was still in use in some schoolrooms of Elizabethan England, to be learned by rote as it had been for centuries before."[16] It is possible to infer, therefore, the broad availability of certain classical texts for larger reading groups, since these texts, such as Solinus, were extant not only in the private libraries of the time, but at the hands of the public in Elizabethan schools.

From the marginal notes of Solinus's account of Greece we learn about "the storie of Arion the Musician, that was brought thether through the Sea upon a Dolphin's backe" (sig. J.i). Arion was the traditional inventor of dithyrambic poetry and master on the cithara employed by Periander, king of Corinth. While returning from Sicily to Corinth he was in danger of being murdered by the sailors for the sake of the valuable prizes he had won, but being permitted to play once more upon his cithara he attracted dolphins around the ship and flinging himself into the sea was rescued on the back of one of them. Arion's adventure was first related by Herodotus (1.24) and alluded to by Virgil, Eclogue 8.56, but the story would be familiar to an Elizabethan or Jacobean audience as a classical commonplace. Sebastian in *Twelfth Night* is described as floating on a mast, "like Arion on a dolphin's back" (1.2.14), barely able to "hold acquaintance with the waves" (1.2.15). The musical resonance of the sea-floating metaphor is attuned to the mythological reference and the location where the shipwreck takes place, the coast of Illyria, which is supposed to be an idyllic land of classical harmony. Solinus also mentions it as "Dalmatia and Illyrick" (G.ii.), inhabited by a people descended from the line of Troy, but who have "grown wilde and savage, and degenerated into barbarous manners" (G.ii.). Shakespeare's Illyria is also a place where vague expectations of Hellenistic poetic harmony and music are blended with the jarring noises of the real world, of carnival, and personality shifts.

In a section about the Sea of Constantinople (the Hellespont), witnessing on the wonderful nature of dolphins, Solinus writes about "another childe named *Hirmias,* likewise riding on a Dolphin's back in the Sea" (sig. N.ii.), who was taken to the shore. Apart from a possible inspiration for Hermia's name, this passage takes us to Oberon's vision, recounted to Puck, about the origin of the "western flower," which the king of fairies saw being born from Cupid's arrow while he "sat upon a promontory / And heard a mermaid on a dolphin's back" (2.1.149–50). The classical allusion has more to it that the mere word-choice similarity because it refers to the mysterious power of art and music, which Oberon could hear, while Puck could not, although he had witnessed that he remembered the moment. Actually, all Puck could remember was seeing Oberon sit on a promontory. Just as Arion the Musician, who was saved by a dolphin drawn by his music in the classical myth, Oberon could hear a mermaid singing on a dolphin's back, and the power of music had redemptory properties. This is a typical example showing how Shakespeare fused classical tradition, names, and places in a way of his own; he displaced them from their points of origin, collated several such stories in a single powerful visual metaphor, and transported it into a new space, the stage, where such scenes could not be shown directly. However, the conceit told more about the myth of origin and the places it summoned to the imagination than volumes of exotic writings, such as Solinus's narrative.

About "Panonie," which is the land of "Austrich and Hungarie," Solinus writes that it is "puissant in men, the soyle champion and rich" (P.ii.). The "Mesians," where the country of "Wallachy" lies (Wallachia was the name of one of the three Romanian provinces), was part of the Roman province Moesia. Solinus reports that the ancients used to call it "the Garden of Ceres" (P.ii.), probably because of its richness, and in the area "toward Pontus" (the Black Sea) he mentions a kind of oil that is called "the Chirurgions Oyle" because, on being set on fire, would burn even more if one attempted to quench it with water. Moving farther south, in North Africa, in the area "of the orchards of the Sisters called Hesperides and of Mount Atlas" (R.iii), Solinus writes of the herb called "Euphorbia," whose juice "cleares the eyesight." In the same paragraph he describes how the place rings with strange sounds and music and dance; the marginal note reads, "These seeme to be all one wyth the Fayries which appeared to men in the time of popyshe darknesse" (R.iiii). It is difficult to identify the voice responsible for the marginal notes, but it is reasonable to suppose that it belongs to the Elizabethan translator or editor, who wanted to make these strange descriptions more familiar to readers. It is impossible to avoid thinking of *A Mid-*

summer Night's Dream when reading this bizarre narrative about distant places, and it is quite plausible that Shakespeare may have had some of these fantastic stories ringing in his head when he conceived the play's plot.

It is not my purpose here to try to demonstrate the influence of Solinus's multifaceted geographical, ethnological, historical, and fantastic account on Elizabethan authors and on Shakespeare. My point in relation to the Latin author's composite method of description lies in the graphic assortment of geographical facts of reality and fictional discourse. In "The Epistle Dedicatorie of the Author Written to the Same Autius," Solinus calls his exposé a "recitall of places," a geographical narrative. He admits to having created a special amalgam of fact and fiction: "For I confesse myselfe to have studied earnestly certaine choyse Bookes, to the intent to digresse further of from thinges knowne, and to make longer tariance in things more strange."[17] The author justifies this explicit insistence on the abnormal and the extraordinary through the ultimate intention to entertain the readers. We find out from this classical Latin text that information is purposefully linked with entertainment. The discursive material is organized in such a way as to please the reader and provide selected and attractive data about various places. Similarly, when Shakespeare uses foreign locations in his plays, his interest is not so much factual as directed to entertainment. Moreover, the theater provides an even more corporeal selection and visualization of the linear narrative of invention than the bidimensional text on page. Real people and their actions grant access to a tridimensional space of fact and fiction. Within this limited conventional extension, geography may be both real and imagined. Thus, audiences access simultaneously several dimensions of the geographic expansion. This always enlarges the cultural range, sometimes in disconcerting ways.

The Eastern European territory occupied by modern Romania contains the Carpathians, the farther end of the Danube, and the western coast of the Black Sea. In ancient times, this was a part of the Greek concept of *oikumene,* the inhabited world. Though within the known world, the Greek and later Roman colonies, and in general that part of Dacia[18] were just at the limits of the domesticated realm of the ancients. As Mary B. Campbell points out, "The limit of geographical knowledge, wherever located, was a point commonly charged with moral significance and, even in pre-Christian times, with divine dangerousness. (The Hades of the *Odyssey* and the Colchis of the *Argonautica,* for instance, are each located in their respective texts at the end of a long passage of geographical *descriptio*)."[19] Marginal places outside the usual ancient routes of commerce had an extraneous and often exotic connotation for the writers of old. They formed the licentious fringe of a geography where extreme events could happen, where excessive winters impeded further exploration, and the inland area was mostly left unexplored because of hard frosts and inaccessible country. Such a territory was the ancient land of modern-day Romania, a country where but few foreigners ventured. When the Greeks extended their commerce there, in the sixth century BC with the Milesian merchants, they did not hazard to settle farther than the western coast of the Black Sea.

It is a known fact that the legend of the Argonauts' initiatory voyage is at the root of the name of the ancient city of Tomis, now the city of Constanta. In Ovid (*Tristia* 3.9),[20] when Medea and Jason fled from Colchis on their way home to Greece with the Golden Fleece, Medea took her brother Absyrtus as a hostage. When pursued by her father, she slew Absyrtus and scattered his body into pieces on the way, to delay her father, Aëtes. The body parts were thrown into the Pontos Euxinos,[21] near what was to become the Greek colony of Tomis. In addition, it is said that Medea's father buried the pieces of his son's body on the shore in the city of Tomis. This vengeful and barbaric act gave the ancient city its name because *τομος* means "cut to pieces" in Greek. Ovid used the legend in his poem to emphasize the fact that he had been banished to a foreign and inhospitable land, and thus to appeal to Emperor Augustus for clemency. Many classical writers took over the Latin poet's laments as undeniable facts, describing the lands on the western coast of the Black Sea as barbarous. Pliny writes about the "territorie of the Istrians[22] . . . and those which the Greeks name Absyrtides, of *Medeas* brother *Absyrtis* there slaine."[23] The general opinion was formed, and everybody agreed that such dismemberment could only take place off the coast of Scythia, a territory where ancient writers thought there were monsters, and local populations were reported to practice cannibalism and other savage activities. This was the image that classical texts created about the regions north and west of the Black Sea, which was available to Shakespeare's audiences: places enshrouded in terror, bloody deeds, and evisceration.

Shakespeare was almost certainly aware of the Argonauts' myth and Medea's anatomization story from his beloved Ovid. We cannot be certain of what Shakespeare read, but, judging from the frequency of the Ovidian influences, we can at least document, as Russ McDonald puts it, "the kind of stories Shakespeare liked."[24] In *2 Henry VI,* Young Clifford, at St. Albans, finds his father slain and vows to have no pity for the House of York. The sanguinary image of his father's dead body recalls the equally barbaric action of Medea, and it becomes an emblem of cruelty and a call for vengeance:

> Meet I an infant of the house of York,
> Into as many gobbets will I cut it
> As wild Medea young Absyrtus did.
> In cruelty will I seek out my fame.
>
> (5.3.57–60)[25]

We see how an appalling image of horror triggered by legendary events that happened in ancient times off the coast of Tomis is used to intensify the consternation provoked by the dead body on stage. At the same time, Young Clifford is given admonitory words against war, which he calls "son of hell" (33), prone to let loose the "hot coals of vengeance." (36) The allusion to Medea's story is from a former pacifist, who, when seeing his father's probably mutilated body, calls for cruel revenge.

According to the familiar Shakespearean tactic of reinforcing the metaphor through a similar or opposed one, Young Clifford summons another classical image, this time drawing on Virgil's *Aeneid* (2.707–29), in which Aeneas carries his aged father, Anchises, on his back on their escape from the burning city of Troy. In his case, however, as Clifford stresses, the son carries the dead burden of his father's body, instead of rescuing his father alive, as in Aeneas's illustration. Both references to classical myth, whether they are accurate to the original or inverted, as in the allusion to the *Aeneid,* summon an image of hatred, death, and destruction brought about by war. Though the name *Absyrtos* seems exotic to English ears, and it may have taken them substantial effort to internalize the strange-sounding conglomeration of consonants, the connection with the Ovidian myth is there to remind the audiences about the implacability of death and the cruelty of internecine war. Mutually destructive action involving conflict in a group generally describes civil wars and entails hacking, slashing, amputation, and reciprocal violence. Moreover, the direct materiality and petrified confusion suggested by the image of the body cut to pieces are dramatically reinforced by reference to the ancient allegory. Old Clifford's slaughtered corpse and the image of young Absyrtos butchered at Pontos call up a strange savage corporeal geography on stage, through which audiences are invited to meditate on cruel things past and present.

An essentially different image evoking the myth of the Argonauts (Ovid's *Metamorphoses* 7.255ff.) has a theatrical tangible representation in *The Merchant of Venice.* Bassanio presents his intended suit of Portia[26] to Antonio as a grand legendary enterprise of important momentum. Classical analogies are of great consequence in the young man's attempt to persuade Antonio to finance him. Portia's hair becomes the "golden fleece" in this mythological and geographical analogy of the body, "her seat of Belmont Colchis's strand, / And many Jasons come in quest for her" (1.2.170–72). In the reference, this country of Asia, south of Caucasus, region of the wild nomad Scythians according to ancient reports, becomes the promised land of wealth for the young would-be winners from Venice and elsewhere. The juxtaposition of Belmont and Colchis anticipates the contradictory peculiarity of Portia's personality. John W. Velz looks to Ovid's representation of Medea in the *Metamorphoses* to explain the complexities of Portia's character. Like Medea, Portia is a shape shifter and "this almost absurd amalgam of innocence and extraordinary competence"[27] is a "hyperbolic juxtaposition of incompatibilities;"[28] thus, as Velz argues, the association between the two heroines is an example of the Ovidian grotesque. Part of this character-related ambivalent topography is illustrated with Portia's body on stage, plus the allusions to distant places drawing on Shakespeare's and the audience's favorite readings.

The parallel between Medea and Portia yields rather disturbing connotations, especially when related to the particular relevance of the allusion to Medea's native place (Colchis), as opposed to Portia's Belmont. Isabella Wheater identifies one of the "sea-stories"[29] lying behind *The Merchant of Venice* in the narrative of Jason and the Golden Fleece that Ovid tells in *Metamorphoses* 7. Wheater parallels Bassanio with Jason and Portia with Medea and finds that Portia, as Medea, had a father who imposed on men conditions that each daughter considered too harsh.[30] Moreover, as Wheater observes, "Jason had a threefold trial, and Medea is closely related with Hecate, 'the threefold goddess' (Met. vii. 94–5)."[31] From this "synthesis" of Aristotle, Christian parables, Ovidian myth, and Horatian lyric emerged, as Wheater argues, a particular "conceptual framework."[32] I would add that a particular geography also emerges from this synthesis, one that is rooted in classical myth and philosophy, but that always keeps the latitudinal and longitudinal coordinates that include the British Isles in the equation. Moreover, this assumption of marginality of foreign distant spaces belongs to traditions, modes, and conventions in the air, dispersed among many books, and not traceable to specific texts. We see how Shakespeare interprets the classical writers and the floating knowledge derived from them retentively and evocatively, reclaiming classical allusions in a positive synthetizing exercise.

Bassanio presents Jason's quest as a story of success and emphasizes the legendary symbol of material wealth that the Golden Fleece has come to represent along the ages. No obvious association with barbarity, dismemberment, loss, and deceit (as suggested by the Medea story) can be permitted here to disturb the expectations of happiness. However, the collocation of Colchis, Medea's homeland, right next to the idyllic Belmont in the text may raise some doubts as to the utter contentment Portia's place can produce. After Bassanio wins over Portia's hand, Graziano reinforces the image of their party as a team of winners: "We are the Jasons; we have won the fleece" (3.2.240). Then again, in the ensuing conversation with Salerio, a pun on *fleece* and *fleet* (3.2.241) reverses the cheerful picture. This is the first announcement of rumors about the wreck of Antonio's "argosies" (1.1.9), and this news brings about the story of loss of fortune, ruination of confidence, deceit, and evisceration (through the pound of flesh argument).[33] According to Alessandro Serpieri, Venice was a "transposed image" (*immagine trasposta*) of mercantile London, a special place for representing "contemporary tensions" (*tensioni contemporanee*), a sign of the city's "actuality" (*attualità*).[34] In my view, Venice is one point of assumed and comparative civility in the geographic triangulation that includes unreal idyllic Belmont and the distant Colchis of the classical myth. All three locations form a constellation of places in which people are expected to act in accordance with the laws of courtesy and honest commerce, but where matters are not always so. Potential atrocity seeps through the cracks of civil understanding, and the classical allusion to an Eastern distant place, famous for cruelty, always rings warning bells.

From a land of milk and honey, as the inexperienced young men Bassanio and Graziano perceived it earlier in the play, Colchis becomes in Shakespeare's theatrical and mythological new geography a region where tragedy is likely to happen and offensive actions are the order of the day, as in Venice. The implied mythological analogy creates a contrast with the remote land of Colchis, north of the Black Sea, where fierce Scythians[35] abide by savage laws. Such a country was seen as being very far from the domesticated and civilized free city of Venice. Even the heavenly Belmont, with its diffuse connotations of eternal wealth and bliss, loses its gilded appearance by association with the distant and savage Colchis of the Scythians. Through dramatic complementariness, Shakespeare uses the classical reference to an ancient myth happening in a distant land to foreshadow a situation of potential tragedy and dismemberment about to happen in a civilized Western European city, where a member of its community, who is viewed as an outsider by some, threatens with the application of an ancient law. At the same time, the allusion to Colchis and the Scythians is used to create a contrast between the civilized Renaissance Venice and the foreign lands where such barbaric acts can conceivably happen. It is likely that the mythological reference to the Argonauts' legend elicited disparaging images of horror and destruction, but also cheating and betrayal, in the audiences, apart from the common suggestion of quest and triumph, and Shakespeare used the insinuation to the classical myth with definite and specific dramatic purposes.

A popular seventeenth-century travel book is William Lithgow's *Discourse of a Peregrination in Europe, Asia, and Africke* (1614).[36] Although the "peregrinations" mostly refer to the contemporary description of places, the narrative is interspersed with references to classical myth and history, as befits a self-respecting travel account. After Paris, Rome, Naples, several islands in the Mediterranean, and Greece, Lithgow proceeded overland to Egypt and finally reached Grand Cairo and Alexandria. He encountered many dangers and difficulties—now shipwrecked, now attacked by banditti, now plundered and maltreated—and he was frequently exposed for days and nights together to the inclemency of the weather. On his arrival at the city of Galliopolis (in the Marmaris region), which was the first town of Europe conquered by the Turks, Lithgow inserts the classical reference to the Medea story and the Argonauts' myth: "As we sailed between *Thracia* and *Bithinia,* a learned *Grecian* that was in my company shewed me *Colchis,* whence *Iason,* with assistance of the *Argonautes,* and the aide of *Medeas* skill did fetch the golden fleece. This Sea *Hellesponte* tooke the name of *Helles,* and of the Country *Pontus,* ioyning to the same Sea, wherein are these three Countries, *Armenia, Colchis,* and *Cappadocia.*"[37] Apart from the references to many interesting places in Eastern Europe and western Asia, the text is mainly informative, with no personal commentary and scholarly additions. However, as was customary in the early modern period, the historical narrative about these places is based on authority of ancient writers such as Pliny, Pausanias, and Strabo, as if all further human activity in these countries had ceased after these historians' accounts. What is interesting about this travel book is the sheer number of the sites visited and described, proudly announced on the title page in italics, which can give a glimpse into the Jacobeans' interest in such travel narratives about faraway lands.

William Biddulph compiled a collection of letters, published in 1609, which describes the travels of Englishmen in the eastern Mediterranean and the Black Sea in the period 1600–1608. Biddulph's *Travels,* edited by Lavender without the author's consent, was sufficiently popular to require two editions within four years. Lavender merged the letters (originally written by William and Peter Biddulph to their brother Beliazel) so as to make them appear to recount the events of a continuous trip, describing chiefly the Greek Islands, Constantinople, and some Levantine cities, with one letter devoted to Jerusalem. Included in these descriptions are accounts of the laws and religion of the Mohammedans and the Jews. Though Biddulph's collection of letters is apparently a firsthand account of travels in the region of the Black Sea, the compilation has a distinct fantastic flavor given by the introduction of classical references to Ovid as an exemplification of the characteristics of the described locales. Readers learn from Biddulph's epistolary narrative about the geographical situation of Colchis in the Black Sea, and of what Ovid had said concerning this sea in his *Tristia.* Transiting from the purely geographical description of the voyage from Constantinople, through the Hellespont, to "the sea called Pontus" (34, sig. G_2), the author cites the Ovidian verse in support of his argument:

> (as Ovid in his Booke *De Tristibus* speaketh,
> *Omnia Pontus erant, deerant quoque littora Ponto:*
> That is,
> All was sea on every side,
> And no firm land could be espied.
> And againe,
> *Nil nisi Pontus & aer;*
> I see nothing but the aire above, and the sea beneath:)[38]

This kind of classical reference, which was a common artifice in most geographical descriptions of distant places, has the telescoping effect of enlarging the perspective of early modern readers about those barely known places. Biddulph gives his readers a photographic image of the Black Sea as seen through Ovid's eyes, which conjures a picture of desertedness and inhospitableness. In fact, Ovid had good reason to create such an atmosphere about the sea because he wanted to impress the officials in Rome with his despondency and unfortunate predicament.

The insertion of allusions to classical myth in the discourse about the real places coexisting with early seventeenth-century Jacobeans makes these locations more familiar and, paradoxically, even more remote for the readers. Biddulph informs them that there is a country named Pontus in the same sea, which contains Cappadochia, Cholchis, Armenia. When the name *Cholchis* is mentioned, another classical parenthesis is in order: "and especially *Cholchis* (whence *Jason* with the *Argonautes,* by the helpe of *Medeas* skil, did fetch the Golden Fleece) is most conspicuous on *Asia* side, to them that saile thorow the sea *Pontus*" (35). The readers of such eclectic texts would form a very vague idea about the Black Sea's northern area. They tend to incorporate real geography and myth in a complex concoction of impressions that had very little to do with the real places. For them, this area represented a distant location expanding over vast stretches of sea and land, where any number of abominable things could happen. Shakespeare took over such polarity techniques and indicated to his audiences that the real place they knew, their England, was no better nor worse than the fictionalized accounts about other distant spaces, be they ancient or contemporary. This pragmatic relation to the reality of performance, clearly connected to early modern England, is one way of Shakespeare's drawing his audience's attention to the fictional status of his stories about distant places, which must be perceived *as if* they were part of the surrounding reality. The only connection between distant Colchis, or the sea Pontus, and the English audiences is formed by the actors' bodies on the stage, which configure an immediate theatrical geography more convincingly than the collections of classical texts can ever do.

There is an abundance of references in classical texts to the northern parts of the Black Sea and their inhabitants, the wild Scythians. Because of their nomad status there is a vagueness of reports relating to the exact region they inhabited, or the names of the various tribes. One of these tribes was called Cimmerians, and they dwelled in what is now south of Russia. Like the space where legendary Colchis was situated, this northern part of the Pontus Euxinos was fabled to be a place of perpetual darkness, where cruel events could occur, and people had the savage habits of carving their enemies to pieces and even eating them. Caius Iulius Solinus reports about the Cimmerians who lived around the Caspian Sea that they had neighborly relations with the warlike nation of the Amazons; they were just as savage and uncontrollable. Their land was famed to be the abode of fierce Hyrcanian tigers, panthers, and leopards.[39] In book 4 (*Melpomene*) of his *History*, Herodotus speaks of the Cimmerians as the former inhabitants of the land of the Scythians. They refused to leave their land to the hostile Scythians and decided to die there, being massacred by the invaders. Herodotus says that these peoples inhabited the eastern and northern parts of the Black Sea before retiring toward the Caspian area.[40] The image the Elizabethans and Jacobeans retained from the classical writers with reference to these nations was that they lived in a remote northeastern region and other savage tribes massacred them during various incursions in their land.

In *Titus Andronicus,* which plays ambivalently upon the issues of expected Roman civility as opposed to alien savagery and terror, Bassianus refers contemptuously to Aaron as a "swart Cimmerian" (2.3.72), meaning swarthy or dark-skinned. The visual opposition between the Moor's dark skin and the Queen's "snow-white" (76) steed enhances the ambivalent image of blackness and dark desire. Historical records mention that the Cimmerians were ancient equestrian nomads who, according to Herodotus, originally inhabited the region north of the Caucasus and the Black Sea, in what is now Russia and Ukraine, in the eighth and seventh centuries BC. They are described in book 11 of Homer's *Odyssey* as living in a land of fog and darkness at the edge of the world, on the shores of Oceanus. As far as the Elizabethans knew, the Cimmerians were a legendary nation in the north of Pontus Euxinus, probably a branch of the Thracians. Their distant region was reputed to be a place where the sun never shone. Therefore, the territory was dark, not the inhabitants. On the contrary then, the natives of these places could be nothing but pale, in total contrast with the dark-skinned complexion of Aaron the Moor, who was from the southern regions of Mauritania. The only relevance that the reference to the Cimmerians could yield was one connected to ferocity and mass murder, as reported in ancient texts. Bassianus's disparaging remark, therefore, instead of referring to a visible reality connected to Aaron the Moor, foreshadows horror scenes to come, which were likely to have happened in such faraway lands to people with strangely melodious names.

Before the entrance of Bassianus and Lavinia on stage, Tamora and Aaron's plotting to have Lavinia ravaged initiates the dark atmosphere of horror and dismemberment. Aaron evokes the Ovidian story of the carnage inflicted on Philomel by Tereus, and Tamora mentions Actaeon's dismemberment by his hounds. Bassianus and Lavinia's arrival cuts short the two plotters' fantasy of horror, and the antithetical representation of Aaron as a dark Cimmerian is meant to prefigure an imminent mental picture of atrocity. The reference to an ancient northern race of fierce people, intensified by the allusion to Tamora as a "lascivious Goth" (2.3.110), another barbarous nation living on the western littoral of the Black Sea, calls up a special geography of outrage and anatomization. The Goths were an East Germanic tribe who, according to their own traditions, from the second century settled Scythia, Dacia, and Pannonia, the area of present-day Russia, Romania, and Hungary. Shakespeare foreshadows the fact that abominable crimes are about to happen, and the harrowing image of Lavinia's mutilated body on stage imposes its ominous presence in advance, by the representation of an expressive geography suggesting horror and barbarity. As in other plays, this spatial contrastive triangulation is again summoned by the savage nations of the Cimmerians and the Goths, set against the supposedly civilized Roman culture, where such atrocities are bound to happen, just as in those remote parts of the world.

In book 1.1, Herodotus[41] attributes to the wild Scythians from the Pontus area an abominable act of horror involving a young boy cut to pieces. A band of Scythian nomads had taken refuge in Media, in the time of King Cyaxares. Because they were considered wise with the bow and arrow, the king entrusted them with a group of boys, who were to be trained by the Scythians in the skills of hunting. When, one time, they returned without the usual load of game, the king rebuked them. In return, the Scythians took a young boy, cut him to pieces, cooked him with herbs, and served him to the king at the feast. The story was taken over repeatedly and in various forms by ancient and later writers, including Ovid in his story of Procne serving Itys to Tereus. Therefore, it is difficult to ascribe one of the many such narratives as a source for the gory feast in *Titus Andronicus*. Katharine Eisaman Maus avers that "Shakespeare's Goths and Africans apparently have no history, no myths of their own: instead they invoke and mimic examples provided by their conquerors, just as Renaissance Europeans revived the classical literary inheritance, testifying to its importance in the very acts of reading and imitating it."[42] While perceiving classical Rome as an "anthology of stories,"[43] as Eisaman Maus puts it, Elizabethans and Jacobeans were able to form stereotypical images derived from the classical texts they could read, or the stories they could hear alluded to in the theater.

Concerning the image of outlandishness and marginality summoned by the reference to the barbaric peoples living in the Black Sea area, it is relevant, however, that the Goths, who are at one pole of Shakespeare's story of cultural and racial opposition in *Titus Andronicus,* inhabited the region north of the Danube and near the Black Sea in the fourth century AD, when the play is set. Shakespeare was confusedly aware of this fact when he placed Ovid among the Goths,[44] during the Roman poet's exile at Tomis. The periods are not exactly right, because the Goths inhabited these regions about two centuries later than Ovid's exile at Tomis. The race of people living there in Ovid's time was the Getae, another culture of purported barbarians. The Getae (singular *Geton*) was the name by which ancient writers referred to Thracian tribes living beside the Danube, especially south of the river, in what is today's northern Bulgaria, but also in the Muntenian plain and in Dobruja (modern-day Romania).[45] Shakespeare knew about Ovid and the Getae (or the Goths), probably about the ancient city of Tomis, and he was ready to place a tale of horror and dismemberment in connection with this vague area inhabited by strange people, who would carve their children to pieces and eat them for supper. However, whenever Shakespeare alludes to Eastern European distant places, though these allusions are leaden with specific connotations, the ostensibly alien is never meant to suggest mere otherness, but a disturbing spatial analogy that summons emotions rather than accurate and specific facts and people.

The textual inference favored by Elizabethans and Jacobeans, drawing mostly on Greek authors in Latin interpretations and English translations, was that the peoples living west and north of the Euxine Sea were cruel and inhuman. They did not abide by the values of gentility and honor, and their habits were far from conforming to the Roman notions of civility and deference. Herodotus said they drank from the skulls of their enemies, carved up cadavers of their loved ones and partook in the feast with all their friends, and wore large mantles patched up with human scalps. In Shakespeare's dramatization of the supposedly "civilized" Roman world in confrontation to the "barbarity" of the Goths in *Titus Andronicus,* these stereotypical analogies are visibly subverted. In the opening scene showing Titus's triumphal homecoming to Rome, we see a Roman (Lucius, Titus's son) relish in the cruel description of carving up Alarbus's body with swords and burning the limbs to the bone. Herodotus ascribes such practices to the barbarous Scythians living at the mouth of the Danube:

> They also sacrifice prisoners of war. . . . One prisoner in every hundred is selected; they pour wine over the prisoners' heads, cut their throats so that the blood spills into a jar, and then carry the jars up on a pile of sticks and pour the blood over the *akinakes.* . . . They cut off the right arms of all the slaughtered men—the whole arm from shoulder to hand—and hurl them into the air. Then they sacrifice all the rest of the victims and leave. The arms are left lying wherever they fall, detached from the corpses. . . . Here is how they conduct themselves in war, when a Scythian kills his first man, he drinks some of his blood. He presents the king with the heads of those he kills in battle, because his reward for doing so is a share of the spoils they have taken in the battle, but no head means no spoils.[46]

In *Titus Andronicus,* we see a noble Roman, Lucius, relishing similar barbaric practices when he announces that they will cut Alarbus's body to pieces and burn his entrails as a sacrifice. In reply to Lucius's offensively violent Roman fantasy, we hear the exchange between Tamora's two other sons, Chiron and Demetrius, who are appalled by such cruelty. These descendants of the supposedly rude Goths cannot even compare the barbarity of the Scythians to that of the hypothetically civilized Romans. Chiron opposes the allegedly barbaric Scythia to this horrifying dismemberment: "Was never Scythia half so barbarous" (1.1.131). In reply, Demetrius does not even want to compare Scythia to Rome: "Oppose not Scythia to ambitious Rome" (1.1.132); this might suggest that even the supposedly merciless Scythians were better than what was just about to happen in Rome, namely, the sacrifice and dismemberment of Alarbus on religious grounds. This is just what Herodotus reported that the wild Scythians would do to their prisoners of war. The telescoping image is reversed, and we have two Goths (considered a barbaric nation by the civilized Romans) weigh the cruel act of a Roman against the extremely violent Scythian practices. Even to the Goths, the Scythian habits seemed inhuman. However, in Rome, ambition caused people's actions to seem more offensive than those of the barbarians did. The antithetical scene is brought to a closure when all the sons of Andronicus enter with bloody swords and boast about having performed "our Roman rites" (1.1.143). In fact, the sacrifice and the dismemberment of Alarbus's body are horribly violent deeds, very similar to what the ancients said the barbarous Scythians did to their enemies.

In *Titus Andronicus* we see how the differences between Roman and barbarian are not so clearly and absolutely marked. The traditional forms of piety that underlie Roman civilization are replaced with the barbaric practice of human sacrifice. The moral, historical, racial, and ethnographic ramifications in this scene are conveyed through the mental map of Scythia, a land of a supposedly bloodthirsty nation; through the region of the Goths, the origin land of Tamora and her sons, a place deemed primitive by the Romans, while a certain noble Roman acted with similar bestiality; and through the empire of the conquering Romans, deemed to be urbane and refined, but actually just as sadistic and sanguinary, similar to what ancient writers relate about barbaric peoples. In examining Shakespeare's geography of the "farthest Greece" in *The Comedy of Errors, Titus Andronicus,* and *Pericles,* Clifford J. Ronan confirms Shakespeare's continuing interest in Ovid and illustrates the inscription of space in early modern ideology.[47] Moreover, as I see it, as with many Shakespearean allusions to locations, the audiences are able to adjust their own measurements to a certain dramatic triangulation, according to which places better or less known become syntagmas of multivocal human relationships. This map is drawn with bodies on a stage, and all the props Shakespeare needs to evoke a specific marginal geography are a few bloody swords, a mental picture of violence, and his audience's conjecture of the barbarity of the Scythians, built up from the large compilation of stories that formed their classical grammar-school education.

A Scythian queen with a reputation for savagery is Tomyris, a queen of the Massagetae. According to Herodotus (1.201), this is a branch of the Scythians. Tomyris was a warrior queen, who confronted the Persian king Cyrus. Though she could have stopped the approach of Cyrus at the river Araxes, yet she permitted him to cross, preferring to overcome him in battle rather than to defeat him by advantage of position. During the battle, Tomyris's son was killed. After achieving this victory, Queen Tomyris crossed over into Moesia and built on the western shore of Pontus the city of Tomis,[48] named after her. In revenge for her son's death, she killed the Persian king Cyrus and kept his head in a wineskin filled with human blood. In *1 Henry VI,* the countess of Auvergne is plotting the death of Talbot. She imagines herself in the situation of "Scythian Tomyris" (2.3.6), a merciless and vengeful heroine who would save her people from the invaders, but the violent image is deflated when Talbot appears. The countess taunts him with the smallness of his stature, and her blood-soaked plan fades away because his army intimidates her. Finally, the French Countess acknowledges his power and finishes by inviting him to feast with her. In this scene, the geographic triangulation that has as reference points France, Scythia, and England is used to play on the French superficiality and lack of determination, in contrast with the English valor, symbolically represented by Talbot. The reference to the implacable Scythian queen is placed at a point of dramatic balance, in which the audience's expectation of violence is undermined and then ironically deflated. Shakespeare chooses to do this by manipulating geographical reference derived from ancient authors.

One of the outstanding writers of the Ciceronian period, Sallust[49] is placed in the front rank of Roman historians because of his accounts of the Catilinarian conspiracy and the Jugurthine War. Salustius was widely printed in the latter sixteenth and early seventeenth centuries, both in Latin and in English. In the second part of the historical account relating "The Warre of Iugurth" (chapter 2) the Latin author sets on to describe Africa and its first inhabitants. Apart from the geographical confusion created by the report that some accounts include Africa in Europe, Sallustius details his method of description of the continent and its inhabitants. As with most ancient authors, his discourse focuses only on the nations that have certain connections with the Romans, not accounting for the margins of the African territory. He makes his method explicit to the readers and leaves the rest to their imagination: "But as for those places and countries, which either for their extream rough mountaines, or vast deserts, lie unfrequented, I will but point at random: the residue I will discourse of in shortest manner. . . . Let euery man give credite, as he pleaseth to fancie it."[50] Therefore, in many ancient writers, the absence of detailed descriptions of geographical regions is used as a device to render the text more inciting, stimulating the readers' curiosity. As others, Salustius likes to inflame his readers' imagination by leaving many gaps in his narrative. These gaps resulted from lack of information, but they acted as effective generators of fictions. Shakespeare's contemporaries collected and took over most of these fabricated discourses about remote regions from the ancients, and the theater is the place where this form of intuitive geography can find a distinctly corporeal meaning.

In the first century A.D., the Latin writer Pliny the Elder[51] published a thirty-seven-volume *Natural History*. This was a massive compilation of two thousand earlier works. In the first tome of the 1601 English edition, in Philemon Holland's translation, Pliny writes "Of the Black Sea and Bosphorus."[52] As it was the custom among ancient writers, Pliny takes over earlier Greek narratives about the Euxine Sea, and he describes the savage natives living on its western coast. According to Pliny, "The Sea called Pontus Euxinus, and named by the Greeks in old time, Axenos, for the hard usage that passengers found at the hands of those savage Nations upon the coast thereof, is spread also betwixt Europ and Asia" (42). This information seems commonplace, since so many classical writers took over ideas from each other, especially when referring to faraway unexplored places. A marginal sea of Eastern Europe, bearing several and often contradictory names, the Black Sea lies between two continents, and this fact alone yields connotations of liminality—the space in between. Besides, ancient reports refer to the cruelty of the people living around it. The "unfriendly" natives who were reported to inhabit the shores of the Black Sea have always been the targets of biased interpretations and elusive narratives created by ancient authors. In the same paragraph in which he writes about Pontus Euxinus, Pliny mentions the sea "Propontis" (43), the sea of Marmora, which gushes furiously from the north through the Hellespont, and the straits of Bosphorus.

In the special geography of *Othello,* Venice and Cyprus are placed at the two ends of an early modern west-east Mediterranean divide. Othello mentions the Pontic Sea in a metaphor that encompasses his rage and the obsessive urge to go forward with revenge at all costs:

> Like to the Pontic Sea,
> Whose icy current and compulsive course
> Ne'er knows retiring ebb, but keeps due on
> To the Propontic and the Hellespont,
> Even so my bloody thoughts with violent pace
> Shall ne'er look back, ne'er ebb to humble love,
> Till that a capable and wide revenge
> Swallow them up.
>
> (3.3.456–63)

Othello's anger is like a force of nature and a most convincing metaphor can only be derived from the analogy to geographical knowledge, according to which, as in the ancients' accounts, the icy Pontic Sea is as unfriendly and merciless as those inhabiting its shores. Revenge and savage bloody ways can only arise in those strange parts, reported to host people who kill their enemies and drink their blood. Othello's words visualize an emotional state (violent rage) through the analogy with a distant place, whose coordinates are familiar from ancient texts. Reference to the Pontic Sea, the Propontic, and the Hellespont elicit a physical connection among the enraged hero on stage, his need for revenge (irrational like a force of nature), and a tempestuous alien sea yielding strange names, which scan beautifully.

My view regarding Shakespeare's interplay of marginality and barbaric practices when referring to the Eastern European Pontos Euxinus and the Scythians inhabiting the area is also maintained in Christopher Baker's study "Ovid, Othello, and the Pontic Scythians."[53] Baker traces the implications of Shakespeare's use of the Pontic Sea and Scythians to denote alienation and ethnic barbarism in *Othello,* in the context of similar descriptions in Ovid's *Metamorphoses* and *Tristia,* as well as similar descriptions of Scythian geography, and the supernatural qualities of Scythians in travel accounts. In a similar manner, Jerry Brotton makes the case that the tragedies show an increasing awareness of the dramatic and rhetorical opportunities given by geography; its metaphorical possibilities and its material manifestation in the shape of maps formed a complex background, on which early modern writers drew.[54] I would add that Shakespeare used these geographic and classical allusions as powerful emotional triggers, eliciting various expressive responses from his audiences and later theater interpreters. It is reasonable to believe that ancient names of Eastern European areas, such as *Pontus* and *Scythian,* were more familiar to Elizabethans and Jacobeans than the modern geographical names of the sea and the countries existing at the time, such as the Black Sea and Wallachia or Moldova, the historic regions of modern Romania in early modern times.

The Latin geographer Pomponius Mela[55] has a chapter entitled "Hellespont, Propontis, Pontus, and Maeotis,"[56] in which he describes all these seas and the cities on their shores, with the legends connected with many of them. Mela was contemporary with Pliny, and their accounts regarding the Euxine Sea are disconcertingly similar. The readers get the same image of cold climate and hostile natives, and Mela makes a distinction between the two Greek versions of the sea's name: "The sea is brief, cruel and cloudy; its stopping-off places are few and far between; it is surrounded by a shore that is neither soft nor sandy; it borders on the north winds and it is billowy and tempestuous, because it is not deep. In the olden days, the sea was called the Axenus [Gr. Unfriendly] Sea from the vicious disposition of the inhabitants, but later it was called Euxinus [Gr. Friendly] Sea because of the traffic with somewhat gentler nations" (63). The "vicious disposition" of the natives consisted mainly of cannibalism, blood drinking, boiling the corpses of their enemies and using the bones for fuel, and many such practices. It is hardly likely that Mela obtained his information from firsthand experience, so it can be inferred that he merely repeated what other ancient writers said about the Black Sea area. Self-contradictory statements, anachronisms, and heavy borrowing are typical features of classical texts, especially when they refer to distant places of Europe and elsewhere.

In *King Lear,* the king's irrational fury is inflamed by Cordelia's poor manipulation of rhetoric regarding filial love and duty. As did the ancient barbarians, Lear voices an oath with magic and cosmic significance, but that has deep textual roots in ancient references to the practices of the savage populations inhabiting the Black Sea area:

> The barbarous Scythians,
> Or he that makes his generation
> Messes to gorge his appetite,
> Shall be as well neighboured, pitied, and relieved
> As thou, my sometime daughter.
> (1.1.105–9, Q text: *The History of King Lear*)

Lear's rejection of Cordelia is set in drastic terms, and his onetime beloved daughter becomes a rejected weird stranger, compared to the barbarous Scythians. Lear swears a pagan oath by "the mysteries of Hecate, and the night" (1.1.100), the classical goddess of the moon and the patroness of witchcraft, who was associated with the underworld. Lear's words are a strange mixture of pagan classical allusions to Hecate, the Scythians, and the Saturn myth of the father who feeds on his children (1.1.107–8). The ancient inhabitants of the Euxine Sea are reported to have worshiped the goddess Hecate, connected with magic spells and witchcraft. In the Archeology Museum of Constanta (former Tomis) we can find a number of first-century AD statues representing the triple Hecate, the image of the goddess in triplicate, facing three different directions, with her dog at her feet. This statue used to confer good luck on travelers and was employed in primitive magic rites performed at the full moon.

Shakespeare was fascinated with boundaries of place and time and metaphors summoning liminality. In ancient times, crossroads were considered to be the most magical places, credited with powers of protection and healing, and favored sites for magical spells. Hecate was the divinity venerated at crossroads and images of the deity in triplicate were erected at such locations. Whenever Hecate is mentioned in Shakespeare, the evocative power of the mystic triple goddess acquires a persuasive force that places the stage and the actor who speaks this name in a magic triangle of powerful signification, involving the distant land of Greece, the time projection of the classical reference, and the physical presence of the character uttering it. In the *Dream,* Puck acknowledges the fairies' allegiance to "the triple Hecate's team" (5.2.14) and the night in his final incantation. On the contrary, Talbot in *1 Henry VI* refers disparagingly to Joan of Arc as "that railing Hecate" (3.5.24) when she reacts angrily at the siege of Rouen. Player Lucianus in *Hamlet* utters an incantation about the poisoning plant with which he intends to murder the Player King; to increase its fatal efficiency, this plant was collected at midnight and empowered with a curse: "With Hecate's ban thrice blasted, thrice infected" (3.2.236). I mention only in passing the Hecate scene in *Macbeth* (3.5.1–74) because of the passage's dubious authorship. The Greek goddess of witchcraft is alluded to in episodes of high dramatic tension, usually in connection with a curse or an oath, whose incantatory power is enhanced by the classical image and the strange-sounding name, usually a disyllable, except in *1 Henry VI,* when the name is used ironically. In each case the incantation has great persuasive force.

In Herodotus, the Scythians are reported to share symbolic meals with their dead loved ones, because they believed in the immortality of the soul and thought that, in this way, the ancestors' spirits would be perpetuated to posterity. According to the classical historian, the Scythians would treat the corpse as a guest to the funeral table, partaking in the food with the others: "when one of them died, his closest relatives put his body on a wagon and take it round to his friends, each of whom makes the entourage welcome and gives them a meal at which the corpse is served the same food and drink as everyone else. The corpse of a member of the general populace of Scythia is taken around to his friends like this for forty days, and then buried."[57] Macabre as it may seem, this funeral ceremony was performed with the greatest respect for the dead relative and with the belief in afterlife. Even these days the funeral rites are very important in the region of Dobrogea of present-day Romania and the period of forty days is essential for the commemoration of the dead relative's spirit. Since pre-Christian belief in the immortality of the soul held that the soul hovers among the living for forty days after the body's death, the family of the deceased feel bound to make offerings of food and wine during the entire period. Christianity, which arrived in this area as an official religion in the fourth century AD, with the emperor Constantine's edict, took over this practice and used it for the proper veneration of the dead.

In Lear's theatrical oath that includes the reference to the "barbarous Scythians," Shakespeare acts upon a special ethnographic and ethical geography. According to it, an ancient pagan Briton objects to the Scythians' savage practices of cannibalism, considering them brutal and inhuman. King Lear would have nothing to do with such uncivilized nations, who feast beside the bodies of their fathers, and he rejects his apparently ungrateful Cordelia for the same lame reasons. However, Lear's oath is a visible barbaric practice, and it serves to produce a ritualized spectacle of authority, enhanced by the allusion to Chronos, who feasted on his children's bodies. The reference to classical mythology that Lear includes in order to be more persuasive is, in fact, reversing his argument of child ungratefulness by transferring the blame to the father. The evocation of the carnage suggested by the reference to the Scythians creates an association of repulsion and horror, although the funeral rites of those peoples inhabiting the Black Sea region were performed out of respect for their relatives. Shakespeare's contemporaries may have thought such practices appalling just because they were different; therefore the physicality of the ferocious allusion obscured any positive moral implications. The fallibility of such an assumption is paralleled with Lear's flawed reasoning regarding Cordelia's supposed ingratitude. Geographical accounts of monstrosities, when performed on the Shakespearean stage, produce uneasiness about the validity of our mental constructs. They make us see, in a direct and corporeal way, the ambivalence of truths when predicated from one intolerant side.

Another ancient story involving poetry, savagery, and dismemberment was the Orpheus myth. The legendary poet who enchanted wild beasts, trees, and rocks with his lute, and even put Cerberus to sleep, was of Thracian origin. The ancient province of Thrace occupied what is now southern Romania (the region of the Danube) and Bulgaria. Herodotus spoke about the Thracians as "the largest in the world," and he would deem them invincible had they been united under one ruler.[58] As it was, they were divided into many tribes, among which were the Getae. Speaking of Darius's campaign north of the Ister, Herodotus says that the first tribe to be subjected was the Getae, who pretend to be immortal, and he called them the bravest and most just Thracians of all. Similarly, Caius Iulius Solinus tells "of the manners and customes of Thrace" in an appreciative manner: "Now it's time to take our journeye into Thrace, and to sette sayle toward the puissantest Nations of Europe: which whosoever will looke upon advisedlie, shall easily finde that there is a contempt of life in the barbarous Thracians, through certaine discipline of moother wytt. They agree all to die willingly: some of them beleeuing that the soules of them that decease returne agaīne, and othersome thinking that they die not, but are in most happie and blissful state."[59] According to Solinus, parents wept when a child was born into the world and rejoiced when their loved ones died. The Thracians practiced polygamy, and wives considered it a duty to be burned on the funeral pyre beside their husbands.

An interesting custom prefiguring some sort of women-liberation rite resided in the fact that women were not compelled to marry according to their parents' wish, but they sold themselves at an auction to the highest bidder. The habit of drugging themselves with herbs (probably cannabis) thrown into the fire is also reported of the wild Thracian women. Solinus's narrative concludes the presentation of the Thracian women's extravagant habits with the story of Orpheus's origin and his mystic connection with a special kind of ritual (the tradition of the Eleusinian mysteries): "On the sea coast of Pontus dwelleth the people of Sythony, the renowne thereof is augmented by *Orpheus* the Poet and Prophette that was borne there, who is reported to have practised the secrets (whither it were of his Musicke or his Ceremonies) in the Promontorie Sperchius" (B.iii). Whenever the land of Thrace was mentioned, most classical writers and some of their early modern emulators referred to the Orpheus myth as a focal point. Ovid (*Metamorphoses* 11) tells how Orpheus was torn to pieces by the Thracian Menades during their Bacchanalian orgies, in revenge for his contempt. Later artistic approaches to the myth have reflected an absorbed belief in Orpheus as both an icon of the power of art as well as a symbol of an iconoclastic, alternative power available to the artist within society. Shakespeare's contemporaries exploited both approaches, and a collateral idea generated by the Orpheus story was that his murderers were savage Thracian women.

One image about Orpheus that penetrated the Elizabethans' and Jacobeans' mental disposition more vigorously was connected with violence and dismemberment. In *A Midsummer Night's Dream,* however, Shakespeare uses the reference to Orpheus's tragedy facetiously. The act of witnessing the horrible scene becomes a possible form of entertainment meant to beguile the time. One of the four "sports" proposed to Theseus on occasion of his wedding feast, along with the *Pyramus and Thysbe* play, is "the riot of the tipsy bacchanals / Tearing the Thracian singer in their rage" (5.1.48–49). Theseus dismisses the production as outdated and overperformed. However, the contradictory reference to a well-known ancient story of dismemberment and death in a context of trivial entertainment reverses all the normal expectations of horror and suffering. The grand notion of the drug-induced cruelty of the Thracian Menades, who were seized with a god-inspired zeal, or enthusiasm, during their Bacchanals, is pathetically reduced to the image of a bunch of "tipsy" women, partially inebriated and ridiculous. The *Pyramus and Thysbe* tragedy, another Ovidian tale drawing on the *Metamorphoses,* becomes a composite genre of "tragical mirth" at the hands of the mechanicals. Likewise, the passing reference, in jest, to a region, Thracia, where ferocious events are supposed to have happened is a special geographical marker in Shakespeare's game of reversing the audiences' expectations at any moment and about any place.

A different connotation connected with the reference to the Thracians and Orpheus is in *Titus Andronicus.* This is the most violent scene, when Lavinia's uncle, Marcus, finds her horribly mutilated body. The analogy with the crude reality of Ovid's dismemberment by the Thracian Menades can be seen physically on the stage in the bleeding image of poor Lavinia. While Marcus laments her state, the Ovidian analogy is reinforced through the reference to another story of mutilation from the *Metamorphoses* (6.412–676), that of Philomel, raped and mutilated by Tereus. Tereus himself was a king of Thrace, and therefore his inbred cruelty was explicable. All these classical inferences can be made during

Marcus's lament evoked by images and allusions suggesting Thracian barbarity. When Marcus actually pronounces the name *Thracian,* with reference to Orpheus, however, the atmosphere is one of peace and beautiful serenity induced by the heavenly harmony of music. In an inciting game of theatrical imagination, Marcus suggests that even the cruelty of the monster Tereus would have been appeased: "He would have dropped his knife and fell asleep, / As Cerberus at the Thracian poet's feet" (2.4.50–1). Shakespeare's theater has a way of showing us two different dimensions of the same geography. One facet is deeply rooted in the audience's expectations (like the preconception that the Thracians were a cruel nation), and the other is the actual image of violence on the stage, where Lavinia's mutilated body speaks in dumb expression. The collision between what people know and what they see makes this scene tell us more than it actually does in so many words.

The reference to savage Eastern European tribes and countries in *Titus Andronicus* is closely connected with the idea of revenge and cruelty. In the same scene in which Demetrius refrains even from comparing the barbarous Scythians with "ambitious Rome" (1.1.132), he alludes to another story of revenge involving an allegedly cruel Thracian king. Encouraging Chiron and his mother to wait for the right moment to avenge the death of Alarbus, Demetrius invokes "The selfsame gods that armed the Queen of Troy / With opportunity of sharp revenge / Upon the Thracian tyrant in his tent" (1.1.136–38). The classical story refers to Hecuba, the queen of Troy. According to Euripides, in order to save Polydorus, her youngest son, from the Greeks, Hecuba sent him to Polymnestor, king of Thrace. After the sack of Troy, she was allotted to Odysseus, who, on his way home, stopped at Thrace. Learning there that Polymnestor had murdered Polydorus, Hecuba, in revenge, blinded the king and killed his children. Here again the classical story foreshadows terrible scenes of mutilation and revenge on the children for the sins of the fathers, as well as the image of a motherly queen who turns into a harpy to avenge her son's death. In all cases, Thrace is present as a locus where such abominable acts are likely to happen, a vindictive world of unforgiving people. However, as in many Shakespearean plays, the spatial analogy invokes a double reference: to the world of the play, foreshadowing abominable acts, and a potential dimension of English behavior, since revenge and evisceration appeared to play an important role in local religious and political warfare.

Another classical suggestion about a Thracian king that involves murder and betrayal is in *3 Henry VI* (4.2.6.29). In this dramatic situation, Warwick suggests a way to capture King Edward and he concocts a story of treachery and possible murder, though he denies having such thoughts, which he imparts to Clarence and Somerset. Using a classical allusion, Warwick describes how they would surprise Edward in his tent, just as Ulysses and Diomedes did when they stole "the Thracian fatal steeds" (4.2.21). The reference is to Rhesus, a Thracian ally of the Trojans; his famous white horses were carried off by Ulysses and Diomedes, and he himself was slain in his sleep by Diomedes. The story is related in Homer's *Ilyad* (10.435) and Virgil's *Aeneid* (1.469). Rhesus is chiefly remembered because he traveled from Thrace to defend Troy with great pomp and circumstance, with a chariot drawn by splendid white horses, but died on the night of his arrival, without ever engaging in battle. His fate is considered as exemplary for excessive self-confidence and ambition. In *3 Henry VI,* the allusion to Rhesus plays on both the royal self-assurance and belief in invincibility from the part of Edward, and mainly on the idea of brotherly betrayal and murder. Though the project succeeds, in the sense that Warwick, George, Oxford, and Somerset capture the king, there is no murder involved initially (Edward is imprisoned at the home of the archbishop of York). The prospect of murder and betrayal suggested by the classical allusion remains, however, embedded in the plot, foreshadowing subsequent slaughter. All these notions were made possible through the image of terror and murder that the mere mention of the word *Thracian* would summon in the audiences.

Shakespeare's precious Plutarch, in Thomas North's translation of *The Lives of the Noble Grecians and Romans,*[60] does not write about the distant places around the Euxine Sea and the Ister; nor does he dwell on stories of barbarity and distress. The moralizing purpose of this translated work, which was intended to offer examples of Greek or Roman excellence, precluded many repulsive allusions or narratives of offensive facts. The emblem on the title page of this edition presents an anchor originating in the clouds, from the wisdom of the gods, and encircled by two olive branches, the symbol of peace. The caption announces that this is "Anchora Spei," the anchor of hope. In this instance of Elizabethan iconography, good expectation can only derive from the wisdom of gods and in good aspiration for peace. In the initial chapter "Theseus," however, Plutarch begins his argument with a reference to the country of Scythia, an ancient distant land, barren and inhospitable: "Like as the historiographers which do set forth the description of the earth in figure . . . are wont to place in the lowermost part of their mappes, the farre distant regions unknowne unto them, and to marke in the margent such like notes and reasons as these: beyond these countreyes are nothing but deepe drye sands without water, full of foule ill favoured venimous beasts, or much mudde unnavigable, or SCYTHIA forsaken for cold, or else the sea frozen with Ise. Euen so in this my historie, I could speake of strange things and more ancient, and further off from mens memorie. But . . ." (sig. A). In this passage, Plutarch dismisses other historiographers' habitual practice of insisting on the description of strange and wonderful things and exposes his serious method of comparison, which had proved to be more reliable and closer to truth. However, in discarding the other historiographers' method, Plutarch discloses an important dimension of ancient geographical and historical texts.

Writing of strange episodes and peoples was meant to excite the reader's *curiosity*. The geographers of the past used this method of leaving unexpected blanks in their narratives, because of the alleged incomplete information about the places, as a form of keeping their readers interested. By declaring the narrative a compendium of marvelous stories, they meant to incite the imagination and develop a certain propensity for fictions. Although Plutarch proposes a more sober method of approach, which would provide good moral instruction, he acknowledges the "sensational" formula as part of the common stock of ancient material relating information about distant places. The rarity and remoteness of the locations described make possible a perception of alien races as primarily significant—even rhetorical. Readers are confronted with an ontological order that lies at the border between the symbolic and the actual. Strange and unbelievable beings and nations are conceived to exist only for the uses to which others can put them. In this sense, narratives of wonders and extraneous spaces and people can have a certain truth value. Solinus clearly explicates that he wants to attract his readers and incite their imagination. With Shakespeare's theater, however, matters are not so certain and definitive. When extant, his references to alien places such as Colchis, Thracia, Scythia, the Pontic Sea, and the people inhabiting those spaces are used to reinforce, subvert, diminish, or anticipate the expressiveness of the representation on stage.

Plutarch seldom refers to scenes of barbarity connected to Eastern European nations in the region of the Black Sea, but he takes over the general idea common to the ancients that these regions were inhabited by brutal and barbarous people. In the *Life of Pericles,* Plutarch writes about the relations of the Athenian governor to the populations inhabiting the eastern coast of the Pontus Euxinus, especially the Greek colonies of Histria, Tomis, and Kallatis, which attained a maximum of development in the Athenian golden period. Plutarch propagates the image of Athenian civilizing power over the barbarous nations inhabiting these places and records a patronizing attitude manifested by the more advanced Athenians toward the backward nations they wanted to control: "And afterwardes, going with a great navie marvelous well appointed unto the realms PONTUS, he [Pericles] dyd there gently use and intreate the cities of GREECE, and graunted them all that they required of him: making the barbarous people inhabiting thereabouts to know the great force and power of the ATHENIANS". . . .[61] Some of Shakespeare's contemporaries learned from these texts that the peoples inhabiting the Euxine Sea were barbarous and integrally impervious to the Athenians' civilizing efforts. However, these barbarians lived and traded in the Black Sea area, in the Greek colonies of Miletus, and the cultured Greeks needed them for commerce because they supplied most of the ancient world's need of grain, honey, wax, and other staple goods.

An interesting reference to the Euxine Sea area by Plutarch, which could have some bearing on Shakespeare, is in the *Life of Theseus,* where the historiographer cites other writers concerning the Greek hero's expedition in the land of the Amazons: "Touching the voyage he made by the sea Major, Philochorus & some other holde opinion that he went thither with Hercules against the AMAZONES: and that to honour his valiantes, Hercules gave him ANTIOPA the AMAZONE"[62] The Amazons were alleged by Herodotus (4.110) to have dwelled in Scythia, in the southern and northern parts of the Black Sea, and the common classical inference about them is that they were a race of female warriors. It is interesting to note that the source passage from North's translation of Plutarch, quoted in the Arden edition of *A Midsummer Night's Dream,* does not refer to the Black Sea as the "Euxine Sea," but as "the sea Major."[63] Another significant source for Shakespeare's representation of the Amazons in the *Dream,* Chaucer's *Knight's Tale,* however, presents the queen

"Ipolita" this time, not Antiope as in Plutarch, as originating from "Cythea,"[64] the country of Scythia in the Black Sea area.

Whatever the name of the queen of Amazons, the origin of this race of warrior women was certain to have been in the region of the Black Sea, where people were notorious for their fierceness and resilience. In Shakespeare, we have various theatrical situations in which the reference to the ancient race of the Amazons is used to impart diversified meanings, according to the specific performative purpose of a certain scene. In the history plays, the parallel with the Amazons appears to designate a special breed of women with warlike inclinations, such as Queen Margaret in *3 Henry VI* and La Pucelle in *1 Henry VI*. In the case of Queen Margaret, only her enemies find it suitable to refer to her as a warlike woman. The bereaved duke of York calls her deprecatingly "She-wolf of France" and "Amazonian trull" (*3 Henry VI,* 1.4.112, 115), appending to her a double metaphor involving cruelty toward her enemies and dubious morality. In a ritualized image of horror, the audiences see a disgraced duke of York, standing on a molehill in a mock-elevated position of power and wearing a paper crown, after Queen Margaret had subjected him to intense humiliation. Playing a pretended game of consideration and liberty, the jubilant queen lets him speak in his defense. After having compared her to a merciless Amazon, York's speech invokes a particular geography of savageness, where images of wolves, Hyrcanian[65] tigers, and fierce women are related to the far northern regions of the "septentrion" and the "antipodes" (1.4.112–69).

Pomponius Mela's description of the Caspian Sea or the Hyrcanian Sea region particularly dwells on the wild animals of this area. In striking cinematic terms, Mela writes: "The forests also bear other fierce animals, but they even bear tigers—Hyrcanian ones, to be sure—a savage breed of wild animal so swift that they easily, and typically, track a mountain rider, even on passing at a distance."[66] Expectations of savageness and swift cruel actions are connected with the image of Hyrcania, the land of Amazons, and finally with Queen Margaret, as a visible embodiment of these beasts and fierce women. Moreover, York calls Margaret more inhuman than cannibals or Hyrcanian tigers (1.4.156) because she could dip her handkerchief in a son's blood and give it to the grieving father. For that reason, the ancient stories about savage places and peoples are not so dissimilar to what the audiences actually see on stage, a bloody cloth and a bloody queen, even more repugnant than the foreign past stories because she is there, in front of them, on the materiality of the stage. Shakespeare's imaginative itinerary of violence seems to draw on ancient narratives of wonder, such as Mela's or Solinus's reports of fierce beasts in far regions of the Black and Caspian Seas area, but these images enhance the metaphor on stage. The audiences' curiosity and revulsion are stimulated, and the intense image of horror in front of their eyes is rendered more vivid through the invocation of these remote places and peoples.

The next reference to Queen Margaret as an Amazon in *3 Henry VI* is made ironically, when the tables are turned, and the duke of York's son is now King Edward IV. On reports of the belligerent queen's intended war against him, with an army from France, King Edward mocks Margaret's attempt at retaliation. He tries to diminish the importance of war with the former queen by using the reference to the ancient race of warlike women frivolously: "Belike she minds to play the Amazon" (4.1.104). The contemptuous remark is contrasted to York's previous reference to Margaret as a warlike and cruel Amazon, thus deflating the queen's ambition to avenge her son's death. However, the king decides to go to war against the French army, disregarding Queen Margaret's threat. In both instances in *3 Henry VI,* when characters refer to the Amazons living in the remote parts of the Black Sea, the images call out war, destruction, and foreign cruelty, in this case in connection to the female population of a faraway barbaric nation. The technique of paradoxical contrast helps Shakespeare use the classical allusion to the Amazons with double signification: one is the expected notion of a barbaric race of cruel women, who used to live in the Black Sea area, and another is the image of the woman warrior in the ironic mode. The tongue-in-cheek allusion, as the references to the Amazons borrowed from the classical texts, plays on the audiences' assumptions about the nation of warrior women supposedly located in a faraway region. Whatever the case, the classical hint complements what the audience sees on stage in the person of Queen Margaret, a cruel and ambitious woman, spurred by thoughts of revenge, but who is finally defeated.

Concerning the reference to Joan la Pucelle, another bellicose French woman, as an Amazon in *1 Henry VI,* scene 1.3 dramatizes a similar geography of violence, but with a different purpose. In this scene of the siege of Orléans, the French army is beaten back by the English with great loss. By contrast to what is being reported about the defeat in the battle offstage, the Dauphin and his party invoke images of the biblical warriors Samson and Goliath, noted for their strength. Amid this atmosphere of glory and defeat, the Bastard introduces La Pucelle. Joan performs the quasi-miraculous recognition of the true king and avoids the intended trap laid out through the identity shift between the Dauphin and René, meant to test her authenticity. The next test is, as in the chivalric contests, the test of war, in which the woman warrior defeats the Dauphin. The conquered Dauphin creates an overstated image of La Pucelle, who incarnates the violence invoked by the injunction "Thou art an Amazon!" (1.3.84), associated to the image of the self-righteous biblical Deborah. Certainly, actors and directors may choose to play this scene and the included reference to the warlike nation of wild women in an ironic note. Whatever the case, however, the physical picture of a violent foreign female race is drawn in every detail, while we are left with uncertain feelings about the veracity of each statement. Hyperbolic images drawing on a variety of classical, Christian, and Islam myths (St. Martin, Caesar's fortune, Muhammad's inspiration, St. Helena and Emperor Constantine, St. Philip, Venus) are agglomerated in just a few lines to raise questions about the truth of Joan's and Charles's overstatements.

Sarcastic undertones concerning the warlike Amazons can be found in many Shakespearean allusions to the ancient female warriors inhabiting the Black Sea area. In *Timon of Athens,* the masque of ladies as Amazons presented at Timon's liberal banquet (1.2.124) is anything but violent. The women dance and play the lute hieratically. The masque is far from inciting harsh images of brutality, and Apemantus calls the ladies' performance "a sweep of vanity" (1.2.124). The scene of these amiable women entertaining a party of men, in a play notably devoid of female characters, shows on stage a corporeal theatrical antithesis, in total contrast with what the audiences had in mind in respect to the Amazons from classical texts. Similarly, in a play concerned with external and internal conflicts and Roman military commotion such as *Coriolanus,* reference to Amazons appears as a testimonial picture. In praising the courage in battle of sixteen-year-old Martius Caius Coriolanus, the general Cominius uses the analogy of the pugnacious youth's "Amazonian chin" (2.2.87), that is, his beardless face, like a female's, as a synecdoche for bravery in youth, opposed to experience in battle. The physical suggestion of the action summoning forth images of war in this scene is achieved in many forms. Besides Martius's name (derived from the god of war Mars), or the narrator himself, who is a

Roman general (probably dressed in warlike regalia), the combative suggestion results from the analogy with the Amazons from Scythia.

The most incompatible figure of Amazon in Shakespeare as compared to the classical myth, however, is the gracious and harmless Hippolyta in *A Midsummer Night's Dream.* The only poor vestige recalling the queen's native untamed distant places of ignominious reputation, where women were famed for their skills in the arts of hunting and war, remains her delight in the noise of the hounds, which Hippolyta perceives as sweet music (4.1.115ff.). This benign Hippolyta is more inclined to believe the stories emerging out of the lovers' fantasies (5.1.23–27) than the skeptical Theseus is. Like the ancient inventors of fancy tales, the queen of Amazons is one who can see the poetic value of narratives of strange and wonderful things. They may transfigure reality to the point that the strangeness of the imagined story becomes irrelevant, while the result of the narrative, the wonder it produces, acquires a special and more constant value than plain truth. Therefore, for Shakespeare, the exact location and customs of the Amazons were less pertinent than the stories produced about them. The geographic and ethnic exactitude becomes volatile, and the more or less appropriate and associated significance is attached to the exotic narrative of wonder. The more extraneous and bizarre the facts, the better they are received by audiences. These are the kind of stories that Shakespeare liked to show his audiences, while they constructed their own conjectures on the places alluded to in the plays.

Jeanne Addison Roberts points out the special cultural correlation induced by the mental constructs of savageness and barbarity in the early modern period. Among the recurring female and male archetypes associated with the idea of the wild originating in outlandish settings, Addison Roberts mentions the African continent as a privileged locus for the representation of such clichés: "The Wild in Shakespeare is associated with Amazons, Scythians, cannibals, and undomesticated animals. Unexplored continents provide mental images of untamed Wilds. . . . In Shakespeare, the imagined Africa is linked with all varieties of the Wild—barbarian, female, and animal."[67] The large number of examples of characters, situations, and metaphorical affiliations relating the African continent to the image of wildness can support such an argument consistently. However, my impression is that the dialectical nature of the theatrical situation allows for no immediate assumption regarding one real place or another as the source or direct reference for the image of the wild in the period. Areas of Eastern Europe and the shores of the Black Sea were as much, or probably more, unexplored in ancient times than the northern African continent, for instance. The wild Scythians, the Hyrcanian tigers, the Amazons, the Cimmerians, the recalcitrant Goths, the wild Thracian Menades, all these fictional-historical creations, were particularly located in the easternmost parts of Europe and in western Asia, especially in the Black Sea area.

Classical narratives of wonder placed the dangerous regions populated by fierce people and ferocious animals at the margins of the civilization borders provided by the Roman Empire. Everything that lay beyond that volatile perimeter was unknown territory and labeled as "elsewhere," outside the domesticated norm. Shakespeare's drama exploits the spatial functionality of these cultural stereotypes of classical origin in a dialogical manner. While playing old and new descriptive conjectures about distant places one against the other, this form of theater questions them consistently, by *showing* the audience that what other people *tell* about these distant locations may not always be true. In addition, he sets these foreign places in contrast with his contemporary England. This alliance between telling and viewing makes the ancient geography represented on stage become more visible and vocal, in many conflicting but convincing ways. The ambivalent mode of Shakespeare's balancing the audience's cognitive assumptions among knowing, showing, and telling has remained a fertile area to be exploited in many subsequent productions of the plays and is partly responsible for Shakespeare's popularity with later audiences on all meridians.

In mapping out the theatrical conditions that afforded the presentation of one or another Shakespearean classical allusion suggesting Eastern European spaces, I have made an incomplete inventory of the references to ancient myth and places of Eastern Europe described by ancient writers that found their way into the plays. The relation of strange historic locations from the area of the Black Sea, the Carpathians, and the Danube to modern Romania is rather vague. The geographical coordinates of the discourses about these places can only determine some relevance to my point. However, it is possible to conclude that the general inferences Shakespeare's audiences could make in relation to these places were connected with the idea of marginality and barbarity. Peoples living at the periphery of the ancients' "civilized" world were expected to be strange and unpredictable, while the atrocities they were reported to have committed seemed to be notorious. Shakespeare's contemporaries had only the reports of others about these places, because very few had ventured to see these locations themselves. However, the playwright found a very direct and corporeal way of sending subliminal theatrical messages that were used either to reinforce or to subvert these assumptions. In other instances, these stereotypes about alien ferocity were used as effective detonators of emotions, because Shakespeare found ways of directing his own plays through the communication of scenes where imagery related to distant places and people had great suggestive force.

The next station in my excursion tracing the coordinates of a Shakespearean geography focusing on classical accounts about Eastern European spaces concerns the special world of the Shakespearean plays drawing on the classics. It would be too much to say that Shakespeare, as had many of his contemporary Elizabethans and Jacobeans, had any special interest in the area of Eastern Europe formerly named Dacia. The trajectory of the heroes in the Roman and Greek plays progressed far from these places, in the more familiar basin of the Mediterranean, the Roman *mare nostrum.* With the few exceptions of passing references and allusions to Eastern European spaces connected to mythology, there can be no justified demand or attempt at demonstrating the existence of a consistent Shakespearean geography that would include at least some of these locations. However, I will try to indicate a special *method* visible in Shakespeare's classical plays, which has a lot in common with Elizabethan translations of the classical reports of wonders supposed to have existed in faraway places.

2

Stage Maps of the Roman Empire: *Julius Caesar* and *Antony and Cleopatra*

I HAVE SHOWN HOW PLUTARCH DISMISSED THE PRACTICE OF CERTAIN ancient historiographers and geographers, who insisted on the fabulous and extraordinary when they reported about distant places, in the hope of attracting the readers and stimulating their imaginativeness. Plutarch[1] suggests a more compact method of comparison, which is intended to parallel important actions and events in the lives of famous people in ancient times, with the purpose of instructing the readers in the good ways of old. Shakespeare thought it profitable to combine those two methods in his plays centered on the classical world. Thus, in drawing the special cartographic conventional lines in each play, we distinguish at least one of the two methods of describing foreign places, or a combination of both. We may look at each play in its individual theatricality, without overlooking, however, the fact that the events the classical plays described were set in an ancient world that the audiences perceived as an anthology of familiar texts. How could an inventive man of theater play on his audience's expectations, and at the same time avoid the uniformity and linearity of the other texts about the ancient world available to them? Probably, he would do it by inventing a totally different method of approach, linked with exploiting the intrinsic materiality of the theatrical space.

When he writes about the role of Plutarch in *Julius Caesar,* David Daniell notices "a plasticity of dramatic potential"[2] in the structure of the *Lives.* The editor of the New Arden *Julius Caesar* points out that the evidence from the references down the ages is that people did not read Plutarch only for the history of Rome, but for the men and women so alive within his pages.[3] Plutarch's vigorous comparative method finds dramatic shape in *Julius Caesar,* because people went to the theater to see what Master Shakespeare did with the ancient writers with whom they were so familiar. They watched how the geography of Caesar's story pointed to the areas of the Roman Empire that had certain significance for the ancient world in those times. The play's active performativity derives from, among other things, the vigorous visualization and material manifestation of imperial geography on stage. Most images are theatrical representations of power through the illustration of the extent of the Roman Empire, and they are inherent in the play's compelling rhetoric. Examining the self-referential discourses of power emanating from Elizabethan geographers and cartographers, in principal the influential John Dee, Lesley B. Cormack[4] argues that these texts originated a complex set of attitudes and assumptions promoting the image of England as the dominant naval power in the early modern world. Likewise, the associations with the Roman Empire extending its power over the Mediterranean basin patronized an imperial theme that was very dear to Elizabeth and her subjects.

In strong figurative language, Cassius wants to suggest to Brutus the magnitude of territorial power in the empire. To this purpose, he creates a hyperbolic picture of Caesar, seen to "bestride the narrow world / Like a colossus" (1.2.135). Cassius's sketch is at once imaginative and material, because it visualizes the aggrandized image of an all-powerful Caesar encompassing the Roman Empire, like the ancient bronze statue of Apollo at Rhodes, which was known to have straddled the harbor. By comparison, all those who walked under its legs were small and insignificant. This visual image of Caesar as a colossus and of all his subjects as small by contrast is meant to inflame Brutus's rebellious spirit and win him to the conspirators, but the analogy contains its paradoxical counterpart. The visible icon of little people passing between the huge legs of the colossus straddling the empire evokes the conquerors' progress through the triumphal arch. It was well known that Caesar had passed many times under the solemn monument celebrating the conquerors' victory, and people wondered at the relativity of all representations of terrestrial grandeur and ambition. If the actor playing Cassius chose actually to make the gesture of bestriding two points of elevation on the stage, the image was even more convincing. We see how the potential of Shakespeare's figurative geography reached its highest manifestation only when the play was being performed. Only then did an abstract foreign territory, in this case the Colossus of Rhodes, figured on a map or a woodcut or described by a geographer's narrative, reach an efficient materialization.

In Antony's oration over Caesar's dead body, Shakespeare makes visible the map representing the extension of the Roman Empire through the metaphor of Caesar's mantle (3.2.168–87). Emphasizing the cinematic power of this scene, Bill Delaney suggests that while the original staging of Mark Antony's funeral oration precluded the audience from seeing Julius Caesar's mutilated body, Shakespeare achieves an even stronger visual effect with the display of his torn, bloody mantle.[5] Moreover, when he performs the dramatic gesture of spreading Caesar's mantle over his body like a map, Antony mentions its symbolic value: the general had put it on when he overcame the Nervi, a northern race of warriors from the family of the Belgae. Antony's funeral oration and the display of Caesar's mantle in front of the populace draw entirely on Plutarch.[6] The impressive gesture is part of the paraphernalia of rhetorical persuasion that Antony uses ingeniously. However, this theatrical movement draws the entire Roman Empire onto the stage, causing it to be spread like a map covering Caesar's body. The enumeration of the wounds inflicted by each conspirator makes visible to the people what Antony wants to imply, namely, that those were just as many wounds caused to the Roman Empire. Such theatrical devices play out for the audiences a physical geography of a world in which domination and authority count absolutely but can be destroyed eventually.

In Shakespeare's dramatic materialization of autarchic worldly power in *Julius Caesar,* the region north and south of the Danube had no meaning for the Romans because at that time these regions were not yet part of their empire. In the first century B.C., the Dacian king Burebista united all the Gaeto-Dacian tribes under his rule and formed a powerful political body, with the capital at Sarmizegetusa. Julius Caesar intended to start a campaign against this powerful king of the Dacians, but his death prevented it. In the same year recording Caesar's murder in Rome, the Dacian king Burebista was the victim of a conspiracy plotted by his confidants. Because of the lack of many written records[7] about these events happening in Dacia, almost contemporaneously with Caesar's murder in Rome, this foreign king's death was mentioned casually in ancient texts as the result of an obscure political intrigue beyond the margins of the Roman Empire. Caesar's death, however, achieved universal proportions because it was multiplied, and its importance magnified, through various texts. This paratextuality of certain events in history was the reason for the construction of many conventionalized ideas in the Western world. One of these texts reproducing Caesar's ignominious murder is the Shakespearean theatrical version, which reverberates "in accents yet unknown" an ancient story of betrayal and assassination that was seen to have shattered the solidity of the Roman world. However, Shakespeare makes us see this historic event differently, by persuading us to consider the ambivalence of our conventional mental constructs about power.

Discussing the rhetorical fabrication of the Roman *imago mundi,* John Gillies notices that it was as much a disposition of eloquence as of factual geography. Rome was the center of the discursive world, and the Greek geographical ideas were used to embellish and transform a potent Roman geographical narrative. Such texts tended to represent the superiority of Rome to the peoples living in distant lands by attributing to the edges of the Roman world "a powerful physical presence."[8] From Gillies's analysis of Vico's concept of geography as an articulation of human perspective, I retain the idea of the monumental physicality concerning the Latin references to places external to the Roman domination. The theater can express this notion of physicality of the distant regions much more effectively than the Latin geographical texts ever could. In order to circumscribe the superiority of the Roman Empire's definition of *orbis terrarum,* world of nations, Latin geographers and historiographers extended their discourse to the limits of the all-powerful empire and left the more distant regions unexplained, or said to be inhabited by monsters. Shakespeare's theater dramatizes the centrality of the Roman Empire in the plays drawing on Plutarch in an operative and corporeal manner. The staged plays realize the figurative presentation of a marginal geography, in which distant regions unaffected by the Roman influence were seen as places of sedition, barbarity, or immorality, or merely devoid of any interest.

In *Antony and Cleopatra,* the play's polarity and parallelism of the two worlds, East and West, Egypt and Rome, have been a subject of intense critical discussion. In a chapter entitled "The Representation of Egypt and Shakespeare's *Antony and Cleopatra,*" John Michael Archer traces "the relation between racial and sexual constructions during the period by reading Shakespeare's text in relation to a number of historical, geographical, and travel writings that became available roughly within a century of its publication."[9] Archer discovers sexual transgression trumped up by a "narrative of degeneration" that "leaves the text open to appropriation by the developing radical and ultimately imperial system of European modernity."[10] It is not surprising to find subversion in such texts, though my contention is that the play is inscribed in a narrative equation of marginality of such foreign lands as Egypt, as opposed to the centrality of, in this case, Rome. However, not even this opposition is clearly structured in Shakespeare, and it remains to be defined in terms of stage practices. In this sense, it is significant to mention Geraldo de Sousa's interesting account of the way habitat, gender, and text ultimately unsettle European narratives of degeneration in Egypt.[11] I see Shakespeare's representation of Egypt as inscribed within a triangulation perspective that includes North Africa, Rome, and Jacobean England, which can never have a definitive interpretation. It is part of a process by which early modern writers developed what Emily Bartels calls "Europe's self-image and self-authorization."[12] The problem is that the early modern notion of Europe would more readily contain ancient North Africa and even the New World within its bounds, rather than its eastern barbaric regions.

Antony and Cleopatra has an active visual component, and the shifting images suggesting various places have the persuasion of cartography. In the introduction to the New Arden edition of the play, John Wilders cites Bradley and Chambers about the two critics' concern with the play's difficulty in being performed because of its frequent shifts of locale.[13] Despite his formidable knowledge of Elizabethan playhouses, Chambers questioned the performativity of a play whose action swings so frequently from Rome to Misenium, Athens, Actium, Syria, to Egypt, with many further subdivisions in the Egyptian scenes. The spatial problem detected by directors and critics[14] might find an elucidation if we think of the method of ancient geographers, mainly visible in Pliny and Pomponius Mela. They used to start in the west of the Mediterranean (usually the rock of Gibraltar) and move in a clockwise direction around the basin of this well-known sea, with occasional incursions into the external regions farther inland. Shakespeare's play starts and ends in Alexandria, but along the course of the action, the audiences travel clockwise around the Mediterranean, and they see significant shifts of locale that might fall into interesting patterns. The order underlying the action seems to replicate the course of ancient geographical accounts of spaces around the Mediterranean, except that everything originates and ends in Alexandria, instead of starting from the west, as did classical geographers. We see a pendulum movement between Egypt and Rome, east and west, graphically depicting Plutarch's comparative method. However, the most frequent shifts of locale concentrate on the eastern side of the Roman Empire, where extreme events happen, as in the wonder narratives of the classics.

Analyzing the social, political, and relational connotations of the ancient Roman Empire for Elizabethan and Jacobean audiences, David Bevington states that the images of Augustus Caesar propagated in the Renaissance came down in two contrasting traditions. One was of Caesar's positive stable rule after the death of Antony and Cleopatra, and another was that of a Machiavellian personality, ready to use all means in the pursuit of power.[15] According to the former view, the Roman Empire was a potential model for Tudor and Stuart rule in England. The play's recurrent locality is primarily connected with those views promoting the extended Roman Empire as a topographic model of ancient civilization. Especially in acts 2 and 3, the frequent shifts of locale confer dramatic shape to an ancient empire that would have been otherwise less visible. The compression of events and spaces contributes to the intensification of this geographic image. In *Antony and Cleopatra,* Shakespeare proposes a theatrical geography of the Roman Empire in which all the significant points are placed on an imaginary condensed map. Alexandria and Rome are the landmarks of the play's imaginative territory. However, the action moves from Sicily (2.1) to Rome (2.2, 2.3, and 2.4), from Alexandria (2.5) to Misenium (2.6) in the Bay of Naples. The easternmost border of the Roman Empire is marked through the action moving to Syria (3.1), with mentions within the text of farther inland territories conquered by the Romans, such as Parthia, Media, and Mesopotamia. This shifting movement suggests potential political instability.

This diverse and material geography in *Antony and Cleopatra* does not develop only through direct tangible action on the stage, but also by *reports* about places belonging to the Roman Empire. Much of the ambivalence of the play derives from the various reports that messengers deliver from one place to another, just like in the ancient geographical narratives, where authors collected their information about distant places from other people's reports. In Rome (2.2), Enobarbus reports of the place Cleopatra first met Antony on the river Cydnus (2.2.196–97). This is a spot in Cilicia, in the southwest of what is now Turkey. While in Rome (3.6), Caesar reports his version of the division of the Eastern Empire by Antony; he made Cleopatra "absolute Queen" (3.6.11) of lower Syria, Cyprus, and Lydia. According to Caesar's account, Antony gave his sons by her Great Media, Parthia, Armenia, Syria, Cilicia, and Phoenicia (3.6.1ff.). Caesar's enumeration of these places from the eastern side of the empire gives an imaginative physical representation of vast territories. The audiences are now able to visualize, on the relatively barren stage, many distant eastern places that, in their geographical catalogue, suggested images of strangeness. For Caesar, this inventory of places is only a manipulation of discourse to justify his motives for turning against Antony, which Shakespeare takes from Plutarch.[16]

In the same scene 3.6, Caesar explains to Octavia how Antony has called up to his help all the eastern kings of the empire (3.6. 70–77). The roll call of Middle Eastern monarchs is impressive, and it includes "the Thracian king Adallas" (3.6.72). According to Walter Cohen, "These lists produce both quantitative and ideological effects in part through their power as sheer sound. In a theater short of scenery, evocative language must have helped deliver to the audience, in the etymological sense, what filming on location provides for the modern movie viewer."[17] In addition, in my view, these exotic Middle Eastern geographic names (*Lybia, Cappadocia, Paphlagonia, Arabia, Pont, Jewry, Comagene, Mede,* and *Lycaonia*) have a way of visualizing distant places about which Shakespeare's audiences were informed from the wonder narratives. In classical texts the presentation of such long listings was a common practice because the enumeration raised the readers' curiosity and drew attention on the passage being narrated. In Shakespeare, we might be tempted at first to think that the repetition is an unfortunate digression, but then we see it serves Octavius Caesar's purpose all too well: he visualizes for his sister the extent of the empire that Antony had signed off to Cleopatra, thus inciting her against both transgressors. To the audience, moreover, the geographic list gives an outlook of the magnitude and impressive power of the Roman Empire. In his dramatic version of physical geography, Shakespeare uses the reference to these distant places as so many jewels in the crown of the extraordinary reasons for which the world would be well won and well lost for Antony.

In *Antony and Cleopatra,* Shakespeare uses Plutarch's comparative method for the dramatization of an Eastern Egyptian space as opposed to Western Rome. In acts 2 and especially 3, which show such exuberant shifts of locale that make the audience's imagination roam to the farthest ends of the Roman Empire, Shakespeare adopts the method of the marvels narratives, which attribute to distant Eastern places incredibly fascinating qualities. In tracing this play's dramatic territory, he uses a method of description characteristic of the ancient geographers, to the effect that the order of the play's action encompasses the progression of the geographic narrative. Thus, the audiences are embarked on a voyage of discovery around the ancient Mediterranean basin, where each traveler can get a taste of love and romance while visualizing distant places. The theatrical physical status of Shakespeare's account of places in *Antony and Cleopatra* provides important graphic shortcuts to geographical knowledge for his Jacobean and later audiences. The process of integration, assimilation, and transformation of the classical sources into Shakespeare's Roman plays, therefore, is not restricted to the actual information derived from them. Since the theater permitted an effective visualization of distant spaces, Shakespeare borrowed the narrative *methods* from his classical predecessors, thus not simply giving his dramatic excursions vigor and materiality, but indirectly inviting the spectators to join him in an interesting journey.

The eclectic blend of geographical and cultural references taken from the classics, the frequent and contrasting shifts of locale, and the comparative or associative methods of description borrowed from the classical narratives show that Shakespeare's use of geographic material exists in conflicting territory. Whether this Shakespearean geography is materialized in setting, character, or allusion, it suggests overlapping orientations and disturbing cultural dimensions. Since geography was known to be the gazing eye of history, these pictorial representations of distant places played on the audiences' cultural assumptions, but they were manipulated as cultural contrasts and a way of mirroring local uncertainties. While Shakespeare was an operative user and generator of national cultural stereotypes and misrepresentations among the early modern audiences' perception of foreign spaces, he used the geographical and historical material borrowed from the classics in specific creative ways of the theatrical medium. Thus, he achieved what Peter Holland calls "the physicalization of nation onstage."[18] Geographic and cultural references, which for his audiences might have seemed disembodied cultural abstractions collated from the classical texts, become real places at the theater, as close to the real thing as the contemporary cartographic images were for some.

It is useful to look at Shakespeare's theatrical representations of distant geography drawn from the classical texts as prisms of refracting political and aesthetic changes in Elizabethan and Jacobean England. Since most classical texts reflected a world in permanent metamorphosis, the principle of change can be applicable to the early modern views about distant spaces. However, Shakespeare's contemporaries adopted many prefabricated ideas about foreign nations from the classical models. The abundance of journals, travel books, geographical texts, and cartographic materials in the early modern period entitled us to think that a totally new view about foreign regions of the earth was being fashioned. However, an attentive study of the Elizabethan and Jacobean texts about distant regions shows that they were eclectic and heavily influenced by classical material, according to the age's fashion. The following chapter shows how early modern texts, whether geographic, travel, or literary, were tainted with prejudice about Eastern European spaces. Shakespeare's theater played on these presuppositions in amazing ways, creating a new relation between the exotic and the domestic. While the plays seemed to posit increasing difference as the distance from England grew, just as his audiences had been trained to expect, we can discern a pattern of conflict combined with assimilation. The farther a place was located in real geography, or in geography and time (as in the classical texts reports), the more appropriate it became for comparisons with potential dimensions of English behavior. Though exotic and often unknown, these places became England.

3

Early Modern Chorographies of Eastern European Regions

THE ENGLISH WORD *CHOROGRAPHY* TAKES ITS MEANING FROM ITS GREEK origin, just as its Latin form, *chorographia,* did for the Romans. In Greek technical literature *khôrographia* typically designates a written description (*graphê*) covering a district or region (*khôros*), perhaps a country, but in any case more than one individual place. *Cosmographia* is a Latinized transliteration of a Greek technical term. A *kosmographia* is a written description (*graphê*) of the world as a whole or of the entire universe (*kosmos*). Greek *kosmos,* as does Latin *mundus,* emphasizes the orderliness and arrangement either of the universe or of the whole Earth. Therefore, *kosmographia* is an appropriate characterization either for a work dealing with the full implications of the Earth's sphericity, or for a study of the Earth's geography in relation to a system of latitude and longitude based on the position of the stars. A *topographia,* in contrast, is a description limited to a single place (*topos*), while in theory *geôgraphia* would have described the whole Earth (*gê*). By genre then, a chorography falls nominally between the two theoretical poles of topography and geography. In reductive terms, a topography is less inclusive, and a geography more inclusive, than a chorography. Considering the early modern texts related to these topics, however, the standard of analysis is often subjective and can be elusive. Readers in the sixteenth and seventeenth centuries had at their disposal a large number of translations from the classical authors describing the parts of the known world. In addition, they could consult a large number of texts digesting for them the basic considerations of ancient and later writers or travelers concerning the regions of the Earth. The early modern assimilation of earlier advances recorded in the domain of geography led to the unprecedented formation of an eclectic accumulation of facts and knowledge about the world. Though issued with the claim to a certain method, these collated texts mainly reconsidered and refurbished the ancients' findings and postulations in geographical science.

In a study examining the ideas that rendered both body and space visible and represented in early modern culture, Caterina Albano exemplifies the analogy between microcosm and macrocosm by referring to an illustration from the 1524 *Cosmographia* by the French cosmographer Pierre Apian.[1] Here, a globe symbolizes geography and is compared to the art of painting, shown as the picture of a human head, while the image of the city appears as the drawing of a single eye and a single ear. In this symbolic illustration, geography is the image of the general and chorography represents a particular place. Both visual representations, however, intersect with the anatomized image of the human body. In the theater, we find a similarly unique concurrence of body and space on the stage, where the general visualization of vast territories or the particular representation of social interaction in the cities can be seen simultaneously. We can only speculate on what Elizabethan and Jacobean audiences saw on their stages and about their cultural assumptions regarding one geographical space or another. We can be relatively certain, however, that they had at their disposal a multitude of texts that described, explained, commented on, and digested facts about the regions of the world. This chapter attempts to reposition our assumptions about the referential significance of geographical and travel texts in the early modern period, with a view to illuminating the eclecticism and the fictive status of the texts available to Shakespeare's contemporaries.

The understanding of the complexity of texts that informed the early modern perception of Eastern European space helps us redraw categorical boundaries in what regards Shakespeare's theatrical representation of distant regions. Looking at early modern England's fascination with, and fantasies about, the area of Eastern Europe, this chapter employs this territory both as a physical and cultural space and as an idea, a site, which challenges boundaries between East and West. By exploring the variety of literary and nonliterary texts produced between the sixteenth and seventeenth centuries as sites of contention, it is easier to understand why these writers emphasized the then Ottoman Eastern Europe and Mediterranean as a place of negative connotation, where any manner of barbaric practice becomes possible. Matthew Dimmock explores the interaction between early modern England and the Ottoman world and observes a radical difference between the situations in the sixteenth and seventeenth centuries. First, there is the Elizabethan and earlier position, when England entered Reformation and started to look for new allies that would enable it to compete against a Catholic power bloc centering on Spain; then, the Anglo-Islamic link was more visible. Second, as Dimmock argues, a rigid definition of otherness started to apply to the Turk only when James I aimed at England's enrollment in a more general tendency toward Christian inclusiveness.[2] This kind of confrontational mythology about the Ottomans,[3] however, which existed in political reality, acquires in Shakespeare a special dimension. He plays on these anxieties but he frequently transposes received ideas and attitudes, and even emotions, into something disturbingly perceptive.

It is necessary to make a distinction between informative accounts about Eastern European locations in early modern texts, which were based on visits to these regions made by various English travelers, and the secondhand reports in the popular geography books, which were mainly inspired by the classical narratives about these lands. However, this differentiation becomes inoperable when speaking of the composite early modern texts. Though many writers produced splendid geographic narratives, adorned with maps and containing substantial information about Eastern European regions, oriented toward the explication of concrete facts about these places, they drew extensively on the classics. Even Ortelius's popular *Theatrum Orbis Terrarum* used references to place-names and nations of Eastern Europe borrowed from classical Latin authors. At least one copy of the 1595 Latin version of Ortelius's atlas existed in the territory that is now modern Romania in the sixteenth century. The atlas is now in the Romanian Academy Library, and one of its seventy maps is a description of Dacia entitled *Daciarum, Moesiarumque, Vetus Descriptio.* The problem is that *Dacia* (the geographical territory containing Transylvania, part of Moldova, and the area north of the Danube) and *Moesia* (the area south of the river and the region of Dobruja) are the *ancient* names of these regions, and many references in this map can be confusing.

Similarly, Bishop George Abbot's popular geographical description (1599),[4] which offers a methodical account of the early modern world of his time, refers to "Dacia" as the region north of the Danube, but he also writes about other countries using their Latin names and even the Latin descriptive phrases "De Hispania" (Aiij), "De Gallia" (Aiij), "De Italia" (Aiiij), "De Dania, Suezia, & Noruegia" (Aiv), "De Russia sive Muscovia" (Av), or "De Graecia" (Avi). These Latin chapter titles and many classical references within the text tell a lot about early modern habits and fashions. In the period when he wrote this text first published in 1599, Abbot had been licensed to teach at Balliol College, Oxford, and the *Briefe Description* was written presumably for the use of his students.[5] Its mixture of fact and comment on geography, politics, and trade, with additional updated information, may explain why it became the most popular of his works, being regularly reprinted, and enlarged in 1605 and 1617. However, it was not until 1634, after Abbot's death, that the book appeared under his name. The book's composition and enlargement indicate the broad intellectual tastes of its author. However, he wrote this book from the seclusion of his own home, with no firsthand experience, and he drew extensively on the classical authors. He relied on information drawing on his library of more than six thousand books, but he never actually visited the places he was writing about. In fact, most writers of geographical texts spiced their accounts with many classical allusions, according to the cultural fashion of the time.

Beginning with the end of the sixteenth century, travel became a fashion, and writing about foreign places was a predilect activity. There was a need of the increasingly cosmopolitan English society to find a reflection of its customs and ideas in descriptions of other lands and peoples. In a survey of early modern travel writing, William H. Sherman identifies a typology of travel writers: editors, pilgrims, errant knights, merchants, explorers, colonizers, captives and castaways, ambassadors, pirates, and scientists. Sherman documents the popularity of the emerging genre and observes its self-reflexive facet: "As travellers made contact with new regions and peoples, authors and editors put the world on paper for the new print marketplace at home: the number of new titles published (and old titles reprinted) during the early modern period suggests that there was a significant audience for travel writing, eager to hear news of the wider world and to reflect on England's place in it."[6] Reading about other peoples and places was thought to contribute to the education of individuals and expand their knowledge beyond the limited local horizon. Despite the obvious advantages of personal development, however, travel and writing about distant places were a challenge that not many Elizabethans and Jacobeans were ready to accept.

Most of the geographical locations, rhetorical forms, and political issues that we now associate with travel writing had appeared in one text or another by the end of the seventeenth century. As more and more English travelers reported about the foreign places they had visited, authors and their audiences learned to write and read the world in books with surprising speed and sophistication. In an early twentieth-century essay surveying early modern English travelers, Clare Howard observes a widespread custom among Elizabethan and Jacobean gentlemen of completing their education by travel, in order to learn modern languages and obtain information about modern history, which represented the newly acquired knowledge of human nature of which the sixteenth century was so proud. Travel became a part of what Howard calls "a widespread ideal of the English gentry."[7] The popular travel writing documents emerging from such travels, however, do not always offer accurate social, political, and economic constructions of Eastern European regions. Centuries of stories about the barbarity of these places had prepared the English to see fantastic creatures there, but also to regard the lands as spaces of opportunity and profit. At the same time, the difficulties of accessing these countries because of the Ottoman occupation exacerbated a sense of English anxiety about economic weakness and a recognition of tropes of civilization and barbarism in these relatively distant cultures.

There was an abundance of journals, maps, and geographical and historical descriptions of various countries, which constituted veritable cultural studies approaches of the regions under scrutiny. Several treatises discussed the advisability of travel as compared to staying at home, analyzing the pros and cons of firsthand knowledge of foreign places versus the examination of maps and geographical atlases, and each writer sought to recommend a personal solution to the reader. It is likely that Shakespeare's contemporaries, assaulted from all sides with repetitive narratives in the same eclectic vein, formed a prejudiced and often unrealistic view about various countries of Eastern Europe, especially the distant spaces in the Black Sea area. Such more or less systematic accounts of European spaces helped in creating a form of cultural communication in early modern Europe, but they were also misleading. Next to the well-organized and sensible facts about these countries, readers are fed subliminal fictional material borrowed from the classics. In their turn, most of the classical writers on whom early modern geographers drew took other people's reports for granted. In this way, we discover a series of concentric discourses pretending to instruct and revise information, but that inadvertently contributed to the crystallization of a deformed cultural mentality. However, the materiality and pragmatism shown by these writers in describing the world, just as the theater, define the boundaries between genders, nations, religions, philosophies, and artistic traditions, even in this form of incomplete and often erroneous description. Just as early modern travelers and cultural mediators dissolved the descriptive boundaries between nations and redefined identities even in the act of transgressing them, these eclectic geographical texts on distant Eastern European regions acted as influential generators of prefabricated fictions.

Thomas Blundeville gives *A Briefe Description of Universal Mappes and Cardes, and of Their Use* (1589), in which he intends to familiarize his readers with the new system of geography that had become so popular in the period. The author is best known as a writer on equestrian subjects, but this work is of particular interest to historical geographers. Observing an increasing interest in people in looking at maps, Blundeville proposes "to instruct those that have not studied Geographie (without the knowledge whereof me thinkes that the necessarie reading of histories is halfe lame, and is neither so pleasant, nor so profitable as otherwise it would be)."[8] In the introductory chapter concerning the basic terms of cosmography, the author writes of the North and South Poles, the parallels and meridians, and the equator, which divides the Earth into the northern and southern latitudes. Blundeville admits that most of the early modern cartography derives from ancient geographical knowledge, namely, "those Cardes and mappes that are made according to the rules of Ptolemy" (sig. Cv), but points out the irregularity of the division into meridians and parallels, and the inconsistency of distances on these ancient maps. The "new" early modern geography proposed by Mercator and others, though derived from the ancients, took into consideration the correct geometrical distribution of the conventional lines, and the right distance between two points. The main concerns for these geographers were, according to Blundeville, to show exactly what parts of the world were known by the ancients and to display the new additions of modern geographic discoveries (sig. C–C3). All efforts of early modern cartographers were directed toward making new geographical information accessible and useful to their public, in a conventionalized and visible form.

The Latin origin of the word *map,* as presented by Blundeville, emphasizes the notion of visibility and material representation of a spatial expanse: "This word *Mappa* in Latin signifieth a Table cloth of lynen to cover a board: of the shape and likeness whereof universall tables, contayning the description of the earth, are commonly called Mappes. And first you have to understande, that every such Mappe is chiefly traced with y. sortes of lynes or circles, that is Meridians and parallels" (sig. B). By stating the etymology denoting a conventional geographic representation of the world, the author stresses the importance of the active visual component in the delineation of the map. Likewise, in dramatizing conventional images connected to distant places, the early modern theater utilizes a strong visual component, which is supplemented by the important factors of action and movement. If we recall the graphic image of unfolding Caesar's mantle representing the Roman Empire in *Julius Caesar,* we can see how the action of spreading the mantle in front of the audience can communicate important political and topographic messages. Directors or actors may choose between the alternative of laying the mantle over Caesar's body, like a tablecloth or *mappa,* or only displaying it frontally to the people and/or the audience. In both situations, audiences are confronted with a precise action that strongly recalls the spreading of a map to their minds.

John Gillies debates the issue of Shakespeare's appropriation of a "new" geography that was also firmly grounded in the ancients, in the conditions when the "theatre was cosmographic and, to an extent, geographic, in its conceptual character," considering the Globe Theater as a case in point.[9] In locating a number of Shakespearean plays and themes in the perspective of the new context of early modern geography, Gillies accounts for the roots of Shakespeare's geographic imagination of difference in the ancient poetic geography and in the hermeneutic model created by early modern cartography. In addition, as I see it, when we examine English stories of the past and the references to faraway spaces they include starting from these two coordinates, we can look at both how British national identity is being reconfigured through history and geography, and at the way in which history and geography are used as a resource in framing this articulation. In both cases, it is possible to identify a sense of tension that exists between center and periphery, especially when this core is England and the periphery refers to less known areas of Eastern Europe.

In classical writers' texts, which were so much revered and imitated by early modern authors in all areas of culture, Britain was at one allegedly uncivilized margin of the Roman Empire, while Eastern Europe and western Asia were at the other extremity. In Elizabethan times, when the sense of nationhood was increasingly present, the English wanted to think of themselves as central to European politics and culture and produced texts that would help their inscription in this order of things. Writing about "Postmodern Hermeneutic as a Comedy of Errors," Thomas Docherty observes that "the post-modern condition of hermeneutic is . . . oriented towards a chrono-political mode, a mode of interpretation which is radically historical."[10] The truth claims of the propositions made in the name of such a method tend toward demystification but can have no claim at verifiability. In my attempt at mapping out the hermeneutic coordinates of an early modern European space, I additionally engage an operational consideration of the physical nature of drama, which is perceived as both text and action. Considering the disruptive heterogeneity of the theatrical space, I see this theater as a spatial combination of word and deed, deriving from an accumulated early modern intertextuality and offering a special concrete manifestation of the action on stage. Because of this combination of texts and action, audiences can better visualize distant places by attending a delightful recreation. This educational and captivating activity seemed to be even more interesting for them than the newly discovered and popular occupation of examining maps, referred to by Blundeville.

In his *Topographicall Glasse*[11] (1611), Arthur Hopton introduces his readers to a compilation of classical ideas from geometry, astronomy, topography, and geography. This is a treatise on surveying by the astrologer, almanac compiler, and designer of instruments Arthur Hopton, who enjoyed a great contemporary reputation. He became the friend of many leading men of his day, before his early death at the age of twenty-six. In the introductory chapter 1, Hopton declares that his geographical "glasse" mirrors the circumference of the earth, the tables of distances between cities and provides astronomical data utilized in establishing the latitude and longitude of a place. Hopton makes the necessary distinctions among topography (which he identifies with chorography), geography, and cosmography, citing the ancient authors for the clarification of these definitions: "TOPOGRAPHIE (with some called Chorography) is an Arte, whereby wee be taught to describe any particular place, without relation unto the whole, delivering all things of note contained therein, as posts, villages, rivers, not omitting the smallest; also to describe the platforme of houses, buildings, monuments, or any such particular thing; and therefore a *Topographicall* description ought to expresse every particular, which caused me the rather to call this instrument the *Topographicall Glasse*" (1; sig. Br). The idea that a topographical description is a form of art, a "glasse," a reflection, or a detailed representation of the real place can summon disturbing connections with the world of the theater, which is an artistic representation created by a king of infinite space while being bound in a nutshell.

Hopton defines *geography* as "an imitation of the whole earth, and his principall and most knowne parts, differing from *Topography*, because it respects but places of note, and from *Cosmography*, because it has no relation unto the circles in the spheare, onely describing the world by hils, rivers, and therefore *Geography* may serve well for a general description of particular places, rivers, etc. in the world" (2–3). The author's observation that geography describes in general mostly places of importance tells us a lot about the amount of interest the early modern writers allotted to the more distant regions of the globe. As does any scientist who intends to define his domain of research and justify his statements, Hopton quotes classical names, such as Vernerus and Appian, in support of his arguments. According to Appian, Cosmography is "a description of the world, which both consist of the foure Elements, and also of the Sunne, Moone, and all the other starres both eraticall and fired, with all things else that be contained within the concavity of the heavens" (3). Despite his pretense of clarity and method, however, Hopton does nothing else but collate several texts belonging to the ancients regarding these definitions. An interesting characteristic of Hopton's *Glasse* is that he also tries to illustrate his terminology with charts and maps. In "A Demonstration of Topography," he presents a chart of England's regions and counties, and a sketch of a city's battlements. (2) In "A Demonstration of Geography," Hopton draws a semiconventional map of the world, in gross disregard of any geometrical projection. (3) This attempt at drawing a specific visualization of space in early modern geographical texts comes to supplement and enlarge the existing linear geographical narrative.

The *Commentaries* by Andrea Cambino (translated from the original Italian by John Shute, London, 1562) on the Ottoman Empire is a fifteenth-century text describing the wars with the Turks. The preface by the translator contains a long illuminating discourse of the principles of military discipline. Cambino notes a conflict between the Genovese merchants and the sultan in relation to the taking of the city of Caffa. This city was an important center of trade for the

Genovese in the Black Sea, and the Turks wanted to impose their control over the commerce in the area. Sultan Mohammed prepared an attack both by land and by sea. On the way, the army passed through Wallachia, one of the provinces of medieval and early modern Romania. Cambino records how the sultan "commanded a great number of horsemen to passe into Wallachia and to spoyle & destroye there what they coulde."[12] Those English readers happening to consult such texts of recorded history were especially interested in these affairs because they were related to the Turkish threat for the Christian world, and especially for the regions of trade in Eastern Europe belonging to Western European companies. Readers would get a vague impression that there was a country called Wallachia in Eastern Europe, on the Black Sea coast, which somehow was on the way of the invading Turkish army.

In addition, when Cambino refers to the Black Sea, he writes that the Crimean city of Caffa[13] lies "upon the sea called Euxino, which at this daye is called the greater sea" (31). The marginal note also explains that this is "Ponto Euxino." The need of referring to the sea's ancient name signifies that this was more familiar to early modern readers than the current one. Moreover, Cambino narrates how the Genovese, on hearing of the Turkish threat to the city of Caffa, were reluctant to send help to the merchants living there because they considered that the journey was long and "the passage perilous, through the countreys of so many barbarous nations" (31). Finally, a troop of one hundred and fifty soldiers left Italy and passed through "Hungarie," then through "Polonia," and finally through "Scythia, which at this daye is called Tartarie" (31). On the same page in this narrative we see that the ancient name of a country is placed before the contemporary one, in order to suggest an accurate location. In the end, as Cambino narrates, the city of Caffa, "which had ben of a longe tyme possessyd by the Genouveses, became subiecte to the tiranouse gouvernance of the Turckes" (32). This reference to the Ottoman siege and occupation becomes quite threatening in the Italian writer's narrative and it must have sounded strange to sixteenth-century English readers. Though the events described seemed to have happened at the end of the civilized world to the average person, the immediacy of the Turkish menace moved these reports of besieging and violence uncomfortably close to Western Europe and to home. If the Turks could threaten the commercial interests of the Genovese, they could do the same to anyone's attempts to trade in those distant lands.

In the anonymous broadside from Venice on May 30, 1597, entitled *Newes from diuers countries*,[14] Elizabethan readers could find out "that the Transylvanian hath overthrown fifteen thousand Turks and Tartars of Valachia and Moldavia" (15). This Transylvanian is the prince Sigismund Bathory,[15] who sided with the emperor of Austria in the war against the Turks. The broadside notes an alternative opinion, according to which this province of modern Romania had offered to host the conclusion of peace between the two empires: "But others affirm that there is a treatie of peace, and that the Prince of Transylvania will be a mediator between them" (12). The publication records the resistance of the three provinces of modern Romania to the Turks, and the large amount of human loss registered among their armies, in a period when Western Europe was seriously menaced by the Ottoman aggression: "And they had intelligence that the Turke having sent 6000 Janisaries to assure the passages through Transylvania, Moldavia, and Valachia: the Transylvanians and Valachians ioyning their forces, had encountered and foilde the first Squadron, in such sorte that fewe escaped, and that they went forwarde to serve the other Squadrons in like manner" (12). Queen Elizabeth and her subjects were interested in these maneuverings of international politics because the issue of peace or war with the Turks in Europe was a sensitive subject in the period. In these texts, we see that at least some Elizabethans were informed of the anti-Ottoman position of the three early modern provinces forming modern Romania. The pacifist inclination of their princes and the competence in the battlefield were the relevant issues of this description regarding the inhabitants of a region considered by some as remote and uncivilized.

There was a special breed of reporters in early modern times, which we may safely call globetrotters. Their accounts are studded with exceptional events and particular descriptions of places and customs, as they perceived them. No philosophical affectation of cultural ostentation could bother their narratives, and the common claim in their titles was that they related the "most wonderful" things ever experienced or seen. One of these travelers, Edward Webbe,[16] was an adventurer who became the master gunner to the king of France. He spent years as a galley slave of the Turks after traveling in Russia in the entourage of the English ambassador. His account (1590) is generally regarded as somewhat more reliable than many contemporary voyagers' tales, and it gives interesting insights into the manners of the Eastern European and Middle Eastern regions. Since a traveler was an alien in all places, Webbe recounts with equal piquancy how he was a prisoner to the barbaric Turks, and then, being able to escape to Christian Italy, how he was submitted to incredible torture by the papacy because he was treated as an English spy. Having spent a significant portion of his time in Russia and then in Turkey, Webbe describes comparatively the two nations' ways of dealing with debtors, which is not in any of these people's favor. About the Russians, Webbe comments that they are "a kind of tyrannous people,"[17] and he relates that if a debtor does not pay his arrears, the officers may forcibly enter the house and imprison the bankrupt. In the case of the Turks, however, the situation is even more dramatic. Webbe reports that "the Turks also useth to beate debters with a mallet, but not in that sort, for in Turkey they are beaten for debt upon the soles of their feet with a cane or cudgel if payment be not made by a day" (sig. B). By comparison to these merciless and barbarous practices, Shylock's menace of extracting a pound of flesh from Antonio might seem indulgent and unpretentious, more psychological than physical in nature.

Early modern English travelers and geographers contributed to the creation of an almost axiomatic Eurocentric mythology according to which the countries of Eastern Europe belonging to the Ottoman Empire were marginal and the sultan himself was evil. This is the period when Western Europe started to imagine itself politically, philosophically, and geographically at the center of the world. Other societies, deemed "non-Western," started to be considered as peripheral to the concert of European states and their cultural satellites. Daniel Goffman succeeds in demystifying the long-lived Western assumption that the Ottoman state was thoroughly martial, which had emerged in the sixteenth century. While inviting us to consider Süleyman's campaigns in Hungary and his sieges of Vienna and Malta in the mid-sixteenth century, Goffman also observes: "Nevertheless, alliances, commerce, and the movements of peoples more and more institutionalized and complicated relations between other European and Ottoman civilizations. In fact, in the economic, political, and even religious spheres the Ottomans assumed many of the duties that previously had characterized Byzantine relations with Western Europe."[18] Then again, a distinction must be made between the attitudes of northern and Mediterranean Europe regarding the Ottomans. In addition, those Western Europeans who experienced the Ottoman Empire firsthand often regarded it with respect and even apprehension. In the democratic environment of the London theaters, however, where the emphasis was on the reality of performance rather than on forming opinion, such emerging preconceptions were played upon, but also subverted, and the audience had the chance of seeing many places and ideas from different perspectives.

Western travelers to Eastern Europe were eager to produce interesting accounts about these regions, fascinated by the stories of luxury and decadence emerging down from the Ottoman Empire. In his *Navigations into Turkie* (1585),[19] the French traveler Nicholas de Nicolay informs his Elizabethan readers on the customs of various nations, their laws, religion, and manner of living. The book contains wonderful illustrations of popular costumes from various regions of Eastern Europe and Africa. However, despite the note of authenticity given by these *cartes à figures,* the sensational note of the events narrated raises doubts about their accuracy. Moreover, many of the stories about the Thracians seem to be taken straight from Herodotus, and they are communicated for their attractiveness and eccentricity. In the prefatory note, dedicated to Sir Henry Sidney and Sir Philip Sidney, Nicolay stresses the importance of firsthand knowledge derived from travel, as opposed to secondary information obtained from books.[20] According to the recurrent image of the world as a theater, it is important for a person to know the diversities of various countries, the differences of their peoples' manners, and the concrete examples of everyday life. The best way to obtain this kind of knowledge, in the author's opinion, is seeing the places and then filtering the impressions through personal discernment and understanding. The book and the map are only conventional illustrations of actual places, "which differ as much in moving the imagination and other faculties of the mind, as the representation of a thing in a glasse or a paynted table, doth vary from the thing represented" (sig. q3v). The author recommends live and direct knowledge of a foreign country, instead of the study of maps or geographical texts.

Despite the claim at authenticity, and the declaration that the author has "seen and observed" the places personally, this treatise is a collection of fictional stories gathered from classical writers. In book 4, chapter 24, which offers a "Description of Thracia," the reader finds mostly the ancient names of the places and a lot of confusing information: "Thracia which first was called Perca, and since Scithion, is a province in Europe (counted amongst the regions of Scithia), most ample and of great compasse, but of an yll temperature, the ayre being unwholesome, & not healthfull, the ground also barren enough, except it be in the places neere unto the sea. It was named Thracia, after the name of Thiras the sonne of Iaphet, or els as others say of Thrax the sonne of Mars . . . at this present day is called Romaine" (139–40). The apparently accurate geographic information traces the northern limits of Thracia to the "river Istre," which is the ancient name of the Danube. The "tribes" inhabiting the region up to the "sea Euxinum," the Latin name of the Black Sea, are the "Bulgares," who live "from the East into the sea Euxinum" (139). All these geographical names draw directly on classical authors and give an expected aura of respectability to these lands where fierce and uncivilized tribes are known to live.

The readers become even more bewildered when, next to the contemporary reference to Macedonia, the Danube, and the Bulgares, they understand that this land of Thracia was much celebrated for the sacrifice of Bacchus and "through the congregation of the Menades under the conduct of the Poet Orpheus" (139). This is a narrative seeming to descend from the classical Solinus, and further chapters expand the spectacular character of the stories about the corsairs under the jurisdiction of the patriarch of Constantinople and about Mount Athos; about what Herodotus said regarding the Persian king Xerxes and what Plutarch said in the life of Alexander the Great. In chapter 26, describing the "Manners, lawes, religion, and auncient order of living of the Thracians," Nicolay seems to have copied straight from Herodotus, replaying the classical stereotypes of cruelty and barbarity. The Thracians "have byn esteemed amongest all the other people of Europe the most cruel, spiteful, and inhumane" (145). In Nicolay's text, the Scythians are "a people most barbarous: their eyes are hollow, their countenance furious, and the sound of their voyce fearefull, exceeding all others in bignesse of body and force of members" (145). The Thracians are reported to sell their women and children to foreigners, and "live in idlenesse without doing of any thing, or els in theft and stealing" (145). According to Nicolay's report, the natives of this region consider any kind of work demeaning, and all they like to do is drink wine and get drugged with poppy seeds burned into the fire, which make them dizzy. It is essential to remember that all these descriptions are from Nicolay, who was the royal geographer during the reign of Henry II of France. He was part of an embassy to Constantinople in 1551, and his reports of scenes and customs are an important source of sixteenth-century Europe's knowledge of the Near East.

In chapter 27, "Of the auncient opinions of the Tharcians touching the immortalitie of the soule," Nicolay repeats the classical stories about polygamy, wives being buried with their husbands, animal sacrifice to the one god "Zamolxis" (146), primitive burial practices, and the democratic election of kings by their people. Zamolxis was the name of the primitive Dacians' deity in pre-Christian times, while in the sixteenth century the local population the narrator speaks about was fully Christian for about a thousand years. Nicolay's entire narrative is borrowed from ancient writers, and it emphasizes the extreme and unbelievable events, in order to attract the readers' attention. At the end of the chapters describing Thrace, which are nothing else but a compilation from ancient authors, Nicolay makes an attempt to get down to reality, but his account replays the usual theme of the degradation of the land as a result of the Turkish occupation: "But at this present their speeche, their garments, religion, manner of living, miserable calamitie and servitude, is conforme and like unto the other Grecians, which are under the same puissance and tyrannous obeysaunce of the Turke" (147). Contrary to the claims advanced in the Preface, which highly recommended the firsthand knowledge of places derived from traveling instead of that from books, Nicolay's inconsistent text does exactly the opposite. It gives readers diversified digested information about the Eastern European regions, but it seems that the narrator never traveled there. All he offers is a composite presentation gathered from other people's books, which creates a very confusing image of the real places around the Danube and the Black Sea, and the people living there.

Bishop George Abbot wrote an important geographical compendium, whose popularity is proved by the existence of seven subsequent editions, besides the original one. *A Briefe Description of the Whole Worlde* (1599)[21] aims at describing methodically the early modern world as it was known at that time. The author wrote this work from the comfortable seclusion of one of his many places, and he enunciates some curious conclusions about America. Abbot relied more on classical and biblical sources than on sixteenth-century works. However, his *Description* appears to have had far more appeal to the public than the well-founded accounts of recent geographical discoveries. In the manner of the ancient geographical narratives, Abbot divides the Earth into zones of sea and of land, and he admits "the North-partes of Asia, and Europe in olde time were but little knowne and discouered."[22] The geographer borrows the method of the narrative journey from the ancients, starting from the western part of the Mediterranean, usually the straits of Gibraltar ("De Hispania"). He continues in clockwise order and writes of France ("De Gallia"), of Germany and Italy, "De Dania, Suezia, & Noruegia," "De Russia, sive Muscovia," "De Prussia, & Polonia" (sig. Aiiij). In the chapter entitled "De Hungaria & Austria," Abbot notes the fact that "the kingdome hath beene a great obstacle against the Turkes coming into Christendome: but especially in the time of Iohannes Huniades who did mightily with many great victories repelle the Turke" (sig. Avi). *Iohannes Huniades* is the Latin name of Iancu of Hunedoara; his family's origin was in the Romanian region of Banat, and he was a *voievod* of Transylvania (1446). He achieved many victories against the Turks and was an ally of the Western coalition against the Ottoman invasion.

In the late sixteenth century, however, Abbot notes that the earlier situation of relative independence of the three Romanian principalities was no longer valid. In his description of Hungary, Abbot deplores the decay of Christianity under the repeated offensive of the Ottomans. Abbot's methodical journey from the western side of Europe to its eastern borders continues with the chapter entitled "De Graecia," devoted to southeastern Europe. Here, the reader learns about the three principalities of the ancient Roman province of Dacia, but Abbot finds nothing of importance to say about the region and its people: "On the south side of *Hungary,* and Southeast, lieth a countrie of Europe: called in olde time *Dacia,* which is large & wide, comprehending in it *Transylvania, Wallachia, Moldavia,* and *Servia.* Of which little is famous, save that the men are warlike, and can hardly be brought to obedience" (sig. Avii). Despite their inclusion among the nations of Europe, only aggressiveness and insubordination distinguish the people of Transylvania, Wallachia, and Moldavia, and the author uses mostly negative terms with reference to them. This influential Elizabethan view, as do others, lies at the basis of the emerging mythologizing stories about the countries belonging to the Ottoman Empire as alien, barbaric, and insubordinate, an idea that was perpetuated in subsequent narrative layers and was transformed into a persistent ideological obstacle to the understanding of these peoples and their society.

The remnants of ancient classical narratives of violence and disorder related to these marginal parts of Europe survive in Abbot's geographic account, despite the efficient organization and objectivity of his treatise. Nowhere else in Abbot's exposé can we find so many negative comments about a nation, except probably when he speaks of the Tartarians, deriving from the ancient Scythians, whom he calls "rude of behaviour" (sig. B2). Abbot borrows from the ancient writers the method of describing Europe from west to east, but he also embellishes his comment with a number of national stereotypes collected from his classical readings. Although he gives pertinent information regarding contemporary events in international politics, and the geographical discourse is factual and unadorned, Abbot's *Description of the Whole Worlde* is no less ambitious than it is influenced by his numberless classical sources. This kind of imaginative topographical manipulation of the readers inscribes Abbot's work among the many similar geographical accounts in the age, which, while being very popular and reprinted several times, succeeded in creating a pool of floating knowledge that accounted for many stereotypes and stark inventions taken as truths. What else but images of disruption and violence could the Elizabethan and later readers summon up about the countries lying in the eastern parts of Europe? When such a critical and supposedly impartial description of the world categorizes the nations inhabiting the area of the Danube and the Black Sea as recalcitrant and uncouth, what can be expected from other heavily partial rhetorical discourses about these places?

Hakluyt's *Principall Navigations*[23] is a thorough and vivid record of English commerce, travel, and international politics through the sixteenth century. The compendium includes firsthand accounts of voyages to the New World, the Holy Land, Russia, Africa, and Asia, as well as a lengthy description of the English fleet's encounter with the Spanish Armada. It reveals correspondence, patents, and passports written by English monarchs and their foreign counterparts, including the emperor of Russia, and the "Great Turke," ship manifestos and trade documents. Hakluyt is one of Shakespeare's acknowledged sources. In a catalogue of the English voyages made to the southeastern parts of the world, Hakluyt documents "The Privilege of Peter the Prince of Moldavia graunted to the English Merchants" on August 27, 1588 (290). The treaty concluded between the prince of Moldavia and the English ambassador stipulated the legality of English merchants to trade freely with the province of Moldavia. Petru Şchiopul, the prince referred to in this text, promoted intensely a number of political and commercial relationships with Western Europe. Hakluyt further describes Edward Barton's ambassadorial visit to Constantinople in the period 1593–95 and the passage via Moldavia (306).

An elaborate network of trade and cultural correlation connected the early modern world and, from this perspective, the Romanian principalities were at the intersection of the main routes of commerce leading to Western Europe. The Ottoman Empire may have conducted a policy of aggression against the Christian West during the sixteenth century, but the sultan actively promoted the rules of free trade and international profit more or less successfully, according to the political situation at the time. Therefore, the three Romanian provinces' strategic geographical position was always a cause for disputation and frequent military aggression. On the other hand, we have an interesting opinion of an English traveler, Fynes Moryson, referring to the period 1605–17, about the constant state of subjection of these peoples of Eastern Europe under the Ottomans. As Moryson observes, "But the Turkes, and especially the Christians subject to them, being borne and from infancy bred under the yoke of perpetuall slavery, and having never tasted the sweeteness of liberty, doe beare with ease this burthen, which we thinke unsupportable."[24] This is a surprisingly sympathetic opinion about the peoples under the Turkish domination, from a traveler who had seen many nations and compared their customs, family relationships, buildings, trade, coins, and so on. Moryson's view is that of a matter-of-fact person, who observed accurately the travel and lodging conditions in the countries he visited, and who dwelled less on political or social matters. This remark is even more surprising because it reveals an unexpected openmindedness and compassion for the fate of these peoples, and an understanding of their mentality of subjection.

The *Travellers Breviat* (1601) by Giovanni Botero[25] is one of the early modern narratives meant to popularize facts about the countries and nations of the world. Botero was an Italian thinker, priest, poet, and diplomat, whose political philosophical work was able to shape at least some of the policy among the European states of the very troubled seventeenth century. The impersonal tone and the impressive quantity of information make it one of the earliest tourist guides designed for the itinerant Englishmen and women. Such works as this were intended for the entertainment of those who stayed at home and for the instruction of those who desired to widen their experience by travel. This *Breviat* is general and historical in tone; its extensive descriptions of India, China, Persia, Tartary, and eastern Africa may indicate the new eastern interest as a motive that induced Jaggard to bring it up in print. However, the presentation of southeastern European countries in the Ottoman Empire added a note of exoticism to the narrative, because the Ottomans were geographically close to Western Europe, yet they were quite apart in culture or religion. Besides, most Western European travel writers, including Botero, tended to include the peoples from the Ottoman Empire in the global misconception of tyranny and savageness summoned by the mentioning of the Turk, without allowing for individual cultural characteristics. The result was, for example, the false impression that the entire area belonged to Islam, while the populations in most countries were mainly Christian.

In the section about "The Great Turke,"[26] readers are informed about the Ottoman power on land and at sea. While the Turks are less powerful than the Portuguese are at sea, their extension on land is impressing. A series of facts and figures include the warlike Ottoman capacity and the battles in Hungary, the siege of Malta, and the battle of Lepanto. Osman Bassa is renowned for having led huge armies through Europe, and Botero mentions three characteristics of the Turkish army with which they have terrified the world: large armies, military discipline, and huge army supplies. The superiority of the Turkish army is compared to the Roman legions: "They go far beyond us both in discipline and numbers; herein giving place no not to the ancient Romanes; much less to any moderne nation how warlike foeuer" (48). The army's extraordinary discipline is explained by the fact that no drinking is allowed among the soldiers, they are instructed to give total obedience to the higher military rank, and women are forbidden to accompany the army. Silence, resilience, and extreme punishment for theft and disobedience have led the Ottoman army, according to Botero, to a high degree of excellence. Armies are never quartered in towns, meritorious soldiers are rewarded and cowards are severely punished, and there is no fear of death among them, because they believe in preordained destiny. This latter aspect is similar to what ancient writers related about the inhabitants of ancient Thracia, a land now conquered by the Ottomans, who had no fear of death because they believed in the immortality of the soul.

Botero goes on to explain the countries neighboring the Ottoman Empire. To the north, the Turks neighbored the "Polaques" (50); that means that the more southern principalities of Moldavia and Wallachia were considered to have succumbed to Ottoman rule, for one thing, and that they were not Christian, for another. However, the author notes that the Turks feared the Polish and gives the example of "the warre which *Iuonia Voyvod* of Walachia made with the Turkes, wherein great numbers of Polaques served" (50). It is interesting how the writer mostly disregards the merits of the Wallachian prince who initiated the war and defeated the Turks, focusing on the Polish mercenaries who only served in this Romanian-principality army. Moreover, Botero notes the superiority of the Ottoman armed forces to those of its neighboring nations. The Polish kings were irresolute and unwilling to deal with the more skilled and disciplined Ottoman army and the Austrians preferred to strengthen their borders with heavy German and Bohemian troops. The Venetians, however, maintained an amiable conviviality with the Turks by treaties of peace and exchange of presents, rather than by open war.

Botero's *Breviat* describes at length the corruption existing in the Ottoman Empire at the highest levels. The Bassas and their officers would take bribes from the people and defraud the sultan's treasury. The sultana took money from pilgrims wishing to go to Mecca, and the sultan himself would not receive ambassadors or generals unless they were loaded with expensive gifts. In general, all high offices were bought, and Botero gives the example of how the princes in the three Romanian provinces gained their offices: "The Vaivods of Valachia, Moldavia and Transilvania hold their estates by vertue of this briberie, and yet they are often changed. For the estates are given to the best chapmen, who again to make good their daies of payment, oppresse the people, and bring the commons to extreme povertie" (42–43). The practice of bribery in high offices was, and is, a common habit of the regions under Levantine influence. The authenticity of the information contained in the *Travelers Breviat* cannot be questioned, especially with respect to the moral degradation and the corruption of public offices at all levels in the Ottoman Empire. However, the tone of the chapter and its conclusion shows us that the text was meant to justify the expenses of the emperor of Hungary in raising an army against the Turks. In "seeing the Turke like an unsatiable dragon" (68), the Western reader was prompted to be cautious of the alarming Ottoman expansion and back those who would fight against it, both financially and morally.

A text apparently showing the opposite opinion, from the side of the sultan, is a set of letters translated and publicized in all countries of Europe, in order to increase the public opinion's reaction against the Turkish visible aggressiveness and arrogance. The 1606 *Letters from the Great Turke,* addressed to the pope and all kings of the Western world, contain a vituperative verbal attack on the Western nations from the presumptuous Sultan Achmed. One letter starts with the announcement that it was composed in Constantinople "from whence wee banished thy first fathers, having most cruelly slaine them with their wives and children, ravishing the women and widdowes for the accomplishing of our pleasure."[27] Following this impressive image of horror and slaughter, the sultan menaces the princes of Christendom, indicating that he has at his disposal an entire army of three hundred thousand Christian renegades, who would fight for the defense of Islam. Half of these men are reported to have already crossed the Danube, marching through Wallachia and Transylvania to invade the kingdom of Hungary, while the other half is going to assault the stronghold on the island of Rhodes. This imposing display of military force is meant to result in the total submission of Western Europe to the Turkish power. The sultan's menacing tone and self-assurance are meant to intimidate the Western countries. It also suggests that, from the Ottoman perspective, the western part of Europe is considered barbaric and uncivilized. After crossing the Danube to attack Hungary, the one hundred and fifty thousand highly trained "Ganessars" had to cross Wallachia and Transylvania on their way west. However, these mercenary soldiers in the Ottoman army were recruited from the young boys taken by force from their families in the countries under Turkish jurisdiction, including the three provinces that now form modern Romania.

Regarding the threat posed by the Ottoman aggression for the Western world, Edward Topsell's *Historie of Serpents* (1608) offers an interesting allegory of the Turkish expansion as the seven-headed Hydra. In fact, Topsell mentions an artistic image of the Hydra, which was taken from Turkey to Venice and was exposed in a public place. The inscription on the engraving suggests that these monsters announce a disaster for the Christian world, under dreadful menace from the Turks.[28] The foreboding message, annexed to a no less terrifying image, was meant to convey an atmosphere of impending doom and activate the Venetians' hatred of the Turks: "Therefore seeing the Turkish empire is grown to that height, in which estate all other former kingdoms fell, I may devine & Prophecy, that the danger threatened hereby, belongeth to the Turkes, and not unto us in whose gouverment this Monster was found to be bred: and the hinder part of his head seemeth to resemble a Turkes Cap" (202). Investing himself with the power of prophecy, Topsell actually makes a political prediction concerning the increasing threat of the Ottomans for Western Europe. In addition, the horrifying image of the seven-headed monster, and the fact that its heads were adorned with Turkish turbans, was meant to spread terror among the readers and invested the text with powerful, almost apocalyptic significance.

Following an authentic early modern empirical spirit, according to which these fabulous and inflammatory discourses stood no chance of conforming to truth because they had not been verified, Topsell calls these statements impossible. He considers a different perspective by questioning the biased view according to which the Turks were the agent of evil: "But let it be as it is, how doth he know that this evill doth more belong to the Turkes then to the Christians?" (202) An alternative outlook suggests that the Turkish threat is a punishment by God of the unfaithful and corrupt Christians in Western Europe. In describing the mythology created around this seven-headed monster, and its destruction by Hercules, Topsell calls the notion a mere allegory of envy and vice, a legendary warning against the dangers of succumbing to sin and moral corruption. Despite the heavily resonant admonition, Topsell's analysis is important because it invites open-mindedness and impartiality. What the political circles of the time were taking as an undeniable fact, namely, that the Turk was an enemy, ergo a monster, Topsell argues and places under the sign of doubt. Topsell's *History* was published at a transitional time in science, and intimations of what we would now call the proper scientific method are clearly visible. However, Topsell is also anxious to defer to the authority represented by classical sources. This results in the situation where we have exotic attributes being assigned to well-known animals as well as fantastic creatures. Readers in Topsell's period accepted these stories because they were circulated by the cultural authorities of the time and relied on the even higher authority of the classics.

However, not all geographical and travel texts attempted to offer unbiased opinions about different areas of Europe, all the more so when these places were in the far eastern regions, where the revered classics said there lurked incredible dangers. In addition, the fact that these territories were under Turkish domination in the early modern period was a further motif of worry for Western Europeans, including the English. In a book containing useful practical advice for travelers, *An Essay of the means how to make our Travailles more profitable* (1606), Sir Thomas Palmer[29] promotes a conservative defense of the educational value of travel. The author concentrates on

Europe, demonstrating the singularly insignificant impact on contemporary attitudes in this respect of the New World. In analyzing the "causes of civility or barbarousnesse," Palmer makes a clear distinction between the civil and barbarous nations of Europe, leaving no room for debate or controversy as to the polished and the rude peoples on the Continent: "And first, therefore, the Travaillers consider, whether the people in generall be civill or barbarous: and that whether by discipline (the best Civilian Master) or by naturall temperature of bodies. Such are the Grecians, and those of the Iles of *Iapan* and *Chios:* as on the contrary side, the people of *Africa, America, Magellanica,* and those of Northeast *Europe* and *Asia,* by nature barbarists. . . . Secondly, that barbarous people are never good faithful friends, but for their profit, being ever wavering and treacherous, nor if enemies other than mortall; yet if their power be not over-great, are easily vanquished."[30] The classical tradition of considering the Greeks as highly civilized is enriched with the addition of the Japanese people. According to Palmer's argument, barbarity went hand in hand with treachery, and therefore all uncivilized peoples were seeking to profit from the others for their own selfish ends.

Interestingly enough, Palmer sees these foreign peoples' incivility as closely connected with their lack of power at the international level. Probably by not adhering to an accepted norm of the community, these peoples' strength is undermined from the interior, which makes them vulnerable. Although Palmer includes the Eastern European nations among those whom he considers uncivilized, the critical observer of human nature is forced to admit that there are many differences in the nature of peoples, and there is no pure example of civility or barbarity. By comparison, "the English, Scottish, French, Italians, & Spanish, which are the most reformed & courtlike people, are tainted with some blemish of barbarousnesse, the which of other heathen nations they might learne to reforme" (62). Palmer observes that the English, "we here," are right to consider themselves the most civilized of the cultures mentioned, yet their "entertainment of strangers" (62) leaves much to be desired; in this sense, Palmer cites the example of the Lithuanians, who were treated with hatred and spite by the English commoners. In opposition, Palmer holds that the English nobility, just like the nobility of Poland, are "more humane towards strangers" (63). A mark of high civility is found in the "great respect the Turkes, Tartarians, and Persians give to their Princes" (63), while the French are famed for the opposite attitude. Palmer's composite discourse is marked by absolute statements and timid attempts at honest critical stance. It is easy to see how ethnographic and cultural generalizations in Palmer's report were seriously affected by class issues and hierarchies of power; these statements were made by a member of the nobility, who could not accept the dissimilarity of individual situations and who embarked upon unwarranted general declarations.

Regarding the behavior toward women, Palmer sets the savagery of the Italians, who are famously jealous and imprison their women, against the courtesy of the "Parthian heathen" (63), who are kind to their wives and are never jealous or suspicious. In fact, this is a mirroring practice of past and present, because the Parthian Empire was the name given to Persians by the Romans. The notion of pagan Parthians is derived from the classical texts, but Palmer opposes this inherited stereotype to a refined attitude toward women displayed by the Persian men. With this East-West positioning, a series of examples of Western uncivilized habits follows, mingling classical culture with cultural, matrimonial, and libation practices of Western Europe. One of these, for instance, is the comparison of the Western nations' habit of excessive drinking with that of the Scythians, "that cruell nation" (64), who used to drink their enemies' blood, but whose princes dare not drink wine before their king does. The author seems to overlook the fact that the Scythians as a nation no longer existed in the early modern period, and he appears to ignore that most of his information about this ancient Eastern European and Asian population is derived from classical sources. This illustration of the savage Scythians' courteous behavior is brought into contrast with the contemporary Dutch habit of mounting drinking contests, regardless of the circumstances, and forcing all to drink way over their measure, as a form of complying with house rules. Palmer's tourist guide achieves its purpose only partially because the information he offers is useful in most cases, but often tainted with classical borrowings and improper generalizations.

In a paper analyzing the culture of violent commerce in early modern England, Daniel Vitkus focuses on the figure of the venturing hero, such as Thomas Stukeley, the Shirley brothers, the renegade pirate John Ward, and on their images in early modern English drama. Vitkus argues that the way the stories about these heroes were represented, altered, and reproduced encouraged later accounts of a self-confident, outward-looking, and even aggressive image of English subjectivity. As Vitkus observes, "English subjects were attracted to compensatory fictions and fantasies that glorified a violent commercial agency, while punishing the unruly renegade who took that agency too far."[31] This assertive self-image, however, I would add, is enhanced and magnified by the unflattering and often distorted presentation in these texts of the nations having contact with the overseas adventurers. While extolling these English heroes' valiance and commendable endeavors in the service of Christianity and the promotion of English national and commercial interests abroad, the savageness of "the Turke" and the peoples under Islam jurisdiction was repeatedly emphasized as a reversed cultural model, in opposition to the English establishment. This particular form of cultural modeling, I believe, had its roots in a similar manner of dealing with the foreign and the unknown in ancient texts. In addition, however, the narratives about English explorers in distant places were refashioned along the pragmatic outlook promoted by the increasing possibilities of trade with these distant nations.

A travel book describing the activities of the Shirley brothers,[32] Thomas, Anthony, and Robert, in their eastern adventures is an attempt at producing popular patriotic literature in England. Anthony Nixon's *The Three English Brothers* (1607) relates how "Master Robert Sherley" is employed in the wars of the Persian king against the Turks. During the 1602–18 Turkish war with the Persians, the English brothers Sir Anthony and Sir Robert Shirley completely reorganized the Persian forces. Sir Anthony had a diplomatic mission to Europe to secure cooperation. Nixon praises the general's valor and describes Sir Robert's first victory over the Turks. Because his brother had been taken as a hostage, however, Shirley threatens to kill thirty of the prisoners of war, since the Turks had refused the exchange of prisoners. The horrid action is related as a justified retaliation and Palmer describes a gory image of the Turkish commanders' heads being carried in the Persian soldiers' swords, as was the custom of the land.[33] This cruel exploit of retribution in war is described as a just reward for the Turks' unwillingness to comply, and Robert Shirley emerges as a valiant English soldier, whose courage is rewarded by marriage to the king's cousin. Robert Shirley, this epitome of English courtesy transferred to the east, is reported to have tried to educate the Persian king and his subjects in the ways of Christianity and to have converted many infant souls to the true religion. When reports of savagery on the part of the members of Western European nations become known, therefore, the narrator's discourse turns toward a brave attempt at justification for the sake of faith. On the other hand, there is no reference to the religion of the nations under the jurisdiction of the Turks, such as Wallachia and Moldavia, whose populations were mainly Christian.

Early modern English travel writers saw the eastern areas under Ottoman rule as presumably dangerous places, where foreigners were expected to face mysterious hazards. In the countries under the power of the sultan, many Christians from the West, who had managed to live there for a while, engaged in businesses, or even raised families in those places, were described as having developed the depraved habits of the land. In William Biddulph's *Travels* (1609), the readers learn about the city of Constantinople and the region of Thracia, "which is also called the countrey *Romania* in *Europe*."[34] Describing the situation in the Ottoman Empire under "Sultan Achomet," the author mentions some examples of marital relationships of Western European Christians and local women. The foreigners would choose local ladies (except for the Turkish women, because any relationship with them was punished with death), who would live with them as husband and wife for the duration of their stay in the country. At the point of departure, these men abandoned the concubines and their children, leaving them in great material need. Biddulph comments that good Christians adopt the bad habits existing in "Heathen Countries." For this writer, and probably for most of his readers, "non-Christian" and "Heathen" spelled evil and subject to corruption. Biddulph's explanation for such reprehensible marital practices was that "they which dwell long in wicked Countries, and converse with wicked men, are somewhat tainted with their sinnes."[35] Many Western Europeans thought that the countries under Turkish occupation were "heathen," non-Christian, and barbarian. In fact, in the entire region north and south of the Danube (the area that covers modern Romania and Bulgaria), the major part of the population was Christian, striving to preserve their religious and national identity under the Ottoman economic pressure and the spiritual assault of Islam.

Biddulph presents what he suggests to be a noncommendable tradition regarding Christian women in Constantinople. Divorce seemed to be a common practice among the wives of the Greek merchants who lived there. According to Biddulph, these women were accustomed to be richly dressed in taffeta, satin, and gold and wear much jewelry. As Biddulph puts it rather coarsely, "They care not how they pinch their bellies, so that they may have fine apparel on their backs" (80). Therefore, before marriage, women would set these requirements in some sort of prenuptial legal contract sanctioned before the patriarch of Constantinople. If, subsequently, the wives complained that this aspect of the settlement had not been accomplished, they were entitled to a divorce and free to remarry, while the husband was at liberty to take another wife. There followed the example of a woman who had three husbands living and was married to a fourth under the protection of this unwritten law. Biddulph observes that this practice was well spread and famous among men, "to the disgrace of his countrie, and slander of Christianitie" (81). It is impossible to avoid making a comparison with what Herodotus narrates about Thracian women, whose freedom of spirit and custom made it possible for them to sell themselves to the highest bidder. However, what Herodotus took as an interesting ancient custom revealing a form of accepted servitude, Biddulph sees it as a degrading habit that goes against the Christian principles of monogamy and decent life. By representing the vilified mores of Eastern countries under the influence of Islam, the early modern traveler disseminates an image of reverted exemplarity meant to contrast good practices at home.

Various editions of Abraham Ortelius's monumental *Theatrum Orbis Terrarum* provide sundry and often contradictory information about the ancient region of Dacia, lying within and around the arch of the Carpathians up to the shores of the Black Sea to the east. Hungary was the northwestern neighbor of the province of Transylvania, and at that time western Hungary was under the control of the Austrians, while the province of Transylvania in the east of Hungary was a principality largely independent of the Turks. Ortelius's description of Hungary, in the early 1603 English edition, gives the impression of a subdeveloped region, much damaged by the frequent Turkish invasions. Ortelius writes about the people of Hungary, "Theyre languadge is the Scythian tongue, different from all the other languadges rounde about them," and "they are of verye discurtious and rude behaviour, more apte for the warres then for peace."[36] Apart from the connection of the Scythians with barbarity, derived from the classics, Ortelius adds the observations of his contemporaries to the idea that the Hungarian population of Finno-Ugric origin was rude and warlike. The richness of the land and hunting fields in Hungary is admitted, but it is recorded that most of the population lives in the country and only the rich live in large houses, while the poor live in rude cabins and do not sleep in beds until they are married. Another sign of incivility about the Hungarians seems to be that the only dowry they give women when they are married is a garment and nothing else. The general idea conveyed by Ortelius about the people of Hungary is that "they are inconstant and covetous, nothinge delighted in any art nor trafficke" (93).

The main reason why Ortelius instilled the idea of the Hungarians' barbarity in language, lifestyle, and manners is that the passage ended with the idea that the country was even worse at that time than it was before because of the invasion of the Turks. This information is inserted in an almost subliminal manner and is meant, through repetition, to convey the impression of a barbarous people living under the repressive regime of an even more dangerous enemy, the Turk. Ortelius moves from west to east in the description of countries and the farther east he moves, the more uncivilized and hard to contain within the borders of normality the peoples become. In the same large edition of Ortelius's atlas, there is no transition from the description of the fallen state of Hungary under the Turks to the description of Transylvania. The readers learn that "Transylvania is deuided from Hungarie by certayne mountaynes, which enclose the same rounde lyke unto a walled towne" (93). This description is geographically accurate, because the Carpathian mountain chain encloses Transylvania from three sides. Further topographical facts include the length and breadth of the country (four days' journey), the narrow paths of access between the mountain ranges, and the fortified castles guarding the main points of entrance in the region. All these are precise observations based on local facts, not confabulations derived from the ancients.

Ortelius mentions Transylvania as a country rich in corn, cattle, and wine, having excellent horses. The mines of gold and silver were known ever since Roman times, and Ortelius says that "in some rivers they finde some lumpes of golde, which waye a pounde waighte" (93). Ortelius documents the complex blend of populations in this region: "The lande is well peopled, beeing for the moste parte all Saxons, whose languadge they use, unlesse in some fewe places where they speake Hungarishe" (93). The German-origin population immigrated to Transylvania in the twelfth century, and Ortelius fitfully records the ethnic composition in the area. The readers find out that a Christian prince rules Transylvania. He used to pay tribute to the Turks but now leads many wars against the Ottoman aggression. In the same edition, however, in the chapter dealing with "The Empire of the Turke," Ortelius mentions Wallachia, Moldavia, and Transylvania among the countries that are tributary to the Ottomans

(100). The text about Transylvania mentions several cities (Alba Iulia, Bistrita, Cibinio, and Fagaras) and the populations of German and Swiss origin inhabiting those cities but does not record the Romanian population of Transylvania, who speaks a Romance language, totally different from Hungarian or German. This may be justified by the fact that this population, constituting the majority in these parts, was mostly of agrarian and pastoral occupation. They were producing that corn, cattle, and wine the country of Transylvania was most famous for, or extracted the gold and silver from the mines. They did not produce many texts about themselves, and this is probably the reason for the poor or nonexistent records about the Romanian-speaking population in Transylvania.

Moving farther to the east, Ortelius's description of Russia gives the same impression of rough people having fallen even worse than their previous state. From the start, the reader is informed that only the so-called white Russia, which comprises the "Moscovian Empire" (101), will be described, although the prince of Muscovie proclaims himself the "Emperour of all Russia," including Polonia and Lituania. Therefore, the geographer begins by undermining the authority of the local ruler by implying that political pretense is only a formality. After setting the political boundaries, Ortelius passes to the climate, which is very cold (no more than three months of summer during the year), and the mostly marshy territory, because of the large number of rivers. As with the other countries, the richness of the land is emphasized, this time corn, cattle, fruit, honey, and minerals. As the narrative moves toward lifestyle and manners, the tone becomes more critical and the general impression is that "the people are of small worthe" (101). In Moscow, princes hold court in a palace built in the Italian manner and there are as many as sixteen churches in town, a sign of respect for religion; some churches are made of stone, and some are made of wood, a difference that speaks of social inequality. Common people live very "miserablye" (101) because the widespread idea among the population is that celebrating Sundays and other pleasures belong only to the nobility. The general idea about the Russians given by this earlier edition of Ortelius's atlas is that "they are subtill and deceitful" (101), which is not very flattering. However, this negative idea makes a suitable transition to "The Empire of the Turke," described in the next chapter.

As in ancient narratives, the enumeration of the countries under the Ottomans, and the various sultans having conquered these countries appear as an artifice in order to impress and give an image of the extensive borders of the Ottoman Empire. At the end of this long account of Turkish victories, Ortelius subtly applies a warning to the Western countries that Sultan Selim II, after having conquered cities in Hungary, "threatens to do worse if God inspire not the hartes of the Christian Princes unitedlye to resist him" (102). The Ottoman threat looms large over the entire text and it is obvious that international policy takes the place of geographical account in this section of Ortelius's atlas. The final idea is that the Turks as a people are "false" and "inconstant" (102), although the author admits their fidelity to the lord, their horsemanship, working potential, and frugality. All these national characteristics recommend the Ottomans as a nation with all the qualities of conquerors, but the implication is not at all laudable. It is rather a form of subtly instilling the notion of a threatening force looming at the borders of the Western world. It is advisable for Western nations to try to contain this power, though nobody seems to take into account the Christian peoples already subjugated by its force, who tried hard to maintain their national identity amid all the religious and political pressure. We can see how similar practices had different interpretations according to the needs of their authors. While Ortelius regarded Hungarians and Russians as bestial and unskilled, the Turks were described as deliberately austere, much as the English viewed themselves.

In the 1606 edition, Ortelius moves from west to east, in the usual manner, and the first country of the present-day central Europe he describes is Bohemia. Quoting Joannes Dubravius,[37] Ortelius writes that the country "is in the forme of a Theater environed around by the forest of woods of Hercynia."[38] Moving farther east, he writes of "Hungary," whose name comes of the Huni, "a people came out of Scythia" (95). Making a very common confusion, Ortelius includes the entire ancient country of Dacia in Hungary, when at that time only the province of Transylvania was a principality in some relation to the Hungarian kingdom. From this huge folio edition of Ortelius's geographic compendium, the reader finds out about Hungary that it "containeth almost both the Pannonies, the countries of the Iazigies, and the Daci, now comprehending Transsylvania, Wallachia and Moldavia" (95). In the section about "Transsylvania," Ortelius takes his information from one Antony Bonfinius,[39] who wrote a history of Hungary. The secondhand source of Ortelius's information about this part of Eastern Europe might explain the confusions, omissions, and historical blunders in the description of the Romanian-speaking countries, probably due to the biased recording of his source. The political rivalries between the Romanian principalities in the early modern period created a large number of misrepresentations and territorial appropriations among Transylvania, Wallachia, and Moldavia. While Austrian and Hungarian princes claimed Transylvania as theirs by right of supremacy, the Romanian princes fought to have the region under their domination, claiming the right of the majority Romanian population. In this conflicting political position, it was understandable for a Hungarian chronicler to describe the ancient Roman province of Dacia as being part of Hungary.

In his geographical atlas (the 1606 edition), Ortelius used whatever sources he had at his disposal, including the classical texts. About the region of Transylvania, Ortelius quotes Bonfinius, but he uses the ancient Latin name of the province, *Dacia:* "Beyond the Carpathian mountains, saith he, is the uttermost province of Dacia, extended even into the river Axiaces. This now vulgarly is known unto the name of Transsylvania, they call it Siebenburgen. . . . It is a most fertile country of cattel, wine & corne: also of Gold & Silver. . . . This country is inhabited partly by Scythians, partly by Saxones and Dakes: these are more humane and civill, those more rude and churlish" (97). According to Ortelius's source, the population of German origin (the "Saxones") living in Transylvania is civilized and amiable. The same are the Dacians ("Dakes'), the local inhabitants existing before the arrival of the Romans. By contrast, the Hungarian population, of wild Scythian descent, displays a "more rude" social behavior. The implication of wildness and uncivilized manners related to Eastern European nations is still extant in the sources of early modern geographers. However, my impression is that this huge folio edition of Ortelius's atlas cannot have been so accessible to many English readers because of its bulky and unmanageable size. The information contained here, and the detailed but very large maps in Latin representing Transylvania, Wallachia, and Moldavia, must have been unappealing and hard to handle, probably less popular than other editions of Ortelius's atlas.

The 1610 edition of Ortelius's atlas seems to be more accessible in size, and the information it presents is more documented and objective than the previous editions. The front page shows the two Earth hemispheres, carefully designed according to the Mercator projection. The preface to the reader clearly states that the information concerning the regions of the Earth presented in this new geography book was secured from "experience and proof (and not belief and faith)."[40] The empirical method of scientific research becomes visible in this later Jacobean edition of Ortelius's text, and all the earlier misappropriations and exaggerations are carefully edited. In line with the old habit of quoting a classical author as a revered source of wisdom, Ortelius quotes Cicero in stating the educational purpose of his geographic compendium. The first page features the Ciceronian maxim "The horse is created to beare and to draw: the ox to til & to labor the earth: the dog to hunt and to guard the hous. But man to consider & contemplate with the eyes of his understanding the disposition of the whole world" (1B). The new empirical spirit of the early modern form of the new geography, as well as the practical instructive aspect of the geographical accounts, makes early seventeenth-century atlases different from the classical narratives of wonder. While in the accounts of the classics about the remote regions of the Earth the tone acquired a mysterious and even rhetorical function, in the clearly informative early modern geographical treatises the unexpected and unexplained had no relevance for the topic under discussion.

This splendid 1610 edition of Ortelius's atlas gives an accurate map of Transylvania, with its towns and rivers. The text on the opposite page is equally factual and instructive:

> This country called in Latin *Transylvania:* is of the Germaines called *Sevenaberger Lant,* that is, the Seven-hily country, of seaven principall hilles where with . . . this county is envyroned. It confyneth on the west side with *Hungary,* & hath *Moldavia* and *Walachia* ioyning to it on the northeast & southeast.
>
> The country albeit mountainous is very good, yielding both corne and wyne & cattel very aboundantly. There are in it wyld oxen which have beardes under their chinnes, and wyld horses whose manes do hang downe to the ground. Mynes there are also both of gold and silver.
>
> The chief citie is called *Hermenstat,* but *Alba-Iulia* is the oldest. The people are very valiant, & have beene very victorious against their cruel easterne neighbours the Turcks, from whose invasions they are much defended through the mountaines that environ the whole countrie even as a citie is environed with a walle. . . .
>
> The prince of this country is called the *Voyevode* & these voyevodes were wont to bee placed there by the kinges of *Hungaria.* (N5)

The factual tone of this early modern description of one of the Romanian provinces makes this presentation relatively unattractive, when compared to other narratives drawing on exceptional acts of violence. However, these accurate texts have an important role in counterbalancing the inflammable and mostly incredible narratives of earlier times. Accounts of everyday social and political life replaced the ancient stories of wonderful things happening in strange eastern lands inhabited by barbarous peoples. This interference of texts and practices, old and new, wonderful and factual, made people see their world as an immense tapestry on which almost everything could be woven and displayed in good order and in full complexity.

The frontispiece of George Sandys's *A Relation of a Journey Begun An: Dom: 1610 (. . .) Containing a Description of the Turkish Empire, of Egypt, of the Holy Land . . .* (1615) shows VERITAS and CONSTANTIA, Truth and Constancy, as the patrons of the book. On each side of the classical structure, there are the symbols of the regions described. The image of the goddess Isis represents Egypt, and the bull Apis or Osyris is in the medallion referring to religion. On the side representing the Turkish Empire, viewers can see the sultan "Achmet, sive Tyrannus." The Turkish "tyrant" holds the globe in his left hand, and in his right hand he leans on a yoke, the medium of subjection of the peoples in Eastern Europe and Asia. The sultan tramples on the instruments of science (compasses) and of learning (the great books of Judeo-Christian culture, the Torah and the Bible). In the medallion referring to religion in the Turkish Empire, the symbol of Christianity lies defeated ("Victa iacet"). This cognitive setting announces the geographical narratives referring to various regions in the Ottoman Empire. With their discernment so heavily influenced by the images opening the book, readers might not notice that most of the information draws on the classics, and the relevance to their age is all but nonexistent. However, this was one of the most popular travel books of the seventeenth century. It contains much valuable information about the countries around the eastern Mediterranean he visited, because Sandys was an unusually acute observer. The book constituted the basis for many iconographic and scholarly representations of eastern Mediterranean regions and many writers in the period referred to it.

Writing of the "Adriatike Sea" and Illyria, Sandys notes that forceful storms are frequent in those seas: "A sea tempestuous and unfaithfull, at an instant incensed with sudden gusts, but chiefly with Southerne winds."[41] Although the book appeared on the market too late for us to be able to draw certain relevance for its influence on the shipwreck off the coast of Illyria in *Twelfth Night*, the general idea that this sea is raided by sea storms must have been part of the collective cultural unconscious. Moreover, these places existed in the Jacobeans' minds as lands devoid of specific localizations, more like shade images projected on a lighted wall, whose contours are very clear but whose defining elements are hidden. From this perspective, it is so easy to suppose that a bush is a bear, or to ascribe certain characteristics to a country with a strange name, heard of vaguely. A similar projection and assimilation process must have given birth to the story according to which the city of Mitylene on the island of Lesbos, also under Turkish domination in Jacobean times, had a strong castle and a garrison that helped, according to Sandys, "to scoure these seas infested greatly by Pirates" (17). All these places mentioned in the geographic and travel texts of Shakespeare's time and after gained an authority mostly inherited from ancient texts; later additions embellished and enriched them with historical fact, delightfully and incredibly blended with mythologized accounts from past and present. This cultural outlook partly responded to the need of the English to construct stories about themselves. Drama would enlarge and expand these stories, offering an additional dimension to them: that of the physical dimension of geographic space, which borrowed the features of the actors and events populating the stage.

With reference to the Black Sea, Sandys gives the already common description and the etymological definition. He notes that "the Black Sea is distant some fifteen miles from Constantinople, so named of his blacke effects, or for the thicke mists that usually hang over it, or as some say, of a princely Bride-groome and Bride that therein perished" (38–39). The author recapitulates the ancient stories drawing on Herodotus about the rough climate of the sea and in the entire area, as well as the barbarity of the population inhabiting its shores:

> First called Axenus, which signifieth unhospitall: by reason of the coldnesse thereof, and inhumanity of the bordering Nations, who accustomed to sacrifice their guests, to eat their flesh, and of their *skulls* to make drinking-bolles. But after the *Ionians* and *Greeks* had planted certaine *Colonies* thereabout, and displanted the barbarous, it was called Euxinus, which hath a contrary interpretation. Of this the exiled Ovid:
>
> > Me the cold coasts of Euxine Pontus hold,
> > More fitly tearmed Axenus of old. (Ovid), *Trist*, 4, Eleg. 4

> The forme thereof is compared to a Scythian bow when extended. (39)

As did many early modern writers, Sandys propagates the confusion created by contradictory ancient reports about this sea. Ovid's testimony in support of the thesis regarding the inhospitable coast of the Euxine Sea is presented as a final word in matters of geographical description, when we know that the Latin poet's position was drastically biased because of his situation as an exile from Rome. The only visible advance of this account, as compared to others, is the comparison of the shape of the sea to an extended bow. The wild Scythian people are said to have been very good at mastering the art of archery, and even this analogy, which is meant to allow readers to visualize the geographic contour of the Black Sea, has deep connotations of war and violence.

Sandys lists the vicinities on the western coast of the Black Sea, bordered "by a part of Dacia, and the hither Moesia, separated by Danubius, and the remainder with Thracia" (39). Again, these are the Latin names used in the classical texts with reference to these regions. As reported by many classical writers, this sea is often frozen and ice storms are frequent. Several Latin poets testify to this biochemical and meteorological statement:

> This Sea is lesse salt than others, and much annoyed with ice in winter.
>
> There were stiffe winter which no spring remits,
> With bonds of ice the Scythian Pontus knits.
>
> (Lucan)
>
> Here the Turke prohibiteth forraines to trafficke, there being no other passage thereinto but by rivers. (39)

The abrupt transition from facts of science to poetical fictions, and then to the situation in contemporary history, makes the statements in these eclectic texts highly improbable. However, this was the information about the eastern parts of Europe available to English readers in the sixteenth and early seventeenth centuries. As far as they knew, the lands in the Black Sea area were hardly accessible, the climate was cold, the population was rude, and, above all, the Turkish occupation precluded any trade relations with the countries in the area. Many texts in the early modern period created, disseminated, and expanded this negative and unfavorable idea about the region of the Black Sea.

The name of the Turks became synonymous with cruelty and disaster, while Islam was the antagonistic evil other of Christianity. In William Lithgow's travel book entitled *A Discourse of a Peregrination in Europe, Asia, and Africke* (1614), the interested reader could find out a lot of instructive information about the Middle East and the western side of the Black Sea. The 1614 edition is the first issue of what was to become, in its various editions, one of the most popular of the seventeenth-century travel books. Though extremely valuable for the insights it gives into people and customs, it suffers from its violent denunciation of popery. The reader learns, among others, about the origin and outgrowth of the city of Constantinople, the customs and religion of the Turks, and the exploits of Sultan Mohammed. According to Lithgow, ambition and presumptuous desire to enlarge his empire led Mohammed to besieging the city and massacring the population. The Turks are referred to as "Infidells" and the author offers a catastrophic representation of terror after the 1453 fall of Constantinople: "In the mercilesse fury of these infernal imps, the Emperour *Constantine* was killed, whose head being cut off, was carried upon the point of a Lance through all the Citty, and Camp of the *Turkes,* to the great disgrace and ignominy of Christianitie. His Empresse, daughters, and other Ladies were put to death, after a strange forme of new-devised torments."[42] Lithgow's persuasive discourse aims at creating an image of horror and mutilation in relation to the Turks' habits, not far from the truth, and yet incomplete and definitely biased. Even in the seventeenth century, Western European writers emphasized the heavy blow given to Christianity through the Turkish occupation of Constantinople, and the permanent threat to the values of European civility posed by the Ottomans.

Seventeenth-century travel writers succeeded in instilling into their readers' minds subliminal information about the Ottomans' barbarity and cruelty. While admitting to the Turks' military superiority and organization, Western European writers never tired of producing catastrophic images related to the inclemency and oppression raging in the areas occupied by the Turks, probably in the hope of providing some positive contrast to the relatively stable Western European ways. It is true that people were impaled, burned, or tortured, during public spectacles of horror, in Western Europe as well, but the narratives of horrors happening in Eastern European distant locations added exotic flavor to these stories and gave them higher marketable value. It likely, therefore, that Shakespeare appropriated and incorporated these mostly fictitious and improbable stories of distant lands in a geographical discourse with eccentric connotations. While early modern nonfiction texts used exotic stories to describe fictionalized spaces, Shakespeare's theater—though the product of literary imagination—offered a realistic and objective account of Eastern European or eastern Mediterranean regions. From *The Comedy of Errors* and *Titus Andronicus,* to *Othello* and *Antony and Cleopatra,* and to the ubiquitous romances, Shakespeare's plays show an amphibolic world in which dramatic comparisons and contrasts intervene to question and undermine orthodoxies and stereotypical interpretations. It is not relevant whether Shakespeare traveled in reality or not; most of his plays seem to be expert travel compendiums, much better documented than the texts available in his time. They offer audiences a direct and impartial view of people and distant lands. Shakespeare did not need to append to his titles the usual note reminding that this is a "true and extraordinary" account, because audiences along the centuries have seen for themselves that they can learn many true and wonderful things from the dramatic encounter with Shakespeare.

Many early modern travel writers sought to produce best-selling books by offering "true and delectable" discourses of faraway places, spicing their narratives with incredible accounts of atrocities that could happen only in distant lands, where nobody could verify their validity. Other authors extolled the benefits of staying at home and enjoying travel vicariously, through books. Joseph Hall's *A Censure of Travell* (1617) is perhaps the best known work in the period attacking travel, either as an element of education or as a means to satisfy mere curiosity. Hall sees travel for commerce no more than a necessary evil, and he maintains that one can gain useful knowledge about other countries' government, manners, and ways of raising taxes by reading the books of accredited authors about these places, which offer a synthesizing and coherent image of the area. "I have knowne some that have travelled no further than their owne closet, which could both teach and correct the great Traveller, after all his tedious and costly peregrinations, what doe we but lose the benefit of so many journals, maps, historicall descriptions, relations, if wee cannot with these helps, travell by our owne fire-side?"[43] This passage might sound like some great marketing advertisement for travel books, written by authors who "have spent themselves in bolting out the truth of all passages" (32), while ordinary travelers, in this view, cannot see everything and spend themselves in tiresome journeys.

Hall's censure of travel and his arguments in favor of reading well researched competent geographic and travel books comes as a surprise in the concert of early modern writings. Authors hoped to attract readers by pretending exactly the opposite, that all the foreign places were described from firsthand experience, while this was very rarely the case.

Fortunately, no tourist companies at that time could protest against providing unpaid-for publicity to scholarly travel books, to the detriment of travel agencies. Communication through knowledge and books was perceived metaphorically as light in early modern times, and Hall praises the ready availability of a large quantity of information about the most distant places: "This age is so full of light, that there is no one countrey of the habitable world, whose beames are not crossed and interchanged with other; Knowledge of all affaires, is like musicke in the streets, whereof those may partake, which pay nothing" (33). Nowadays, when everything has a price, people might pay for the music in the streets, though not so consistently for the products of knowledge. Extrapolating this metaphor to Shakespeare's theater, and the way in which it plays upon and enlarges the audience's knowledge of remote places, we could say that the Shakespearean allusions to far-off spaces are like music in the streets for the audiences' ears. Though they pay to attend the performance of a Shakespeare play, they secure good value for money, because the plays compress and expand suggestions to outlying spaces, people's customs, and culture in such a way that the places become real in front of their eyes. Despite the important amount of intelligence derived from books about all the parts of the known world in the early modern period, however, the area of Europe under the influence of the Turks provided a ready source of radical discourse and negative connotations for the English.

An Itinerary written by F. Moryson (1617) was one of the most compendious encyclopedias of travel published in the seventeenth century. It illuminates European and English conditions and attitudes from an English perspective, and it appeared in both Latin and English editions by the same author, containing plans of several cities in the text. In part 3, book 3, chapter entitled "Of the Geographicall Description of Turkey, the Situation, Fertility, Trafficke and Diet," Moryson enumerates the provinces of the Turkish Empire in Europe at the time, namely, Illyris, Albania, Epirus, Graecia, Macedonia, Tessalia, Thracia, Mysia, Dacia (or Transylvania), and Hungaria. The readers learn that "the Lower *Mysia* is divided into three parts, *Bul-*

garia, Wallachia and *Moldavia.* In *Bulgaria* the River *Danubius* beginnes to be called *Ister,* which fals into the Euxine Sea, with foure strong and three lesser channels. *Dacia* or *Transylvania* was of old possessed by the Saxons, who there built seven Cities or Castles, of which the Province is called *Septem-Castrensis,* vulgarly *Siebenburgen,* and of old it belonged to the Kingdome of Hungary, but at this day is tributary to the Turks."[44] In all the 891 pages of Moryson's impressive *Itinerary* dealing with the manners, customs, and government of the countries in Europe, there are only a few lines describing the Romanian provinces under the Ottoman occupation. Though the Turkish customs and manner of dress are described at length and in detail in this account, the countries under their jurisdiction seem to have no national identity, no customs of their own. It is as if Moryson assumes that, once part of the Ottoman Empire, these regions exist only geographically on the map and are totally subsumed economically and culturally to the Great Turk. Even the geographic information is not very original because it reproduces what many authors before him had said. Despite all this negligence, common to travel writers in the period, English readers could form a vague idea about the territories in the Turkish Empire.

John Hagthorpe was a minor poet and friend of Captain John Smith, who, apparently, had also been a seaman. He wrote an unusual book in prose and verse, *Englands Exchequer or A Discourse of the Sea and Navigation* (1625), dedicated to the duke of Buckingham, which advocates England's interest in the colonies and overseas expansion. The arguments for the benefits of trade with the West Indies are somewhat bizarre, considering that Hagthorpe tries to defame the situation of the current trade routes with the Middle East, invoking the reason that these regions are under Turkish influence. Admonishing the English habit of luxury clothing, with velvet, silk, and taffeta materials being imported from these Eastern Mediterranean regions, the author gives a lucrative argument related to the international division of labor, very actual in the contemporary trade and workforce policy as well. Hagthorpe puts it as a "case of conscience" for the English to reconsider using imported materials from these regions, since this Eastern market would "set so many thousands Turkes, infidels, and hereticks at worke, whilest our brethren here at home perish for want of imploiment."[45] Defining the trade with the Turke as "unsettled" (30) because of the many wars and the mysterious menace in the area, Hagthorpe commends the commerce with the West Indies as more profitable and safe.

Would America need a more persuasive advocate for the successful mercantile exchange with the Continent? Whatever the case, this author, too, joined the chorus of most early modern writers who, for various reasons of religious, military, economic, or cultural extraction, were intent to vilify the entire eastern European and eastern Mediterranean area, for the specific and unmerited excuse of being under the Ottoman influence.

These detrimental accounts about Eastern Europe tended to impress the idea of an imminent Turkish threat upon the readers. Peter Heylyn's *A Little Description of the Great World* (1631)[46] was one of the most popular manuals of geography issued during the seventeenth century, as evidenced by its frequent revisions and reissues. Dedicated to Prince Charles, it is, in many respects, an epitome of the polite learning in the subject regarded as necessary for every gentleman. The author concedes relatively little space to the three provinces of Eastern Europe now forming Romania, but he mentions each of them with reference to their etymology. "Transylvania, so called because it is penetrable no way but through woods" (369) is to the west of "Moldavia, so called for Mauridavia, i.e. nigrorum Davorum regio" (371). Wallachia is "called more properly Flaccia, from Flaccus, a Roman, who here planted an Italian or Roman Colonie" (372). An idea deriving from Heylyn's account is that a common feature of these three provinces is the Latin origin of their names. The Roman occupation had left a strong imprint on the language and customs of these nations, despite the subsequent Slavic and other influences of the migratory peoples. According to Heylyn, "The people speake the Latin tongue, but so that it is much corrupted, and can hardly be understood" (373). These are mere laconic references to the Romanian provinces, covering only a few lines on three pages, out of the almost eight hundred folio pages of this large geographical and historical compendium. However, the fact that these provinces are mentioned among the countries of Europe in the early modern period is of no little importance. Heylyn's treatise handles history, geography, etymology, mythology, and many other domains in the description of the world and is focused on accurate reports of countries and nations. This is a systematic and controlled view of the world, so different from the ancient narratives of wonder or the earlier Elizabethan and Jacobean geographic narratives.

As the readers' tastes advance toward a clearer and more practical grasp of the main features delineating distant places, and the new science loses its ballast of fabulous classical discourse about regions of the Earth, a more compact form of writing emerges towards the mid-seventeenth century. Through the practical guide entitled *The Marchants Mapp of Commerce* (1638), Lewes Roberts wants to come to the aid of the ambassadors to foreign countries, or of travelers who go there for pleasure or for business. Drawn up by a practical merchant and onetime director of the East India Company, this is one of the earliest systematic treatises in English on mercantile affairs and principles. The author attempts to eliminate all unnecessary information about the places described, focusing on the countries' resources and potential for commerce. The classical references are inevitable, but even those interpolations tend to be practical and historically oriented, devoid of all exaggeration or inflated description. In chapter 49 "Of Pontus and the Cities thereof," Roberts writes: "On the North side of *Bithinia* is *Pontus,* wherein is found the ruines of *Tomos* to which Ovid was banished . . . here also ruled *Mithridates,* who for 40 Yeeres withstood the *Romanes,* not more excellent in Warre then learning and memory, who spake 22 languages, and invented that *counterpoyson* from him named *Mithridate.*"[47] Roberts still spices his description with the Latin names of the places, including reference to classical literature and mythology, but the style is more factual and the information borrowed from the classics less evident, being counterbalanced by important and documented practical data.

Though the text provides much information from ancient sources, the factual style and the accent on history, geography, and learning make it more reliable and attractive. Roberts reserves the description of trade in Europe for the last chapter. He considers that, in following the custom of merchants, it is better to "shew the best last, and the worst first" (I, sig. Aa2). The methodical ordering of this guide calls for a division of Europe into fourteen provinces: (1) Spaine, (2) France, (3) Italie, (4) Belgia, (5) Germanie, (6) Denmarke, (7) Norway, (8) Sweden, (9) Moscovia, (10) Poland, (11) Hungarie, (12) Dacia, (13) Slavonia, (14). Grecia. The mode of approach in the description of these countries respects the classical clockwise orientation from west to east. The enumeration of the eight "Seas" of Europe, however, is from east to west, in clockwise manner: (1) Greeke Seas, (2) Egean Seas, (3) Cretan Seas, (4) Ionian Seas, (5) Adriatique Seas, (6) Mediterranean Seas, (7) British Seas, (8) Northerne Seas. This classification and ordering make the description more attractive, interesting the reader in the evolution of the story as a journey, in which geographical distance and narrative space become one. The prevalent information, however, is focused on natural resources and trade. In the section dedicated to the kingdom of Hungary, in which he includes Transylvania, the merchant mentions that the country is so rich that it could feed all Germany, so that the inhabitants sell to their neighbors an important quantity of cattle, copper, tin, corn, honey, wax, and other commodities.

The author makes his narrative more inciting by adding the testimonial component: "and from hence to *Constantinople* I have seene *Hides, Butter* & *Cheese,* that in great aboundance have come out of these parts through the *Black Sea*" (177). This kind of trade from Hungary to Constantinople could only be possible by land through Transylvania and Wallachia, and then through the port of Constanta (ancient city of Tomis) to Turkey via the Black Sea. Another route would be through the Danube, since the lower river area was navigable. Readers learn from this section of the map of commerce that certain countries in Eastern Europe are very rich, but the center of trade for them is via Constantinople, having few direct relationships with the Western world. In the section entitled "Of Dacia and the Provinces and Cities thereof," readers can find one of the most accurate descriptions of the three provinces forming modern Romania, with their vicinities, rivers, and important cities:

> Dacia is bounded on the East with the *Euxine,* on the West with *Hungary,* on the North with the *Carpathian mountaines,* on the south with *Hemus* dividing it from *Greece.*
>
> The rivers that inrich this Countrey are *Danubius,* 2 *Aluta,* 3 *Salvata,* 4 *Cockle,* 5 *Morus,* and some others.
>
> The commodities that this countrey affordeth for merchandise, is *Butter, Cheese, Hony, Wax, Hides, Oxen, Tallow,* and *warlicke horses* of great worth.
>
> The provinces are these, and are under the command of the *Grand Signiour.*
>
> *Transylvania,* the chiefe townes thereof are, 1 *Wisenberg,* 2 *Clausenberg,* 3 *Bristitia,* 4 *Fogares,* and others, and now in possession of *Bethlem Gabor* the *Voievode* thereof.
>
> *Moldavia* is the next, the chiefe cities are *Saccania,* the second is *Falsing,* 3 *Kilim,* 4 *Chermon,* &C. under a *Vaivod* who is tributary to the great *Turke.*
>
> *Valachia* is the third province, the principall townes whereof are 1 *Salnium,* 2 *Praclaba,* 3 *Tergovista,* the *Vaviods* seat, who is tributary to the *Turke.* This countrey abounds in mines of *Gold, Silver, Iron, Salt.* (177)

Roberts uses the Latin name of the country of Dacia, probably because it was more comprehensive, including all the three Romanian provinces of the time. The author gives the Latin names of the rivers, probably inherited from earlier maps in Latin. However, the rest of the information is accurate and devoid of any rhetorical persuasiveness.

The Marchants Mapp of Commerce gives a realistic picture of the situation in the three provinces on the territory of modern Romania, with the exact geographical, topographical, and political situation. Such a guide was very different from the ancient confabulations about these places, though no less distant in tone. The exact description and the system of enumeration give the impression that the narrative is factual and precise, with no deviation from reality. We perceive, however, certain indifference toward these regions, always at the margins of the map, in all cases at the end of any coherent representation of the Continent. In the initial summarized exposition of the regions of Europe, these countries are connected only to southernmost Greece. The inference is that all these areas, being under the direct jurisdiction or only under the influence of the "great Turke," are predestined to ostracism. They were excommunicated from the family of European nations for obscure reasons having to do with their subjection to a foreign power for which they did not ask. These mid-seventeenth-century geographical or travel discourses materialize the growing taste for factual intelligence and the practical necessity of travelers and merchants to learn useful tips for their trading routes. This need existed in the earlier Elizabethan and Jacobean periods as well, but the majority of texts failed to rise to the time's necessity, steeped as they were in the pool of classical fashions. Although the more factual texts by Lithgow (1614), Hall (1617), Moryson (1617), Hagthorpe (1625), Heylyn (1631), and Roberts (1638) cannot have influenced Shakespeare, their presentation is necessary to document the evolution of the reading public's taste and to show how the British were encouraged to see the Eastern European area.

While Elizabethan and Jacobean readers were assaulted from all sides with various texts, by classical or contemporary authors, which narrated, digested, explained, and exhorted on all sorts of subjects, the theater offered them something else. Dramatists, who were engaged in the making of fictions, were well placed to see through the process by which fictions of meaning were made. Therefore, they could play with various views and move toward an objective representation of the worlds they knew or had only heard. As Julia Briggs points out about drama in Shakespeare's time, "The ability to retain opposing points of view in a volatile synthesis, the refusal to ignore contrary evidence or to reject refutations of their strongest convictions, is a source of great power for all these writers."[48] Both tragedy and comedy tested inner convictions against the assumptions of the day, sometimes arriving at potentially subversive conclusions. In dramatizing the national and cultural stereotypes of his time about Eastern European spaces, which posited notions of liminality and barbarity inherited from the classics, Shakespeare uses these ideas in a contrastive mode, questioning their partiality and generating opposing views through historical and locality shifts. Thus, he devises pragmatic ways of talking about things and places or, to use a term from Docherty's chronopolitical theory of interpretation, he constructs "secret narratives."[49] By providing not an allegorical revelation or a demystification of the obscure and partial discourses about distant places, but rather contradictory versions of those texts, Shakespeare construes a dramatic interpretation based on questioning and parody, whose orientation is proleptic.

4

Early Modern Drama about Central European Spaces

IN BEN JONSON'S *EVERY MAN OUT OF HIS HUMOUR,* THE TWO CHARACTERS playing the role of chorus, Cordatus and Mitis, discuss self-referentially the structural properties of the comedy about to begin. After a learned excursion in the history of comedy, they analyze the importance of setting in comedy and the observance of the classical rules regarding the unity of place, time, and action, among which the unity of space is essential. In this context, as Mitis wonders, "In some one play we see so many seas, countries, and kingdoms passed over with such admirable dexterity," and, as Cordatus explains, "The authors can travel in their vocation, and outrun the apprehension of their auditory."[1] By opposing this comedy, which observes the unity of place, to the plays of his contemporaries, Jonson makes the essential distinction between his more classically structured plays and the frequent spatial dislocations and geographical shifts preferred by other playwrights.[2] In an article on Ben Jonson, Shakespeare, and the Italian theorists, David Farley-Hills argues that Jonson employs the neoclassical theories of Cinthio and Ludovico Castelvetro as he criticizes Shakespeare's negligence of the laws of time, place, and characters. In addition, Farley-Hills considers *Eastward Ho* as an attack on *Hamlet; Everyone in His Humour* as an attack on *1, 2,* and *3 Henry VI, Richard II, Henry IV, Henry V,* and *King Lear;* and *Epicoene, or the Silent Woman* as an attack on *Antony and Cleopatra.*[3] Whatever may have been Jonson's critical intentions, he states clearly the idea of representing geographical space with specific dramatic purposes.

This chapter analyzes the perception of Eastern European geographic space in early modern drama in terms of types of plays, sources, scenes, action, nationalities represented, and customs depicted. With a selected corpus of early modern plays as a basis, aided also by an examination of the political situation in Europe and the relations between England and the countries under discussion, it is important to determine how extensive and how accurate the knowledge of Elizabethans and Jacobeans was regarding this area of the world. In addition, we can learn how much the theater could influence and use such stereotypes in order to convey certain information or metaphors. In his seminal study on the complementarity between *locus* and *platea* and the performative force of drama in production to localize and visualize space, Robert Weimann writes of the "self-propelled modes of theatrical signification, the unsettling capacity of the theatre for disrupting the fixture between signs and their meanings."[4] This power accounts for "the movable, audible, visible extension in the use of signs, symbols, localities in rapid succession and interaction."[5] This apparent anomaly of early modern theater's manipulation of space becomes more visible when we look at the paradoxes raised by the representations of foreign locations, spaces that were not so familiar to Elizabethan and Jacobean audiences. While taking into account the potential of drama as a medium of instruction as well as entertainment, it is easy to see the diagonal and often incredibly thwarted relationship between the geographic and historical realities of the places mentioned in plays and the metaphorical treatment they generated in the theater.

The geographic narrative in this chapter starts in the conventional manner, borrowed from ancient texts—from west to east—looking at the inscriptions of Eastern European geography, sometimes straightforward and accurate, sometimes allusive and extravagant, in Elizabethan and Jacobean comedies, tragedies, and tragicomedies. The order is not chronological but geographic and cultural, with the mention that when we examine the plays from this perspective, the context in which the references to geographic space appear becomes less important than the general knowledge transmitted. It is clear, therefore, that the farther we move to the east in the description of places in early modern plays, as in ancient texts, the suggestion regarding the barbarity and marginality of these spaces becomes more evident. Although national and political boundaries about Eastern European countries and regions are accurate in most cases, the discourse moves toward the alien and the negative as the place is more eastward, or *Eastward-Hoe,* to paraphrase the title of the comedy by Chapman, Jonson, and Marston (1604). By examining references to these countries and peoples in popular drama, we learn how early modern English playwrights contributed to the construction of mental maps about places and nations they had never visited. It is a known fact that one's local area is almost always viewed positively, so it is reasonable to believe that English playwrights, despite their critical stance toward the mores in their own country, were tempted to look more favorably at the places closer to home and invest the rest of the world with notions of often objectionable foreignness. These investigations of mental maps show that drama coverage and stereotypical discussions, as well as geographic and travel texts about these Eastern European places, had a major effect on the Elizabethans' and Jacobeans' perception of the world.

Critics have well documented the references to Italy, Spain, France, Denmark, the Netherlands, and other Western European countries in early modern drama.[6] In addition, these allusions and settings far exceed in number the references to Eastern European regions just because the Western world was more familiar to these playwrights. However, when a note of foreignness, violence, or extreme suffering in unfamiliar lands was needed, the reference to an Eastern European place became necessary. Even in the context of the city of Venice, the icon of Western commerce and spiritual intrepidity, the Adriatic Sea on whose coast the city lies becomes a site for suggesting threatening vicinity. In Marlowe's *The Jew of Malta,* as Barabas conjectures, the Turkish fleet that his fellow merchants had seen intends "to pass along / Towards Venice by the Adriatic Sea."[7] Although the other Jewish interlocutors in the debate sense the threatening proximity of the Turkish armada, Barabas's self-serving strategy makes him suggest that there is no obvious threat. Moreover, the mentioning of the Adriatic route inserts an intimidating note in the conversation. Even more upsetting appears the reference to this sea in Jonson's *Every Man in His Humour,* where Brainworm claims, "I have been at Marseilles, Naples, and the Adriatic Gulf, a gentleman-slave in the gallies."[8] The Venetians and the Turks employed prisoners of war as galley slaves. In fact, Knowell's servant brags about his exploits, and the long list of his foreign adventures includes participation in the wars of Bohemia, Hungary, Dalmatia, and Poland, and the siege of Vienna in the past fourteen years. All these Eastern European countries appear as hostile places where war and destruction are at home.

In *Locrine* (1595), a play vaguely connected with Shakespeare's name,[9] the dying Brutus narrates his exploits prior to the foundation of the city of Troynovant (London) and the nation of Albion, supposedly descended from Troy. Unsurprisingly, Brutus's narrative contains many inaccurate geographic references and anachronisms, but the general metaphor of bloody battles waged in mostly strange places is constantly present. After seeking refuge in Greece, Brutus's party sailed "through the boisterous Hellespont" (the Dardanelle strait) to the fields of "Lestrigon," a legendary race of man-eating people who, in the *Odyssey*[10] book 10, were intent on sinking Ulysses's ships. Similarly, Ovid in his *Metamorphoses*,[11] book 15, mentions the Lestrigon. This possibly northern wild race, which Herodotus places in a land with long nights, may be located in the north of the Black Sea. However, Brutus's peculiar geographic narrative cannot be trusted as accurate because, in the next verse, he describes how the Trojans "passed the Cicillian gulf" (Sicily) "And so transfretting the Illirian sea, / Arrived on the coasts of Aquitaine."[12] It can be argued that the author of this play knew little of geography, but it is also possible that the enumeration of these geographic names (*Hellespont, Illyrian Sea*) is meant to cast a note of adventure and peril on the brave Trojan party, who suffered extreme dangers before settling on the comparably safe haven of the English land. Here, as in other Elizabethan and Jacobean plays, foreign locations and seas, as well as long listings of strange-sounding names, have the role of making visible a kind of bizarre geography in which ancient and contemporary space names blend in a confusing amalgam that may impress the audiences through sheer strangeness and the rhetorical power of repetition.

Like the more eastern Euxine Sea, the Adriatic or the Illyrian Sea is famously rough and tempestuous, therefore threatening. Placed between Italy and Illyria, this sea has the reputation of being raided by pirates and the enemy Turk or having caused many shipwrecks, as is implied in *Twelfth Night*. In *The Taming of the Shrew*, the seemingly imperturbable Petruccio says about Katherine that her alleged unconventional behavior cannot move him, "were she as rough / As are the swelling Adriatic seas" (1.2.70–71). Although such reference might seem natural for an Italian, whose closeness to this sea might explain a certain familiarity with its climate, there is more to it than mere comparison. The metaphor foreshadows the roughness of Petruccio's relationship with Katherine, in plain contrast with Bianca and her suitors, who exist in an Italianate setting devoid of any apparent controversy, a conventional Renaissance world of sweet music making and poetry. Petruccio enumerates a famous blackmailing wife from medieval poetry (Florent's ugly love from Gower's *Confessio Amantis*), the old Sibyl of Cumae from Greek mythology, and Xantippe, Socrates' notoriously shrewish wife. All these three classical feminine references are the accredited points of contact on which Petruccio's metaphor of the violent Adriatic Sea relies, prefiguring a conflicting relationship with a woman. As in other allusions to distant places and seas, the geographical reference becomes a point of triangular convergence of the turbulent Adriatic Sea, the classically formal Padua, and the real Elizabethan England, where an arranged mercantile marriage may happen just as it does in any other place in the world.

Illyria is the Greek and Roman name for the area on the eastern shore and inland of the Adriatic Sea. Heylyn defines it as bounded on the east by Dalmatia, on the west by Histria, on the north by Croatia, and on the south by the Adriatic Sea. Ortelius says it is difficult to describe this country, partly because the ancient writers are in serious disagreement about its borders, calling it *Illyricum* or *Dalmatia.* Moreover, as Ortelius observes, "The country people in old time were much given to robberies and thieving but now they be somewhat more civill.[13] The incivility is because of the country's division among various kings who distrust each other and because of the Turks, who are feared by everybody. As do all the geographers of his time, Fynes Moryson, in his *Itinerary* covering the period 1605–17, writes about *Illyris* as part of Sclavonia, subject partly to the Turks and partly to the House of Austria. Moryson mentions the hero Alexander Scanderberg, who had been brought up at the Great Turk's court and then caused the empire so much trouble.[14] Since *Illyria* is the country's ancient name, early modern plays dealing with classical and historical themes and settings mention it in particular. Drama imports these cultural codes of strange and dangerous peoples and locations from geographic texts, which, in their turn, borrow most of the information from classical writers, because of the relative inaccessibility of these regions in the sixteenth and seventeenth centuries. Even the travelers who ventured there, such as Fynes Moryson, did not refrain from taking already processed information about these countries from geographic atlases, which, in their turn, drew on classical texts.

The first play on this list is Marlowe's *The Second Part of Tamburlaine,* whose hero is himself a member of the wild Scythian nomadic tribes that raided ancient Eastern Europe and Asia. The play's popularity and influence on the drama of the 1590s must have a lot to do with the fascination of early modern audiences with powerful and ambitious characters bearing strange names, who are natives of faraway places. In this particular passage in act 1, scene 1, which starts the subplot interwoven in the play's first two acts, three Turkish sovereigns (Orcanes, Gazellus, and Uribassa) agree to an alliance with Sigismund, the king of Hungary, and his two generals (Frederick and Baldwin), in order to combat jointly the encroaching Tamburlaine. Using the artifice of enumeration, which is very effective in drama, Orcanes emphasizes the extent of Tamburlaine's threat by mentioning all the Western European nations fearing him, as well as the other nations ready to enter an alliance against the Scythian: "Grecians, Albanees, / Cicilians, Iewes, Arabians, Turks, and Moors, / Natolians, Sorians, blacke Egyptians, / Illyrians, Thracians, and Bithynians."[15] In addition, Orcanes implies that the Danube, the river that lies at the imaginary border between Turks and Christians, will be red with Christian blood, as will be the sea into which it flows (the Black Sea). However, for the time being, they must all be allies against the common Scythian threat.

This scene from *The Second Part of Tamburlaine,* is an example of how Elizabethan playwrights used history, international policy, geography, and religious debates, interwoven in the plot, in order to address current issues at home. Jeff Dailey's analysis of this scene supports the argument that "the theme of the sub-plot is not an anti-Christian message, but rather a moral one."[16] The passage evidently plays subliminally on the sensitive Christianity-Islam conflict in the period, and there are strong reasons to believe that the compellingly delineated Eastern European geography made visible to the audiences in Orcanes' speech is part of a conflicting rhetoric of war and international politics. In this scene, where the pact between east and west (Islam and Christian) creates a wall against the common enemy, the Danube emerges as the border between two worlds; leaders of both parties mention the river repetitively and it looks as if the kings sealed the pact by shaking hands over its borders. The large number of geographical references in this scene delineates metaphorically the huge extent of Tamburlaine's forces, the power of other Eastern and Western kings, but also a mental map that can become real only in drama. Hungary is near Scythia, Illyria, the Danube, Thracia, Turkey, and many nations and places in Eastern and Central Europe, to remind audiences of political threats past and present, but also to increase the dramatic tension through this kind of visualized geography. The stage is the place where this rhetorical conjunction can happen effectively, and audiences may tend to feel overwhelmed by the sheer number of countries and the vastness of spaces incorporated in the dramatic discourse. This device has the cinematic effect of screen flashes in modern movies and it contributes to the formation of a vague idea about conflicts in these faraway lands.

Shakespeare's Illyria, like his Arden, his Scotland, his Denmark, his wood near Athens, is less of a geographical and cultural location than a space for the free ranging poetic imagination to roam. At times, it seems terribly English: Toby Belch is an overgrown public school boy, spouting endless topical gags. At other times, it is pure fantastic exoticism: Antonio, Olivia, and Orsino grow lyrical, melancholic, and wild with the pain of love. As for Viola, it is hardly surprising that she chooses to disguise herself in a world that seems threatening and alien. Martin Procházka sees Shakespeare's Illyria in *Twelfth Night* and Bohemia in *The Winter's Tale* not as historical, fixed locations but as heterotopias that reflect real sites.[17] In a similar vein, Sara Hanna examines some of the mythical, historical, and geographical associations that Shakespeare may have had access to when he chose Illyria as the setting for *Twelfth Night,* including Greek and Roman representations, its conceptual proximity to Elysium, its geographical and cultural centrality, and its role in various important journeys.[18] Ann Blake examines the significance of location in *Twelfth Night,* finding that the play's Illyria is exceptionally remote and unlocalized, seeing it more as a mood than as a place, and concludes that this lack of localization allows the audience to live in a realm of imagination, undistracted by actualities.[19] Finally, Peter Milward focuses on contemporary religious significances in *Twelfth Night,* arguing that it represents Catholic Italy as well as Protestant England rather than the historical Illyria of the Adriatic.[20] In searching for Shakespeare's localities, the answer to Viola's question, asked at a moment when she is lonely and vulnerable, "What country, friends, is this?" (1.2.1), would be not to locate the geographic reference, but to dislocate it. However, it is possible to discern a threatening note in this harmonious-sounding country name. Shakespeare's Illyria may be a place of festive fantasy, but it also darkens the stage with inauspicious happenings and frightening expectations of wildness.

In *2 Henry VI,* the captain of the pirate ship that captured Suffolk at sea orders that Suffolk be put to death after enumerating the terrible things he had done at the English court. While he cannot believe he could be killed by such low men, the disguised Suffolk says disparagingly, "This villain here, / Being captain of a pinnace, threatens more / Than Bargulus, the strong Illyrian pirate" (4.1.106–8). Cicero, in book 2 of *De Officiis,* a text much used in Elizabethan schools, mentions Bargulus, whose real name was *Bardyllis,* as "Bargullus, the Illyrian robber,"[21] who had great riches. He was first a collier, then a pirate, and finally king of Illyria. Philip of Macedon, Alexander's father, finally defeated Bargullus and killed him. Richard S. Ide finds that, in such plays as *Pericles, Hamlet, Measure for Measure, Twelfth Night,* and *The Winter's Tale,* Shakespeare transforms the conventional device of the attack by pirates into a kind of deus ex machina, and the stereotypical pirate into a symbol of providential intervention[22]—even more so when such devices appear in a history play, where the inscriptions of fate cause frequent shifts of fortune and turn the succession of events. It is not clear whether the Captain who captures Suffolk is a pirate, but the intervention of fate appears in clear terms when Suffolk finds out that his executioner's name is *Walter* and the prophecy was that he would die by water. In this scene happening off the Kentish coast, the allusion to the dangerous Adriatic Sea, Illyria, and savage pirates foreshadows the gory image of Suffolk's severed head and headless body appearing at the end of the scene. Even if Suffolk means his allusion to the Illyrian pirate as a metaphor of a base villain who uses empty threats, the outcome of this scene is unexpectedly gruesome, or rather expected, because the Illyrian hint subtly announces it.

The anonymous *Misogonus* (1577) is an early comedy modeled on the Latin prototype *Acolastus* of Gnaphaeus, published in England with a translation by John Palsgrave in 1540. It draws on the "prodigal son" theme with the general framework and conventions of Roman comedy, in emulation of *Acolastus.* The nominal setting is Italy, but the author of *Misogonus* individualized the somewhat shadowy neoclassic types into English figures of his time. The eponymous young hero leads a life of debauchery, to his old father's distress. However, it appears that Misogonus has an elder twin brother, Eugonus. Immediately after their birth, his uncle carried him off, but it subsequently appears he is in "Polona land" (31) or "Apolonia" (3.2).[23] This is probably the city of Apollonia in Illyria, some eight miles from the sea. Maybe the author means the Illyrian Apollonia, but there are many other cities named Apollonia in Sicily, Crete, Asia Minor, and half a dozen other places. The point in the plot development that is of some interest for my argument is in act 3, scene 2, when Cacurgus, a double-dealing fool who pretends to play the spy for the father and then reports to Misogonus his father's suspicions about him, informs the son at home that he has a lost brother in Apollonia. At this point in the plot, the Illyrian city becomes a threatening place for Misogonus because the twin brother who might inherit his father's fortune in his place dwells there. At the same time, this realization is the first step toward the prodigal son's reformation. Although the text is incomplete, we infer that Misogonus repents and his father forgives his trespassing.

Dalmatia is the southern part of Illyricum on the eastern coast of the Adriatic Sea and this is the ancient Roman name of the region as it appears in classical texts. The Romans first entered Dalmatia in 156 BC, when it became tributary to Rome. The country revolted in 119 and again in 48 BC, but it finally became an imperial province in 34 BC under Augustus. In 16 BC, the Dalmatians made an unsuccessful effort to free themselves and in 11 BC joined the Pannonians in a dangerous revolt and it was not until AD 9 that the Romans managed to reduce the country to subjection. The emperor Diocletian was born in Dalmatia; on his resignation of the purple robe, he retired to his native country, where he spent the last nine years of his life in retirement and died in AD 314. During the sixteenth century, Dalmatia belonged partly to Hungary, partly to Venice, and there were many fights between them about it. In early modern drama, references to Dalmatia appear mostly in plays dealing with Roman history, and these allusions give local color but also emphasize the externality of this region as compared to the centrality of Rome. Such plays have many settings in various parts of the Roman Empire and this geographical dislocation apparently pushes the freedom of observance of the three classical unities to its limits. At the same time, however, it has the role of projecting the audiences' imagination to the farthest edges of the world, while showing them, in an almost physical way, the geographic and cultural extent of the civilized Roman world. Within these boundaries, however, the centrality of Rome is always opposed to the marginality of the other colonies, such as Dalmatia, which is, in fact, not so far from Rome.

Beaumont and Fletcher's or Massinger and Fletcher's *The Prophetess* (folio, 1647) is a tragicomedy set in Rome at the end of the reign of Emperor Carinus, AD 285. The story is about the struggle for power in ancient Rome. Delphia, a prophetess, foretells that Diocles, a mere soldier, will become emperor after he kills a boar. Diocles does not take the prophecy seriously and jokes that, if this occurs, he will marry Delphia's ill-favored niece Drusilla. It turns out that a soldier, Volutius Aper, nicknamed "the boar," has murdered the old emperor, and Diocles kills Aper in revenge. In reward for this action, he becomes coemperor and renames himself *Diocletian.* He ignores his promise to marry Drusilla and courts the princess Aurelia instead. This angers Delphia, who brings a stop to the wedding ceremony by conjuring a storm and a giant monster. She then causes the princess to fall in love with Diocles' rival Maximinian, and the Persians to defeat the Roman army. Diocles realizes the error of his ways, routs the invaders, cedes his half of the throne to Maximinian, and moves to Lombardy with Drusilla. The rising action leads to the moment when princess Aurelia, in love with Maximinian, denounces Diocletian as a "poor Dalmatian slave, a low thing, / Not worth the name of Roman" (3.3).[24] The deprecatory remark suggests not only the contempt that Aurelia feels for Diolcetian, artificially induced by the prophetess's charms, but also the bad reputation and discrediting opinion the Romans had of those not living Rome but in the closer or more remote parts of the empire.

Shakespeare's references to "Pannonians" and "Dalmatians" in *Cymbeline* have produced intense critical debate. In a study on *Cymbeline* and modern Europe, James R. Simon considers how the play locates its characters among competing and interacting claims of religion, nation, empire, ethos, gender, and economy. Simon suggests significant homologies to the overall topography of real and potential locations of dispute in the European world.[25] Similarly, Erica Sheen analyzes how the act of reading in *Cymbeline* displaces narrative meaning in relation to the "Pannonians and the Dalmatians."[26] However, the play's historical context allows for several ambiguities regarding the allusions to these peoples and their anti-Roman struggle. The reference is to the revolt of the Pannonians and the Dalmatians in 34 BC, which Holinshed gives as a reason why Augustus did not extract the tribute withheld by the Britons in the tenth year after the death of Julius Caesar. Cymbeline takes their revolt as a "precedent" (3.2.72) for not paying tribute to Rome, which should incite the Britons to do the same. These populations fought against the domination of Rome, just as the Britons in *Cymbeline* confronted the difficult choice between war and peace. In a parallel scene shifted to Rome this time, a Roman senator announces, "The common men are now in action / 'Gainst the Pannonians and Dalmatians" (3.7.2–3). Here the war appears from the Romans' perspective. As in many plays, Shakespeare uses a triangulation view, which includes the central European peoples of the Pannonians and the Dalmatians on one side, the Britons on the other, and the Romans as the third point. Thus, audiences can see that boundaries among nations and cultures become blurred and nonspecific when perceived from the corporeal direction of drama, and that the theatrical discourse juggles with national stereotypes, preconceptions, and historical or political meanings in significant and always inciting ways.

Like Dalmatia, Pannonia was a province of the Roman Empire lying in the angle to the west and south of the Danube, north of Illyricum, corresponding roughly to the territory of the present-day countries of Austria, Croatia, Hungary, Serbia, Slovenia, Slovakia, and Bosnia and Herzegovina. Augustus partially conquered it in 35 BC and Tiberius finally made it a province AD 8. The Pannonians were a brave and turbulent people and often caused trouble for Roman emperors. Roman writers described the inhabitants of Pannonia as brave and warlike, but cruel and treacherous. In the early modern period, all countries in this area were, in various degrees, under the rule of the Ottoman Empire. However, when reading various editions of Ortelius's atlas describing this region, the references are only to classical authors, such as Solinus, Ptolemy, Florus, Strabo, Dion, Plinius, Aristotle, Diogenes Laërtius, Appianus Alexandrinus, Clemens Alexandrinus, Theophrastus, Ovidius, or Cassiodorus. This means that, in the general frame of mind accessible in the sixteenth and seventeenth centuries regarding these geographical coordinates, these countries existed only in their classical referential structure. It is not surprising, therefore, that the populations in this area enjoyed a reputation of brave and savage people, who drank wine from the skulls of their enemies (as reported by Polybius), but there was little or no information regarding the present political status of these countries, their religion, or the inhabitants' current way of life.

Early modern drama took over these classical stereotypes and developed them into even more established cultural constructs by popularizing these ideas on stage. It is true that mostly the plays dealing with Roman or classical subjects used references to these peoples and the province's ancient name, but the contexts are always those of ferocious opposition against the enemy, of conquering and subduing extended territories, or heroic valor of characters measured in combat with these warlike peoples. In the anonymous play *Nero* (1623),[27] there is an oppositional reference to the Illyrians and Pannonians. The first mention appears in act 1, scene 1, when, in the introductory manner common to plays drawing on Roman history, a group of Romans compare Nero's triumphal image on his return from Greece with mythological exploits or previous victories of Rome's golden Augustan period. The second Roman narrates how he heard his father relate "the triumphs / Which in Augustus Caesar's times were shown / Upon his victory o'er the Illyrians; But it seems it was not like to this" (1.1). We cannot know exactly in what manner Nero's triumph could measure up to that of Augustus, but we can infer that the people compared the two scenes in history in a sycophantic manner for Nero. However, as the other characters exeunt, the First Roman comments that Augustus's triumph was for good cause, suggesting that all people are flatterers, "all ears and eyes": all live in confusion of senses, unable to distinguish wisdom and goodness from their opposites. Therefore, through subtle suggestion and a historical reference to a famous Roman victory over the Illyrians, the play draws a basic distinction between matters present and past, redrawing the historical allusions with the help of geographic landmarks.

In the next scene, Poppaea, Nero, Nimphidius (Poppaea's lover), and others extol the emperor's artistic exploits in Greece, while the inference is that he overlooked famine and suffering. The audience has an alternative view of Nero's exploits in a private conspiratorial discussion in Scaevinus' house, where Seneca and other leaders of Rome discuss critically the crimes surrounding the emperor's accession, from his father's death, to his brother's and wife's murders, and finally to his mother's death. Scaevinus describes Nero's abominable deeds by comparing them to the actions usually attributable to Scythians, Moors, and other barbarous nations:

> Nay, what can you say for him, hath he not
> Broached his own wife's, a chaste wife's, breast and torn
> With Scythian hands his mother's bowels up?
> The inhospitable Caucasus is mild;
> The Moor, that in the boiling desert seeks
> With blood of strangers to imbrue his jaws,
> Upbraids the Roman now with barbarousness.
>
> (1.4)

We can see the predictable inclination of attributing meanings of cruelty to the Scythians or Moors; the implication is that even the Romans have become merciless under Nero's influence. These remote places and their inhabitants are personifications of barbarity, while a geographic triangulation makes it possible for audiences to see that even in Rome, the supposed haven of civilization, such things can happen in times of decadence.

In a similar racial association with implications of cruelty and lack of feeling, in act 3, scene 3, a senator describes Rome on fire and says that even the most ruthless nations would feel sympathy at the terrible sight, enumerating among them "the Getes," the "men of Colchis," the "Scythian," and other far-off populations of poor reputation:

> O Rome, the envy late
> But now the pity of the world! the Getes,
> The men of Colchis at thy sufferings grieve;
> The shaggy dweller in the Scythian rocks,
> The Mosch condemned to perpetual snows
> That never wept at kindred's burials,
> Suffers with thee and feels his heart to soften.
>
> (3.3)

The enumeration has a rhetorical purpose and appears at the close of the scene in order to leave the impression of extreme cruelty happening in the center of the world, Rome, not in some out-of-the-way corners of the empire, where such events might be expected. This apocalyptic scene of the fire in Rome contrasts with the apparently peaceful setting in Nero's palace, where the emperor declares his love to Poppaea by comparing the victory of extracting a kiss from her with a conquest of "the fierce Pannonian" (4.1). In fact, in his delirious fantasy, Nero takes the credit for victories he never achieved, but the Pannonians he mentions remain famously violent and brutal. At the end of this act, in a thoughtless act of violence, Nero himself strikes Poppaea to death. In the end, however, the revolt in the Western European countries, Britain, Spain, the Germanic tribes, and France, causes Nero's fall from power and his subsequent death.

Belgrade was among the European cities under the Ottoman rule in the early modern period; therefore, all the references to it in drama draw on the anti-Ottoman conflict between West and East, Christian and Islam. The capital of Serbia, lying at the junction of the Save and Danube, Belgrade was under Hungarian jurisdiction in the period from 1086 to 1522, but it was the center of wars between Hungary and the Ottomans during the fifteenth and sixteenth centuries; in 1522, the Turkish sultan Solyman conquered the city after several assaults. In Middleton's *Roaring Girl*, Trapdoor claims to have served "in Hungary against the Turk at the siege of Belgrade" (5.1).[28] When Lord Noland asks who served with him, Trapdoor lists "many Hungarians, Moldavians, Vallachians, and Transylvanians, with some Sclavonians (5.1). After the war, Trapdoor says the Venetians took him prisoner, so he traveled all over Italy, and there follows another list of Italian cities and provinces. This conversation looks like an image on a map, with the Eastern European countries on one side, and Italy on the west. However, there is no historical accuracy; as Moll Cutpurse, the heroine of the play, was born in 1584, Trapdoor must have been a centenarian to have been at the siege in 1522. Certainly, this conversation is just vain and empty boasting. In Trapdoor's mental geographical construction, however, the enumeration of Eastern European mercenaries was a way of adding spicing interest to his self-serving narrative because the names of the Eastern European nations must have sounded remote and exotic to his interlocutors, as well as to the audiences of the play.

Theatrical representations of Islamic power took the stage during a time when the Turkish Empire was expanding rapidly. As Daniel Vitkus observes, "English images of Islamic culture often exhibited exaggeration and demonization, but increasingly these images were based on real contact with Muslim peoples in the Mediterranean."[29] In Greene's *Selimus* (1588), for instance, English audiences get a glimpse of the eastern regions from the perspective of the Ottomans. However, the play insists on the fickle fortune theme and we infer that no power is permanent and absolute. In this play, the son, who is already the rightful heir, comes into conflict with his father. Bajazet makes an offer to Selim, sending it through the messenger of Selim: "We give to him all great *Samandria,* / Bordring on *Bulgrade* of *Hungaria,* / Where he may plague those Christian runnages / And salve the wounds that they have given our states" (1.507–10).[30] This was in 1512, but Selim refused the offer, saying, "Here the Hungarian with his bloody cross / Deals blows about to win *Belgrade* again" (3.543–44). Historically speaking, Bajazet's offer is a little premature, as Belgrade was not in the hands of the Turks in 1512; only in 1522 did Selim's successor take the city. Since this play deals with Christian-Turkish wars in the area and the internecine conflicts for the throne among Bajazet's sons, Selim necessarily mentions the Eastern European nations opposing the Ottomans, including "the Hungarian with his bloody cross" and the "mightie Emperour of Russia" (546). Selim's ambition goes beyond the traditional borders of the Ottoman Empire because he wants to bear his father's crown and rule the world, as he confesses in the same scene to the sultan. Nothing can stop him in his stride, and the geographic references to Eastern European nations standing in the way of the Turk are there to emphasize Soliman's insatiate wish for power. Yet, we may notice that, in this play about the Turkish Empire, all characters use too many metaphors from classical Greek mythology; this artifice makes the play pagan, indeed, but not Ottoman at all.

It seems that the kingdom of Hungary as presented in early modern drama is a country lying at the imaginary border between East and West, Muslim and Christian. Geographically, its territory corresponds roughly to the Roman province of Pannonia. The Romans abandoned it to the Goths in AD 247. Successively, the Huns under Attila and the Lombards under Alboinus, or Albovine, the hero of Davenant's play, took possession of the country about 530. At the close of the ninth century, the Magyars, a Mongolian people, crossed the Carpathians and overran Hungary and Transylvania, where they formed the ruling caste that would dominate the country for centuries. Magyar kings ruled the country from Stephen the Saint (1000) to the death of Andrew III in 1301. Then Wencislaus founded a dynasty that lasted until 1527, when Hungary fell into the hands of the House of Habsburg. The Turks, after the capture of Constantinople, attacked Hungary, and ultimately Solyman the Magnificent utterly defeated the Hungarians at the famous battle of Mohacs in 1526. The sultans held the greater part of the country until 1686. The prevailing idea in early modern England about Hungary was that it was a rich country, but the people had fallen into decadence and corruption because of the constant fighting against the Turkish sultans and the subsequent Ottoman occupation. Geographers and historians constructed images of dissolution because of the Turks; the few travelers venturing in those places took back stories of dangers and wars waging the country, and theologians emphasized the resistance that Christianity must present against the invading Ottomans by means of these bordering countries. Drama staged these stories of violence invoking images of kings opposing the Turks and creating powerful alliances, or mercenaries who fought in the numerous wars in the region.

The focus related to Hungary in early modern drama is on the kings who fought against the Ottomans. In Marlowe's *The Second Part of Tamburlaine,* Uribassa mentions the king Sigismond, who reigned from 1386 to 1437 but was defeated by the Turks at another famous battle of Nicopole in 1396.[31] In *Selimus* we are told about the "*Hun-*

garian with his bloody crosse" (544), a sign of a king fighting for Christianity. In Middleton's *Roaring Girl,* Trapdoor claims to have served in all the wars in Hungaria, and in *Every Man in His Humour,* Brainworm makes a similar claim. In Glapthorne's tragedy *Albertus Wallenstein,* the emperor of Germany Ferdinand II orders Lord Questenberg, "Despatch a trusty messenger unto the King of Hungary" (1.2),[32] who is his son, Ferdinand. The emperor enrolls the king of Hungary's help in the fight against the rebel Wallenstein, in a play dealing with Western European politics but involving supportive kings from more eastern parts of the Continent. Moreover, the emperor expects the useful Hungarian troops to train his own army (2.3), probably because they were more experienced in battle.

Most references to the Hungarians in the tragedies deal with a significant king or nobleman's taking up arms against the Ottomans. In Webster's *The White Devil,* the conspirators Lodovico and Gasparo disguise themselves as "two noblemen of Hungary,"[33] who had served against the Turk at Malta and had then joined the order of the capuchins in Padua (5.1), while Francisco appears as Mulinassar, a Christian Moor. Impressed with their "honourable service 'gainst the Turk" (5.1.47) Brachiano even grants Mulinassar a pension. However, later, Flamineo says it is only an empty assurance, because he had heard of pensions promised to soldiers who had fought against the Turk, which were never paid, and even if they were, were barely enough to pay for new wooden legs and fresh bandages for their maimed limbs (5.1.144–48). We see how all attitudes toward anti-Ottoman struggle in these plays relied on deeply ingrained negative preconceptions regarding the Turks. In addition, images of war and destruction, mutilated bodies, and tortured souls emerged about the regions of Eastern Europe under Ottoman jurisdiction. It is as if the plays contributed to the general opinion existing in Europe, namely, that all things Turkish were dangerous and not to be trusted, while these foreigners' actions attained incredible levels of cruelty and ruthlessness. Péter Dávidházi discusses Hungary's singular perspective on the cloud scene in *Hamlet* (3.2), which stems from the country's history of subordination to an oppressive regime.[34] In fact, Dávidházi means communism, but it is possible to extrapolate the metaphor to mean all the historical periods of subordination to a foreign power that had marked Eastern European countries. In early modern times, the Ottoman threat loomed large over political relations in this part of Europe, and English drama of the time rendered this situation accordingly, playing upon images of peril and destruction.

It is important to consider all these characters' references to Hungary in their respective dramatic context, according to their genres and the period of composition. However, what remains in general about this country is the image of a region ravaged by war and led by kings fighting for Christianity. One reference to Hungary in *Measure for Measure* is rather doubtful in both meaning and authorship. Right at the beginning of 1.1., Lucio makes a remark regarding a vague political situation of potential enmity: "If the Duke with the other dukes come not to composition with the King of Hungary, why then, all the dukes fall upon the King" (1.2.1–3). The First Gentleman replies, "Heaven grant us peace, but not the King of Hungary's!" (1.2.4–5) The play's temporal setting is rather indefinite and we cannot give a specific explanation for this political situation. Moreover, the Oxford editors believe that this is an interpolated passage by Thomas Middleton,[35] therefore not relevant to the plot. However, this reference to potential political trouble with the king of Hungary, and even some controversy on "grace" (1.2.24, 25), only hinted at and not continued in the play, may suggest religious conflict and foreshadow the announcement of Claudio's arrest and possible death, as well as the imagery of animalism, horror, and pollution that follows. If we may push speculation even further, the passage implies disobedience and breach of authority on the part of the king of Hungary, because the kingdom of Hungary was supposed to be in cordial political relations with Vienna. Whether a meaningful reference or an insignificant interpolation, this passage announces war, sedition, or moral corruption, usually associated with the eastern parts of Europe, in this case the kingdom of Hungary.

In a more facetious note, early modern playwrights use the term *Hungarian* with a punning allusion to *hungry*, to mean a famished, needy, narrow-minded person. Dramatists reworked the references to foreign nationalities into English dramatic and cultural stereotypes to produce humor, mostly in the comedies. In *The Merry Wives of Windsor,* at the Garter Inn, Pistol addresses Nim, "O base Hungarian wight! Wilt thou the spigot wield?" (1.3.18). The disapproving remark is in jest, but the term is a pun and also a suggestion of foreignness and wildness. In *The Merry Devil of Edmonton,* Blague, the merry host of the George, says, "I have knights and colonels at my house and must tend the Hungarians" (1.4).[36] The host's conversation relies mostly on quibbles and he refers to his hungry guests here. The play is a crossbreed of a reversed comic *Dr. Faustus, The Merry Wives of Windsor,* and *Measure for Measure,* with a young daughter sent to a nunnery and a scholar disguised as a friar. Another deprecatory reference to Hungarians appears when Blague says to his companions, Banks, Smug, and Sir John, who are very much in Sir Falstaff's or Sir Toby's league, "Come, ye Hungarian pilchers, we are once more come under the Zona Torrida of the forest; let's be resolute; let's fly to and again" (p. 244). The editor W. Carew Hazlitt quotes Tollet in a note to this passage, with the following remark: "The Hungarians, when infidels, overran Germany and France, and would have invaded England if they could have come to it. . . . Hence their name might become a proverb of baseness."[37] Moreover, since the Host's remark is an incitement to action, because they are in a hot spot and should escape from the thorny situation, it is reasonable to say that the Hungarians, as had other people from the eastern parts of Europe, had a bad reputation for indolence and tendency toward sluggishness.

A pun on *Hungarian* and *hungry* appears in Brewer's *Lingua* (1603), where Appetitus says, "Give me no sceptre but a fat capon's leg, to shew that I am the great King of Hungary" (2.1),[38] namely, the king of hungry fellows. Though he is a lean fellow, Appetitus's name suggests the gratification of the senses; the conversation he has with Mendacio opposes the pleasures of eating and drinking with the enjoyment of scholarship, and Appetitus proposes an academic subject on cookery. In Massinger's *The City Madam* (1619), Luke reprehends the city madams' aping of court fashions, reproaching the women for their love of foreign fashions and speaking of "your Hungerland bands and Spanish quellio ruffs" (4.4).[39] Considering that the surrounding text mentions imported fashions from other parts of Europe (France, Italy), it is possible that "Hungerland" should mean Hungary and the reference would be to a special kind of ribbon produced there. In this case, the irony addresses superficiality and addiction to fashions. The scene in Massinger's tragicomedy *The Picture* is set partly in Hungary, partly in Bohemia, or as the author states, it draws on "true Hungarian history"; in this play, Mattias, a knight of Bohemia, on going to war with the Turks, parts with his wife and shows her substantial reasons why he should go (1.1).[40] The impression of Hungary as a land where people wage serious battles for Christianity is present in most of these plays. We see, therefore, various aspects of early modern dramatists' relation to the more Eastern European kingdom of Hungary, none of them flattering for the region. Comedies used puns on the country's name and the treacherous fashions emerging from there, while tragicomedies and tragedies played on images of war, dissolution, and opposition to the threatening Turkish invasion.

Bohemia is a famous landmark in early modern geography in drama because of its connection with the setting of *The Winter's Tale* and all the ensuing discussions. Early modern audiences would know from geographic atlases that Bohemia is a kingdom in central Europe, once part of the Austrian Empire. Massinger's *The Picture,* as mentioned earlier, is set partly in Hungary and partly in Bohemia, during the reign of Ladislas of Hungary, in the latter half of the fifteenth century. Mathias, a knight of Bohemia, is the hero of the play, and the author probably refers to Matthias who became king of Hungary on the death of Ladislas in 1457, and in 1469 became king of Bohemia. In Marlowe's *The Second Part of Tamburlaine,* King Orcanes of Natolia, together with other kings, had crossed the Danube to form an alliance with Sigismund king of Hungary against the threat of Tamburlaine. This scene of the pact rings many warning bells because it might be associated with the pact with the kings of Hungary against the Turks in early modern times. Actually, instead of dealing with his future ally Sigismund in peaceful terms, Orcanes boasts of his warlike exploits against European kings, when he claims to have so battered Vienna with his cannon that "the King of Boheme, and the Austrich Duke, / Sent heralds out, which basely on their knees, / In all your names, desir'd a truce" (1.2.2420). This exchange happens in the presence of Frederick and Baldwin, lords of Buda and Bohemia, who are conspicuous in their silence, but who later in the play (2.1.2795–2820) complain about the destructive wars of the Anatolian king and instigate Sigismund to retaliate, despite the previous alliance. The reference appears to be to the defeat of the king of Hungary and his allies at Nicopolis in 1396 by Bajazet I. The king of Bohemia, then, was John the Fearless, but there is no evidence that the Turks reached Vienna at this time. However, the reference to the king of Anatolia's exploits bears a threatening reference to the early modern audiences of the play because of the constant Turkish danger.

The city of Prague is the capital of Bohemia on the river Moldau. During the reign of Charles IV (1346–78), it became one of the most important towns in Germany, and Charles IV founded the city's famous university. In the sixteenth century, Copernicus and Tycho Brache made their home in Prague. For early modern dramatists, Prague was rather distant from their center of interest; because of so many war stories, the city would give the impression of a site of conflict. In Rowley's *A Match at Midnight* (1633), Carvegut says that he served last "at the battle of Prague" (2.1).[41] This battle was at Weisenberg, near Prague, November 18, 1620, and was fatally decisive against the elector Palatine, who, in consequence of it, not only lost his new kingdom of Bohemia, but also was deprived by the Emperor of his hereditary dominions. In this comic context, however, the discussion takes place in a tavern and Captain Carvegut is rather confused; he cannot remember in what regiment and under what colonel he fought, and the Ancient's questions become more and more embarrassing for him. Finally, he avoids needless details by saying that true soldiers scorn pointless discourse, especially in taverns. This easy way out does not get him out of the tight spot he is in, and the Ancient accurately characterizes him and his companions as "tavern rats" (p. 332). The general idea the audience gets, however, about the city of Prague is that there was a war there, where many soldiers died or returned home with confused minds and ruined lives.

In *Twelfth Night,* Feste, disguised as Sir Topas, discloses his mask and spurious authority to Sir Toby, just before going to Malvolio's prison, through a curious and illogical parable: "*Bonos dies,* Sir Toby, for, as the old hermit of Prague, that never saw pen and ink, very wittily said to a niece of King Gorboduc, 'That that is, is.' So I, being Master Parson, am Master Parson; for what is 'that' but 'that' and 'is' but 'is'?" (4.2.11–14). Douce identifies this hermit with a certain Jerome, born at Prague, who became the hermit of Camaldoli in Tuscany, but the reference to Gorboduc is mere nonsense. In fact, it is irrelevant who the hermit of Prague was exactly, because Feste intends his anomalous quibble as a sign of false authority and counterfeit identity. Starting from the false and incorrect Latin (or Spanish) "Good day," through the inexistent hermit of Prague and the fictional niece of King Gorboduc, Feste creates imaginary stepping stones to the deceptive identity of Sir Topas, while using a phrase that is a parody of the divine symbol of absolute selfhood. The biblical "I am what I am" is intentionally twisted into "that is, is," and this philosophical principle is split into semantic units of sophistry. Like in many Shakespearean manipulations of place and time, it is irrelevant, therefore, who the hermit was, or where the real Prague was located; what counts is that this location can be put to creative uses in the dramatic context. In this particular situation, we see the dubious truth value of ambivalent statements drawing on unwarranted assumptions. Moreover, the reference to Prague might summon the image of an Eastern European city that may easily distort any claim to truth because of many unverifiable existing rumors about it.

Poland or Polonia is another country in Eastern Europe mentioned frequently and in many contexts in early modern drama. In the sixteenth century, it was at the height of its power under Sigismund I and II and held its own against both the Russians and the Turks. Dramatists used the country's name for various purposes, but especially in the sense of a country serving as a bulwark of Christianity against the Ottoman advance. In the play offering a perspective of Europe through the eyes of the Turks, Greene's *Selimus* (1588), Selim says of Samandria: "Here the *Polonian* he comes hurtling in / Under the conduct of some forraine prince / To fight in honour of his crucifix!" (Sc. 4. 540–43).[42] In Kyd's *Soliman and Perseda* (1588), the knights from Christendom and Turkey assemble for the celebration of the prince of Cyprus's wedding. The introductory scene creates an interesting array of nationalities, with a marked note of cosmopolitanism attributed to mercenary soldiers. The Englishman served in Scotland, France, and Ireland; the Frenchman fought in Italy and France; the Spaniard's combat cry is "Golden fleece"; Basilisco was born in Germany and claims the Earth to be his country; and the Turk, Brusor, fought for Soliman in Persia, Africa, Asia, Portugal, and Spain. After this presentation of a multinational assembly at a jousting game, the next scene shows Soliman, who states his intention of withdrawing his troops from Persia and Eastern Europe in order to mount an attack on Rhodes. Haleb advises Soliman against it: "I hold it not good policy to call / Your forces home from Persia and Polonia."[43] The general impression conveyed about this area of Europe to Kyd's audience was that Poland, like other Eastern European countries, was under Turkish siege, if not yet tributary to the Ottomans, as the more southeastern principalities of Wallachia and Moldavia were.

Poland as a cold and wintry country and the Polish primitive trading arrangements are other ideas communicated to Elizabethan and Jacobean audiences. In *The Comedy of Errors,* Dromio of Syracuse says of his kitchen wench, "Her rags and the tallow in them will burn a Poland winter" (3.2.96–97), meaning that the greasy rags will burn a long time, the length of a winter in Poland. Dromio continues his geographical metaphor by saying that Nell is "spherical like a globe" (114) and he could find countries in it. However, the countries mentioned in the question and answer session between Dromio and his master Antipholus of Syracuse are mostly in Western Europe: Scotland, France, England, Spain, Belgia, or the Netherlands. Viewed from the perspective of the Syracuse characters, as well as of the English playwright, these countries were more familiar because they were nearer to home, in Western Europe. The mention of America and the Indies provided all the exoticism the poor confused Dromio could assemble in his metaphorical map reading. In opposition, it seems that Flamineo of Webster's *The White Devil* is a traveled and/or informed person, because he refers to various countries and national characteristics. In this sense, Flamineo says that he would rather "be entered into the list of 40,000 pedlars in Poland" (3.2)[44] than have served Brachiano. This is a sarcasm addressed to the poor trade conditions in Poland, but Flamineo lists other displeasing things existing in Western countries. As if speaking from personal experience, Flamineo mentions traveling through France and being his own hostler, which, on second thought, turns out to be a flattering remark about French accommodation, and rotting in some surgeon's house at Venice, which is not a very positive description of the Venetian medical services of the time.

In *The White Devil,* we find another scornful reference to Polish nationals, this time in a conversation between Brachiano and Isabella. Visibly displeased that his wife sought him in Rome, thus rendering his plans for seducing Vittoria Corrombona more difficult, Brachiano shows his contempt for Isabella's brother, Francisco de Medicis, duke of Florence. Brachiano says he scorns the corpulent duke "like a shaved Polack" (2.1).[45] It is clear that Polish foreigners did not enjoy a good reputation in Rome, the play's setting, or in Jacobean England, for that matter, and people mocked their customs and hairstyles. Another example is in the anonymous *Wily Beguiled* (1595), where the Nurse describes Master Churms, the lawyer, to Sophos and Fortunatus in the following ironic terms: "He does so ruffle before my mistress with his barbarian eloquence, and strut before her in a pair of Polonian legs as if he were a gentleman usher to the Great Turk."[46] It seems that Turkish habits influenced the Polish fashions and the lawyer looked ridiculous in his probably large hoses. However, the Nurse is not to be trusted entirely because her biased opinion also characterizes the lawyer's Latin as "barbarian eloquence," which shows dubious contempt of what passed as high education in those times. The inference from these mostly ironic references to Polish customs and dress in early modern drama is that there was a strong influence of Turkish or Levantine ways, while Polish kings fought frequently against the Ottomans, often with few allies and chances of success, in defense of Christianity. In all situations, then as now, things do not come easy for the peoples in these East European countries.

Cracovia or Cracow is the ancient capital of Poland, where most of the country's kings lie buried. Early modern playwrights dramatized historical events having this city as their center. In Beaumont and Fletcher's *The Knight of the Burning Pestle* (1607), the Citizen's wife gives the Citizen an idea for the next romantic plot for Ralph to perform, as she says, "Let Ralph travel over great hills and come to the King of Cracovia's house" (4.2.36–45),[47] where he is supposed to be met by the king's daughter, who is waiting for him in a black velvet castle, combing her hair with an ivory comb. The implausible romantic story is the wife's idea of a good plot, and the location of Cracovia, which we will later find is in Moldavia, is an exotic location stemming from the wife's geographic narrow-mindedness and preconception. Dramatic reversals introduce considerable irony and some of the recommended setting cannot be fulfilled (for instance, the black velvet castle the wife suggests as the setting of the love story between the princess and the knight). In the next scene, Ralph goes to the court of Moldavia, which is held at Cracovia. Actually, in history, Poland claimed the lordship over Moldavia and had many wars with the Turks about it in the sixteenth century. In this play, however, the wife's mistaken judgment of Moldavia as an idyllic place of romance invariably flies in the face of what actually happens in the scene, where Ralph refuses the princess's love and tips her and her servants for her services, as he would treat an innkeeper. Part of the irony involved in this reference to Moldavia addresses the English merchants' and their wives' limited geographic vision and their willingness to place an improbable romantic story in an imprecise and geographically heterogeneous Eastern European place, arbitrarily called Moldavia, or Cracovia, or any such outlandish name.

Moldova or Moldavia is one of the Danubian provinces lying north of Wallachia and east of Transylvania. Princes called *voievozi* in Romanian governed the province, and, during the sixteenth century, it was under the control of the Turks, who extracted tribute and claimed the right of veto on the appointment of the *voievozi*. England was interested in the Danubian provinces at this time and in 1593 sent Edward Barton as ambassador to the Porte of Constantinople to support the claim of Michael the Brave of Wallachia to independence.[48] Ultimately, after having succeeded in uniting the three provinces, Wallachia, Transylvania, and Moldavia, Michael the Brave was murdered. In July 1578, Hakluyt tells us that William Harborne left London by sea to Hamburg and then traveled to Poland. Dressed in the Turkish fashion, he traveled through Moldavia, Wallachia, and Bulgaria, and he arrived at Constantinople October 28 of the same year. Here he obtained from the sultan trade privilege for himself and his companions, as well as letters to Elizabeth, dated March 15, 1579, which Hakluyt also prints.[49] On September 11, 1581, Elizabeth granted letters patent to the "Company of Merchants of the Levant" formed of twelve members.[50] Although trading with the Romanian principalities was not the main business of English merchants, they certainly passed through these countries on their way south.

There is a rather long list of claimants from the Romanian provinces who asked the English court for diplomatic protection. Some of them were reputed scholars, such as Petru Cercel, but many others, according to the Romanian historian Nicolae Iorga, "carried in their luggage genealogies which no one could verify."[51] Among these visitors from the Romanian principalities, special mention is due to Stephen Bogdan, Iancu the Saxon's son, who was financed and protected by Henry Lello, the English ambassador to the Porte, and is known to have been in London both during Queen Elizabeth's reign and, a second time, during the reign of James I. As stated by several researchers in British archives, a manuscript of safe conduct was given to him by Queen Elizabeth in 1592, and there is also another document, Sir Edward Hoby's letter, dated 1607, which mentions "a prince of Moldavia."[52] Marcu Beza quotes Sir Edward Hoby's letter, which documents how the Moldavian prince asked for the queen's mediation with the sultan for restitution of his inheritance. The queen sent him to her ambassador, but after Elizabeth's death, the Moldavian was sold to the Turks. Sir Edward Hoby documents a story of betrayal and political conspiracy, much suited to the plots of drama. It is plausible to believe that the personal gifts of this prince of Moldavia occasioned the introduction of such a fictional character in Beaumont's comedy *The Knight of the Burning Pestle* and Ben Jonson's *Epicoene: or The Silent Woman.*

Judging by the reference in Ben Jonson's *Epicoene,* a Moldavian prince had visited England shortly before 1609. In act 5, scene 1, La Foole and Clerimont discuss Daw's skill while this one is away to fetch his box of instruments—square, compasses, brass pens, and black lead—to draw "maps" of people. Probably these maps were portraits, but the square and compasses were more in the line of the cartographer. La Foole exemplifies, saying that Daw drew maps "of Nomentack when he was here, and of the Prince of Moldauia, and of his mistris, mistris Epicoene."[53] Considering the fact that "mistress Epicoene" was a boy disguised as a woman, therefore a nonexistent identity, it is difficult to trust La Foole's words, which are characteristically the words of a fool. Therefore, we cannot tell precisely whether Nomentack, the Indian chief from Virginia, or the prince of Moldavia could actually have posed for these portraits. What remains probable, however, is the fact that both names sounded exotic and their utterance converged toward the aporetic limit of impossibility: just as Daw could not have drawn the portrait of a nonexistent woman, he could not have documented in painting the visit of an Indian chief or a Moldavian prince. Yet again, drawing the portrait of a person does not mean ascertaining that person's identity. Consequently, Daw might have drawn the portrait of the boy, even if he pretended to be the woman Epicoene, or of the spurious prince of Moldavia, whoever he was.[54] Maybe he was just an adventurer. The location of the West Indies and the Eastern European principality of Moldavia sounded just as remote and elusive to Ben Jonson's audiences.

These examples of early modern dramatic references to Moldavia point to the partial transgressiveness of the theatrical experience. Just as representations of the "foreign" signified a disjunction from the fabric of everyday life, representations of travel pointed to freedom, not merely spatial but also intellectual and social. As Russell West points out, "Theatre is a way of creating, within the settled stability of the source culture, similar modes of perception to those gained in travel."[55] Travel experience means mobility, intellectual flexibility, and an inquiring spirit; the audiences could gain all these assets by staying at home and enjoying plays at theaters across the river. However, theater was something more than simply a surrogate for travel, which the Elizabethan and Jacobean stay-at-home inhabitants liked to adopt. Because of its intrinsic spatiality and direct human interaction, the theater could perform a similar epistemological and intellectual disruption to that embodied in the voyage, without the inherent unpleasantness of the latter. It was enough for a character on stage to suggest a foreign space, and usually these examples occurred in bundles, and the audience could visualize these places and others connected to them within the narrative perspective. Viewed from this direction, representations of geographic space in early modern drama opened infinitely more varied perspectives to the audiences than the mere travel or geographic narrative because audiences could ascribe a variety of meanings to the places mentioned, in accordance with the specific dramatic purpose. Theatrical discourse entailed a strong sense of spatial imagery, and at times the exact geographic location of the place was less significant than the meanings it could summon for the audiences.

Wallachia was the southern of the three provinces of modern Romania, lying on the north bank of the Danube, between Transylvania and Bulgaria. The names *Vlachs* or *Wallacks* (i.e., "foreigners," "Welsh") originally applied to all the Slavonic peoples of the Balkan region. Even etymology, therefore, places this area of Eastern Europe in a context of marginality and foreignness. Lying between the Turkish Empire and the Hungarian kingdom, Wallachia was constantly involved in their wars, taking the part of Christendom in the Turkish conflicts; however, many times the Turks defeated the country, which became tributary to them. Wallachia reached the highest point of its fame in the time of Michael the Brave (1593–1601), who drove out the Turks and made himself prince of Romania and Transylvania. Though it observed the forms of an Islamic legal code, Turkish rule was an unlimited despotism, suffering from none of the financial and constitutional weaknesses of Western states. With its disciplined standing army and its tributary populations, the Ottoman Empire feared no internal threat, except during the periods of disputed succession. It was typical for the sultan, therefore, to be content with being the overlord of these frontier provinces of Eastern Europe, which acknowledged his suzerainty. Moldavia and Wallachia were, for a time, held in this fashion; in Transylvania, the *voievod* John Zápolya gladly accepted Süleyman as his master in return for support against Ferdinand of Austria.

The province of Transylvania lies between Hungary and the Romanian regions of Moldavia and Wallachia. It became subject to Hungary in AD 1004, but gained its independence under John Zapolya in 1538. The population was very mixed, including Romanians, forming the majority of the rural population; Magyars; Saxons (of German origin); and a large number of gypsies. There are not many references to these Romanian provinces in early modern drama, except for a reference in *Pericles,* which appears in chapter 6 of this study, and the one mentioned before in chapter 4, from Middleton's *Roaring Girl* (5.1). Here, Trapdoor claims to have served against the Turks at the siege of Belgrade, in company of many other Eastern European nations, among them the Moldavians, Wallachians, and Transylvanians. The main impression early modern audiences could gather about this nation of European "outsiders" was that they fought as mercenaries in foreign wars and their country was an alien place of undesirable internecine combat. Moreover, many of the inhabitants of this area died in foreign lands, away from their country, subject to the anomalous sixteenth-century immigration rules, according to which most people who traveled did so forced by circumstances, going to war or seeking a better life through commercial activity. In most cases, Elizabethans and Jacobeans ignored that the majority of the population were Christians and that the *voievods* were fighting against Islam and Ottoman political domination, most of the time unaided by the Western powers. For the purposes of drama, this place of conflict served well for attracting the audience's attention to people and lands of nowhere, bearing unusual names, and whom only bizarre characters claimed to have seen.

The ancient Roman name of the province of Dacia, on the territory of modern-day Romania, appears in a few plays in the sense of a remote and barbarous region. The country of the Getae or Daci became a Roman province in A.D. 104, under the emperor Trajan. It lay along the northern bank of the Danube, among the Black Sea, the river Theiss, and the Carpathian Mountains, thus including the early modern Transylvania and Wallachia, and parts of Hungary and Moldavia. The column of Trajan at Rome was set up to celebrate his victory over the warlike tribes of the Daci. Therefore, the general idea conveyed in English plays drawing on Roman or classical history was that of uncivilized tribes that frequently opposed Roman influence. In Massinger's *The Roman Actor* (1626), the player Latinus complains to his fellow actors about the lack of interest in their plays in Rome, hoping for an emendation of this situation after the emperor's arrival. He announces the triumphal entrance of Domitian in Rome, after having fought with the mutinous tribes: "'Tis frequent in the city / He hath subdued the Catti and the Daci" (1.1).[56] This was at the beginning of Domitian's reign, but this conquest was imaginary and led to nothing. Probably this is why the Dacian tribe appears in the text: to suggest an imaginary conquest of an obscure people at the margins of the civilized world.

In *Locrine,* the main hero is the eldest son of King Brutus, and the plot deals with the wars between the Britons and the Huns. Humber, the king of the Scythians, lands on the shores of Albion and claims that no power on Earth can prevent him from taking this territory by force and making it his and his heirs'. In a geographic span that encompasses eastern and western Europe, Humber boasts, "Nor could the barbarous Dacian soueraigne / Nor yet the ruler of brave Belgia, / Staie us from cutting over to this Isle" (1.1.6).[57] Since the entire story of Brutus and Locrine is purely legendary, we should not look for historical correspondents for the barbarous Dacian king. However, what appears a paradox, in a very Shakespearean manner, is that the king of the Scythians, a population considered barbaric and warlike by Western Europeans, even or especially in those ancient times, refers to the king of the Dacians as "barbarous," which tells us that such qualifying tags attributed to other peoples are invariably biased and contingent on circumstances.

Similar in dramatic use to the reference of the distant people of the Daci is the allusion to the Goths in early modern drama. The Goths were a Teutonic people who first appear in history on the north of the lower Danube in the third century A.D. This area was the ancient country of the Getae, the ancient Dacia, and this fact, along with the similarity of names, caused the two peoples to be confounded. The Getae and the Gothi, or Gothoni, are, however, quite distinct. During the third century, the Goths gave great trouble to the Roman Empire and made several inroads with varying success. In the fourth century, we find them divided into Eastern and Western Goths, or Ostrogoths and Visigoths. For a time, Rome extended its protection to the Ostrogoths, but in 410 Alaric, king of the Western Goths, sacked Rome to the amazement of the entire civilized world. Probably because of this aggressive action, early modern drama references to the Goths involve either barbaric nations or strange lands and people with unfamiliar names. In Ben Jonson's *Masque of Queens* (1609), the Heroic Virtue mentions as one of the galaxy "the wise and warlike Goth Amalasunta."[58] It is interesting that most of the foreign queens who appear in this constellation of martial women have strange and melodious names: Penthesilea, the brave Amazon; Camilla, queen of Volscia; Thomyris, queen of Scythia; Artemisia, the Carian princess; Beronice, queen of Egypt; Hypsicratea, of Asia; Candace of Ethiopia; Voadicea, queen of Britain; Zenobia of Palmyr; and Valasca of Bohemia. As did Amalasunta, the daughter of Theodoric the Great, famous for her learning and capacity for affairs, all the other queens mentioned were from distant lands and had strange sounding names, which would have seemed exotic to Jacobean ears.

The destruction of Rome by the Goths must have seemed a piece of barbarism to people in the Middle Ages, and this idea went down to the Renaissance. Drama took over such preconceptions, and we have frequent references to belligerent exploits by the Goths. In *The Misfortunes of Arthur* (1587) by Hughes and others, the Nuntius relating Arthur's landing announces that Arthur's allies are "Islandians, Goths, Norwegians, Albans, Danes" (4.2).[59] It seems that the reference is to the Scandinavians, whom the messenger names Goths, but the indication is, in any case, to warlike peoples. In the anonymous *The Return from Parnassus* (1602), in a discussion by Immerito; Stercutio, his father; and Academico, the scholar mocks Stercutio's rudeness and the fact that he knows no Latin, which he sees as a common trait of any true Englishman. When Amoretto expresses his admiration for Ovid, Academico replies contemptuously, "Good Ovid in his time lived among the Getes; and now, after his death, converseth with a barbarian (2.4)."[60] The audiences must have known that Augustus banished Ovid to Tomi, a town of Lower Moesia, on the Black Sea, formerly inhabited by the Getae and later by the Goths. In this context, and in Academico's assumption, a barbarian is a person who has no Latin, but also a member of the Getae nation, whom the early modern English considered as uncivilized by comparison to the Romans. Similarly extolling a paragon of English civilization, in Ben Jonson's masque *The Speeches at Prince Henry's Barriers,* the Lady of the Lake compares the architecture in King Arthur's time with the Greek temples, and the opposite appears to be the edifice that "all the ignorant *Goths* have rais'd."[61] In this classically tuned mind, the Goths were ignorant and uncivilized, while the people in King Arthur's time were comparable to the Greeks. This is untrue, historically speaking, but the poet goes along with the general conception of the age about the barbaric peoples living farther east in less known areas of Europe.

There are many examples of situations in early modern drama that posit Latin as a perfectly civilized language in comparison to the vernacular. In Shirley's *The Lady of Pleasure* (1635), the Steward to Sir Thomas Bornwell tells Frederick, Lady Bornwell's nephew, that his aunt intends "to make you a fine gentleman and translate you out of your learned language, Sir, into the present Goth and Vandal, which is French" (2.1).[62] Frederick is fresh from the university and his Greek and Latin displease his aunt, who thinks he cannot court a young woman using these languages, while the Steward implies that French vernacular is a barbaric language, related to the idiom spoken by the Goths and Vandals. In a similar note and with the same meaning, we see the reference to Goths and Vandals as symbols of barbaric language in Shirley's *Honoria and Mammon* (1631). In the Mammon house in London, people perceive learning as some kind of infectious disease. When the scholar Alworth presents his letters of reference for employment in this family, lady Mammon speaks disapprovingly of "your most learned tribe, that think themselves / Brave fellows, when they talk Greek to a lady; / Next to the Goth and Vandal, you shall carry / The babble from mankind" (1.1),[63] and she chases Alworth away. This comedy shows that certain members of seventeenth-century upper classes generally despised learning and preferred patronage of those who would flatter them.

Another example of the preconception regarding basic language as opposed to more sophisticated forms of expression is in Shirley's *The Humorous Courtier* (1631). This romantic comedy is set in Mantua, but the kind of social intercourse pictured is that of the court of Charles I. The duchess of Mantua, secretly betrothed to the duke of Parma, gives out that she means to marry at home and enjoys the spectacle of her lords covering themselves with ridicule in their efforts to gain her hand. Foscari, the duke of Parma, takes the disguise of a court favorite under the name of *Giotto*. During an elegant conversation with several lords (Deprazzi, Crispino, Comachio, and Giotto), in the presence of Lady Laura, the duchess's favorite, the men use "hyperbolizing" language. One of the young lords, Volterre, speaks in both Italian and bad Spanish and Giotto calls it something "between Goth and Vandal Spanish,"[64] meaning uncivilized and incorrect language. Looking at the way humor, irony, and ridicule were used in late antique and early medieval writing, Guy Halsall discusses the concept of the barbarian: "The humour directed against barbarians worked not only simply by mocking the supposed nature of the Other; it also worked by ridiculing instances when the barbarian tried to play the Roman. The language barrier that created the concept of the barbarian in the first place could also be used to create comic difference, and underline a sense of superiority."[65] This sense of superiority was transmitted to early modern drama and transpired in the use of "civilized" or "uncivilized" language.

The idea that the Goths and Vandals, and implicitly their language, are uncivilized, as compared to Latin or English, appears in some plays by Beaumont and Fletcher. In the London comedy *Wit without Money* (1614), Valentine is a gallant crazy about fashion, who had relinquished his clothes to his friends in contempt and remained freezing with cold. Master Lovegood, his uncle, and Lance, an ancient servant to his father, want to mock the young man in what concerns his friends and expenditure on clothes. They give him a bundle of rich clothes and taunt him about his friends who have let him suffer in the cold. Lance uses a series of hyperboles, saying that the entire town should shiver with cold, and all should suffer interdiction, "no more sense spoken, all things Goth and Vandal" (3.5),[66] namely, rough-edged language and probably nearly naked people, until Valentine is dressed again in velvet, gold, silver, and Spanish cotton. This city comedy plays upon the metaphor of clothes as disclosing social status and fine manners. To the barbaric clothes and language of the Goths and Vandals, the play subtly opposes the French fashions and manners, supposedly refined and civilized.

In Beaumont and Fletcher's tragicomedy *Philaster* (1609), the hero is the rightful heir to the crown of Sicily and he is condemned to die for having wounded Arethusa, the usurping king's daughter, who, nevertheless, had accepted death willingly from Philaster because she was in love with him. Since Philaster is very popular, however, there is a mutiny in the city in order to save him and probably restore his inheritance. Dion, a noble lord, and Clerimont and Thrasiline, his associates, are Sicilian courtiers loyal to the prince, who are pleased to see that the popular revolt is helping them to rescue Philaster. Therefore, Dion urges his companions to take swords in this attack, and their deeds will be "chronicled," or else he will reprimand them. Dion utters a strange curse against both the cowards and the too daring in battle. His hyperbolic pathos encompasses all domains, including the language characteristics of the island's inhabitants: "May they know no language but that gibberish they prattle to their parcels, unless it be the goatish Latin they write in their bonds—and may they write that false, and lose their debts" (5.3).[67] The "goatish" Latin is actually *Gothish,* which is the common form of the adjective, meaning barbarous Latin.

It is the nature of drama to represent conflicting viewpoints and the variety of experience. As Julia Briggs observes, "By offering a complex experience and demanding a complex response, the drama could express provisional or relative ways of thinking and feeling, and represent a new consciousness of simulation and dissimulation, both within the self and the others."[68] This is even more so when much of this practice drew on familiarity with a range of different philosophies or outlooks, and the differences among pre-Christian, classical, and Christian attitudes. Apparently, this versatility enabled dramatists to present particular issues, situations, or places from contradictory or even opposing angles. However, since classical writings had influenced so much the geographers and educated travel writers of the period, dramatists took over certain classical stereotypes about Eastern European spaces and peoples extant in these texts and gave them new dimensions, synchronized with their age's mentality. Therefore, much of what was anomalous, marginal, and difficult to categorize aroused suspicion, as did accounts about different spaces, peoples, and customs. Paradoxically, however, the merger of old classical stereotypes and new accounts about spaces that most English audiences had never seen created a special fascination with ethical dilemmas and extreme forms of behavior originating in these places, expanding moral horizons and exciting the public curiosity, in a literal and metaphorical way.

5

Eastern European Geography in Early Modern English Drama

LIKE THE MEDITERRANEAN FOR SOUTHERN EUROPE, THE BLACK SEA IS THE symbolic Eastern European water expanse, yielding connotations of cold and inhospitable places, populated by barbarians. The ancients called it the Euxine Sea, or Pontus Euxinus. The modern name is due to the Turks, who found the navigation on this sea difficult after their experience in the Aegean Sea, with its numerous islands, and so they called it Kara Deniz, or Black Sea. Early modern English writers and audiences would know this sea mostly by its ancient name, *Pontus Euxinus,* rather than the modern name, because of the higher frequency of this term in classical texts. In Marlowe's first part of *Tamburlaine,* Bajazet speaks of himself as "Great King and conquerour of Grecia, / The ocean, Terrene, and the cole-blacke sea," (3.1.942–43).[1] By enumerating these vast expanses of water, the Atlantic Ocean, the Mediterranean ("Terrene") Sea, and the Black Sea, Bajazet intends to impress the king of Fez, and implicitly Tamburlaine, who was supposed to receive the fear-provoking message. In the same play dealing with a medieval Scythian conqueror, however, the sea appears under its ancient name. Ortygius, in the presence of other Persian lords, crowns Cosroe "Chiefe Lord of all the wide vast *Euxine* Sea, / And of the ever raging Caspian Lake" (1.1.175–76). The names of the Black and Caspian Seas follow the enumeration of all the Persian territories supposedly owned by Cosroe. In fact, Cosroe's coronation is the result of a coup involving the takeover of power from his brother, Mycetes. In a parallel geographic reference, Mycetes had complained of his brother's betrayal: "O, where is dutie and allegeance now? / Fled to the Caspean or the Ocean maine?" (1.1.109–10) The invocation of this large expanse of water, especially the Euxine and Caspian Seas, suggests wilderness and the negative moral attributes associated with the peoples inhabiting these areas, such as duplicity and disloyalty.

The Euxine Sea is famously turbulent and dangerous, and its destructive force becomes a metaphor for the implacable power of nature and fate. Chapman's tragedy *Bussy D'Ambois* (1595) features the Iago-like character, Monsieur, who sees himself as a minister of fate against the protagonist's alleged infidelity with Tamyra, Montsurry's wife. In fact, Monsieur envies Bussy d'Ambois and plots his murder in complicity with the betrayed husband, in a revenge ploy involving disguises, ghosts, and devils summoned to reveal half-truths. Expecting the betrayal of Bussy and his fall into a trap laid by the deceived husband, Montsurry, Monsieur meditates on the fickleness of fortune and damaged virtue. In an exchange with Guise, Monsieur says that Bussy, though virtuous and strong, will soon become the victim of bad chance, which is harsher than a force of nature. In a group of metaphors with geographic resonance, Monsieur exclaims,

> Not so the surges of the Euxian sea
> (Near to the frosty pole, where free Bootes
> From those dark deep waves turns his radiant team),
> Swell (being enrag'd even from their inmost drop)
> As fortune swings about the restless states
> Of virtue, now thrown into all mens' hate.
>
> (5.1)[2]

The Euxine Sea ranges among the harsh areas with extreme climate; the high waves' swelling is compared to the perturbations of fortune. Monsieur means in particular Bussy's swelling arrogance, soon to be overwhelmed by the intervention of fate. It seems that Monsieur prefers geographic parallels in the area of this wild sea; this scene has a foreshadowing counterpart in act 1, scene 1, where Monsieur makes a similar comparison, which he discloses to Bussy, regarding the customs of the wild Scythians, a population inhabiting the Black Sea area:

> The old Scythians
> Painted blind Fortune's powerful hands with wings,
> To show her gifts come swift and suddenly,
> Which if her favourite be not swift to take,
> He loses them forever.[3]

Monsieur is a believer in serendipity and taking the chance as it comes, but this particular passage describing the customs of the Scythians, people inhabiting the area around the Euxine Sea, foreshadows the associated image of the fickleness of fortune summoned at the play's climax, when Monsieur lies in wait to catch the unsuspecting Bussy.

In early modern tragedies set in classical times, the Euxine Sea and the land around it were the territory at the extreme end of the world, whose ultimate conquest (usually by Rome) proved that there was nothing else left to take by force. In Kyd's tragedy *Cornelia* (1592), we face the unfortunate destiny of Metellus Scipio's daughter, who lives to see both her husbands (Crassus and Pompey) dead, and then her father, who committed suicide after being defeated by Julius Caesar. The theme of the fickleness of fortune blends with the historical representation of the conspiracy against Caesar, when the first seeds of rebellion germinate in the minds of Brutus, Decius, and Cassius. In act 4, unaware of or vaguely warned by Mark Antony about possible discontent among the senators, Caesar boasts his triumph over the entire world in front of his general; Caesar enumerates the peoples he conquered, and, besides Gauls, Germans, Britons, Moors, Numidians, he mentions the people and lands around the Euxine Sea:

> The faithless Moor, the fierce Numidian,
> Th'earth that the Euxine sea makes sometime, marsh,
> . . . .
> Have all been urg'd to yield to my command.[4]

The marsh is probably the Danube delta, where the Danube flows into the Black Sea through (now) three main channels, but earlier there must have been more. In Caesar's self-aggrandizing speech, the conquest of the territories from the Pontus Euxinus, at the margins of the inhabited world, with harsh peoples and marshy land, was a compelling sign of Rome's absolute power, "An universal conquest of the world."[5] We know that Caesar only intended to take the region of Dacia, but his murder prevented it. Only in the time of Trajan were the Euxine lands and the Danube Delta conquered by the Romans.

Interesting parallel speeches by Julius Caesar in Jasper Fisher's *Fuimus Troes, The True Trojans* (1633) suggest a similar vision of the wide expanse of the Roman Empire to the Euxine Sea as the last eastern point of frontier for the civilized world. In a play definitely concerned with nationalistic British issues, in which the British king Cassibelanus fights the Romans led by Julius Caesar, we hear Caesar, placed on the westernmost coast of the Continent, in full view of Dover cliffs on the British shore, paraphrasing what Ovid had said about the Euxine Sea: "beyond, /Nothing but sea and sky. Here is *nil ultra*" (1.1).[6] In addition, in order to emphasize his conquering spirit, Caesar compares the Dover strait to the Hellespont in the Euxine Sea, boasting to Comius and Laberius, his generals: "I long to stride / this Hellespont, or bridge it with a navy" (1.2). In a similar context, Camillus's ghost warns Caesar of the Britons' valor and incites him to fight against this nation, who had helped the Gauls sack Rome, "then led the Gauls in triumph through Greece / To fix their tents beside Euxinus' gulph" (2.7).[7] The reference is to the Gallic incursions of Brennus in 279 BC, when, after being repulsed from Delphi, numbers of the Gauls settled near Byzantium. What appears interesting here, however, is the constant parallel between the easternmost shore of the Euxine Sea and the coast of Britain in Western Europe. From the Romans' perspective, both shores were at the end of the world, beyond which nothing else was. From the British standpoint, after the Romans' defeat by the allied forces of the British, Picts, and Scots, Cassibelanus compares the fierceness of his Cornish allies attacking the Romans with the violence of the "Scythian wolves" (4.4). In the final reconciliation scene (5.6), Caesar and Cassibelanus join hands and pledge mutual peace. At this point, Caesar gives a final laudatory illustration of the extent of the Roman Empire in Europe, from the Tarpeian rock on the Capitol, a symbol of Rome, to the river Danube ("Danow"), which crosses several countries and gathers sixty rivers until it flows into the Euxine Sea (5.6, p. 454). Thus, the Danube becomes a symbol for the Roman Empire, and the Black Sea is its easternmost point, just as Troynovant, the town of London on the Thames, is its westernmost end.

Unlike the majority of classical references to the Euxine Sea, which suggested foreignness and extreme climate, early modern playwrights invested the great city of Byzantium or Constantinople, lying on the strait of Hellespont at the entrance of the same sea, with the glamour and mystery of the East. *Byzantium* was the name of the ancient Greek city on the Bosphorus, on the most eastern of the hills on which Constantinople or the Turkish city of Istanbul now stands. In ancient times, in 440 BC, the city revolted from the jurisdiction of Athens and joined the Lacedemonians. Alcibiades besieged it in 408, and after a difficult blockade took it through the treachery of the Athenian party within the walls. In *Timon of Athens,* it seems that Alcibiades refers to this siege when he says, pleading for a friend before the Senate: "His service done / At Lacedemon and Byzantium / Were a sufficient briber for his life" (3.5.59–60). Alcibiades tries to present this friend's rash action of killing someone, for which the jury intends to execute him, as an uncharacteristic situation due to drunkenness, and he presents his friend's fidelity to Athens. However, the allusion to this particular siege of Byzantium indicates that this friend must have been among the Athenians who worked from within the city and contributed to its fall, introducing a note of betrayal and dishonesty into the discussion. The term *bribe* reinforces this idea of duplicity and foreshadows the sharp dismissal and banishment of Alcibiades himself by the Senate of Athens. Beside the note of foreignness and disloyalty happening in distant lands, Byzantium and Lacedemon have beautiful sounding names.

The city of Byzantium suffered numerous changes of political and religious loyalty and, from the capital of Orthodox Christianity, became the capital of the Ottoman Empire in 1453, under the name of *Constantinople.* Therefore, the same city has different connotations in early modern drama, according to the dramatic intention. Whenever authors need to invoke its glorious classical past, it is "fair Byzantium," as in Greene's *Selimus,*[8] where Mustapha urges Bajazet, when his son, Selim, rebels against him, to run away to the relative security of their beautiful and protected capital city; however, the term *fair* drastically opposes the dishonesty discovered in the rebel son. When playwrights need to summon images of the Turkish threat and domination, they use the city's early modern name, *Constantinople.* This is the name of the city founded by Constantine the Great on the site of ancient Byzantium (AD 328), which was the capital of the Roman Empire of the East until 1453, when Sultan Mohammed besieged and took it by force. Therefore, dramatic references to Constantinople invariably bear the mark of the Ottoman connection, usually in a negative or derogatory manner. In *Henry V,* in the wooing scene, Henry says to Catherine facetiously, "Shall not thou and I, between Saint Denis and Saint George, compound a boy, half-French half English, that shall go to Constantinople and take the Turk by the beard?" (5.2.193–96). Despite this scene's apparent idyllic note and submerged impression of reconciliation between warring nations, the reference to a fictional king who would fight for Christianity against the Ottomans introduces a note of conflict, wedged between the just temporarily appeased Anglo-French war and the ongoing war of the sexes. In addition, the historical framework appears rather blurred because, when Henry V married Catherine of France, Constantinople had not yet fallen. This kind of temporal, historical, emotional, and moral ambiguity draws some of its persuasive force from the ambivalence of power and religious allegiance connected to this city.

In Greene's tragicomedy *Alphonsus, King of Aragon* (1591), act 3, scene 3(2) takes place at the palace of Amurack, the great Turk, at Constantinople. The self-confident and ambitious Alphonsus, who became king of Aragon after having killed his cousin, had defeated Belinus, king of Naples; Belinus goes to the Turkish sultan to seek support. Amurack grants it and the sultan sends Bajazet to bid his vassals, kings of Eastern Europe and Asia, to go to war and gather at the capital city of Constantinople (act 3, scene 3.2.68).[9] The scene indicates an expectation of the Turk's absolute power, which the immediately following conjuration episode radically subverts. In this scene, the sorceress Medea conjures the spirit of Calchas, who makes Amurath disclose, in a trance, his intention of giving his daughter in marriage to the powerful enemy king of Aragon, instead of Belinus, his supposed ally. We see how fate plays an important part in the dealings of the powerful of this world, and the changeable destiny of the city of Constantinople in history is a case in point. Besides, the play's setting is historically inaccurate because Amurack died in 1389 and the Turks took the city in 1453. However, early modern playwrights relied less on historical accuracy than on the suggestive power of an allusion, and in the case of Constantinople, the city's changing fate replicates the characters' shifts of fortune. Sudden changes of fortune and deux ex machina solutions are typical for such an anomalous play, which is announced "a comicall historie," but in which tragedy, depositions, and killings take place.

Similarly, in Kyd's tragedy *Soliman and Perseda* (1588), set in a mixed Christian and Ottoman eastern Mediterranean world, Erastus decides to fly from Rhodes to Turkey, after having killed Ferdinando. When Erastus arrives in Constantinople, Soliman questions him about his background, saying: "for though you Christians/ Account our Turkish race but barbarous, / Yet have we ears to hear a just complaint" (act 3).[10] As if trying to belie these preconceptions, Soliman receives Erastus civilly, in a city renowned for its cultural greatness, and makes him the captain of his Janissaries. Basilisco, the well-traveled knight who boasts that the Earth is his country, reasserts the low opinion the Christians had about the Turks: "The Turks, whom they account for barbarous" (act 4).[11] Meditating on the alterations of love and fortune, Basilisco informs us by way of conclusion: "The Great Turk whose seat is in Constantinople / Hath beleaguer'd Rhodes, whose chieftain is a woman" (act 5).[12] The paradox expresses an unlikely situation that exists because of sudden changes of fortune: Constantinople, the cradle of Christianity, is in the power of Islam, and the fortress of Rhodes, led by powerful generals, is in the situation of receiving protection from a woman, namely, Perseda. As does Greene, Kyd uses this eastern city's name and setting to suggest dark actions of secret power and betrayal in distant Eastern European lands and the eastern Mediterranean area, in a city whose name is renowned as the haven of civilization. The impersonality of the dramatic medium makes it possible for the audiences to see both sides of the situation. On the one hand, there is the Christian perspective that the city of Constantinople had succumbed from its former glory to the hands of barbarous Turks. On the other hand, the play shows that the Ottoman rulers are keen on having a positive image circulated abroad, especially among the Christians who had heard so many disastrous rumors about the Turks.

Another example of a historically inaccurate allusion to the siege of the city of Constantinople, which brings to mind connotations of Turkish power and fleeting fortune, appears in Marlowe's *Tamburlaine, Part 1.* In act 3 scene 1, Bajazet reports that Tamburlaine "thinks to rouse us from our dreadful siege / Of the famous Grecian Constantinople."[13] In front of his allies, the kings of Fez, Morocco, and Argiers, who rule the North African area of Barbary, Bajazet emphasizes the power of the "invincible" Turkish army and the extension of his empire. In order to maintain the siege of the Greek city, Bajazet proposes to cut off the water supply that is running through leaden pipes from the nearby mountain Carnon, while he mounts an attack by sea. Bajazet boasts to conquer the Greek city thus, while he sends a messenger to order Tamburlaine to refrain from attacking him in the meantime. However, according to historical fact, Bajazet did not besiege Constantinople; Marlowe probably thinks of the siege by Amurath in 1422, which was not successful. In any case, the passage emphasizes the greatness of the city's infrastructure, as well as the numerous and significant attempts of the powerful of the day to besiege it in order to acquire the desired status of masters of the civilized world.

A metaphor suggesting sudden changes of fortune linked to the city of Constantinople appears in Massinger's *The Renegado* (1624), where Asambeg, the viceroy of Ottoman-held Tunis, sends "a well-manned galley for Constantinople" (3.5)[14] to take the news of his niece's apostasy to Amurath. In Tunis, Donusa, Sultan Amurath's niece, was soon to be married to Mustapha, the *basha* of Aleppo, elected by the sultan. However, by the hand of fortune, Donusa fell in love with a young Venetian man, Vitelli, who had gone disguised as a merchant to Tunis in search of his sister, Paulina. When Donusa's betrayal comes out, Asambeg announces that he will await the decision from Constantinople regarding her fate and sends the galley there with a message. Although the play is not set in the capital city of the Ottoman Empire, allusions to Constantinople reinforce the theme of fickle fate and the misfortunes caused by illicit love. The reference to the Eastern city of Constantinople as a place where destinies are settled serves as a point of support for the *fortuna labilis* theme. By opposition, Tunis and the Western European city of Venice, the place of origin of the protagonists (Vitelli; his sister, Paulina; and Antonio Grimaldi, the Renegado), are locations set in contrast during the religious conflict between Islam and Christianity. The fact that the protagonists escape to the safety of Christian Venice, away from the punishment of Mohammedan law, speaks once more in favor of oppositions and dispute based on religious arguments, set in symbolic locations suggestive of subtle oppositions. This time, Constantinople is the city of the East that suffers Ottoman pressure, once the cradle of Eastern Christianity, but now the origin of Islamic absolute power and punishment.

A similar parallel between Constantinople of the East and a Western European city appears in Fletcher and Massinger's tragedy *Double Marriage* (published in 1647),[15] where the unhappy state of the city of Naples, under the Aragon prince Ferrand, has a correspondence with the destitute status of submission of the city of Constantinople under the Ottomans. Virolet is a nobleman of Naples who desires fervently his country's freedom. In act 1, scene 1, in his patriotic zeal, Virolet explains to his first wife, Juliana, that the poor situation of capitulation in Naples can be compared to that of Constantinople. According to Virolet, the sufferings of Naples are so great "as that fair city that received her name / From Constantine the Great, now in the power / Of barbarous infidels, may forget her own / To look with pity on our miseries."[16] Just as Naples was the paradise of Italy once, and of the entire world in the earlier times of the Romans, it was in a fallen state under the Spanish domination, much like the city of Constantinople, once the jewel of the East and of Christianity, now a city that could take pity on its even more afflicted sister, Naples. In addition, the projected suffering of Constantinople for the cause of religion foreshadows Juliana's real torment on the rack for the sake of her husband, whom she does not betray to Ferrand. Considering the tendencies in representing nationhood in early modern drama, Claire McEachern writes, "Differences in national characteristics were attributed to religion, climate and custom, but rarely to race."[17] Therefore, the symbol of Constantinople would ring powerfully to Jacobean ears when connected to a city of divided allegiance and religious conflicts.

Oppression of Constantinople, the former pillar of Christianity, under the Ottomans was a common theme in early modern plays, for instance, Fletcher and Massinger's tragicomedy *The Knight of Malta* (1619). Though set in Malta, the action plays against the background of the fight of the Dutch captain Norandine against the Turks for the Maltese capital, Valetta. Displaying the immediate conflict between the knights of Malta and the Turks, Christianity and Islam, the love-and-betrayal argument appears enjoined with religious issues. In the final reconciliation scene, Colonna, a captive redeemed from the galleys during the combat with the Turks, reveals himself as the Italian Angelo. Born in Florence, Angelo, as he says, had been taken by the Turks and has since lived "in Constantinople" (5.2),[18] where he fell in love with a Turkish lady, Lucinda, and converted her to Christianity. The exotic and dangerous setting of the Eastern European city of Constantinople is set against the western Mediterranean island of Malta; these two locations speak for the early modern concern with both political and religious issues, but the solutions to these conflicts are not easy to find. Early modern playwrights exploited these themes in tragedies and tragicomedies, using the exotic Eastern European spaces and the names of various cities and countries as stepping stones in the construction of romantic plots with guaranteed attraction. Stories about pirates, abductions, betrayals, military alliances, or great cities as centers of absolute power could emerge more convincingly from dramatic representations of such distant lands.

In the comedies, early modern playwrights invested such an exotic place as the city of Constantinople with glamour of the East. Moreover, despite the length of the journey, many English travelers arrived there. It is also interesting to note that the English were also contending with a supposed climate theory that was becoming popular throughout Renaissance Europe. This idea suggested that, within an area, those living in the south and north were destined to be polar opposites in personalities and tempers. The people living in the middle of these two zones appeared to be superior because they were able to incorporate the best qualities of the two opposing areas. Writers in the Renaissance rebelled against this theory, some even going so far as to say that every nation had faults and virtues. For instance, Fynes Moryson, in his *Itinerary,* writes, "We betray our ignorance or our selfe love, when wee dispraise forraigne things without true judgement, or preferre our owne Countrey before others, without shewing good reason thereof."[19] Moryson is critical of undiscriminating opinion and judgmental opposition, seldom backed by facts, but, unfortunately, this is how things stood with the general opinion about foreign lands, and especially Eastern European places, in early modern England. It was still common to ascribe the most unflattering qualities to those who were least like oneself. The English began to develop stock stereotypes for other races and these images often showed up in drama.

Thomas Heywood's tragicomedy *The Fair Maid of the West,* published in 1631, illustrates the English simpleton life and the exciting foreign travel of English sea captains. The plot is complete with pirate sea battles, exotic lands, courageous adventures, and devoted love that reflect the ideas of the period. In this play, we have a prime example of virtuous English characters trying to defend themselves from supposedly more vulgar races. Bess is shrewd, valiant, patriotic, and chaste, just like Heywood's ideal English girl. Heywood's entire play is a commentary on how the superiority of England should be recognized and respected. The example of excellence found in both Bess and Spencer has the ability to awaken the heroic spirit in even the most lecherous people. In *The Fair Maid of the West, Part 1,* Roughman and Forset discuss the ways of conquering the soon-to-be heiress Bess, and Roughman compares her to a treasure trove, similar to the exotic Eastern city of Constantinople. Roughman boasts, "There shall be doings that shall make this Windmill my grand seat, my mansion, my palace, and my Constantinople" (2.1).[20] Thus, the Eastern city becomes a metaphor of wealth and good life. Despite the blatant ethnocentrism, the play also signifies that the English were intrigued by far-off cultures and places.

Ever since the anonymous morality play *Hickscorner,* written about 1500, it is evident that the glamour of Eastern European and Mediterranean cities fascinated the English traveler. Being questioned by Imagination and Free Will where he was from, Hickscorner enumerates many Western European countries and regions (France, Ireland, Spain, Portugal, Germany, Flanders, Britain, Gascoigne), and then he passes to Eastern Europe and the eastern Mediterranean, saying that he had been "at Rhodes, Constantine, and in Babylon."[21] These foreign names had a curious fascination for English audiences, and mentioning them in conjunction with more familiar Western countries gave a larger scope to the symbolic morality meaning. Similarly, in Thomas Heywood's *If You Know Not Me You Know Nobody, Part 2* (originally published 1606), Constantinople is mentioned in connection with the building of the Royal Exchange in London. Two well-traveled lords compare this building with the great places they have visited: the First Lord says that "it is the goodliest thing that I have seen," while the Second Lord says there is no such thing in Christendom, adding: "I have been in Turkey's great Constantinople; / The merchants there meet in a goodly temple, / But have no common Burse" (1.1).[22] Here, Constantinople appears as the pinnacle of Eastern European trade in the Renaissance, and comparison of the London Royal Exchange with the one in this city can only be flattering for the former. The lords mention other such financial institutions in the Renaissance, such as the Frankfort Exchange, the Burse in Rome and in Antwerp and, certainly, the Rialto in Venice, but all are in Western Europe.[23] Apart from being a city of culture, Constantinople was, in Elizabethans' and Jacobeans' eyes, a city of trade and profit making.

There was a chance of making great profits at Constantinople, but the journey was dangerous and it was a common practice to insure one's safe return by putting down a sum of money, to be paid fivefold when the insurer returned; otherwise, the person accepting the insurance premium kept the money. In Ben Jonson's *Everyman Out of His Humour,* Puntavorlo, the vainglorious knight, explains exactly this insurance system. He tells Carlo Buffone and Sordido about his travel plans in the following terms: "I do intend, this year of jubilee coming on, to travel: and because I will not altogether go upon expense, I am determined to put forth some five thousand pound, to be paid me five for one, upon the return of myself, my wife, and my dog from the Turk's court in Constantinople. If all or either of us miscarry in the journey, 'tis gone: if we be successful, why, there will be five and twenty thousand pound to entertain time withal" (2.1).[24] Similarly, in *Epicoene, or The Silent Woman,* Morose, in contemplation of his nephew's ruin after Morose's intended marriage to the silent woman, says that Sir Dauphine Eugenie's knighthood will be brought down, and "It shall not have hope to repair itself by Constantinople, Ireland, or Virginia" (2.5.126–27).[25] The implication might be that voyages to these supposedly dangerous places would gain the returning traveler well-deserved fame and fortune, thus repairing any damaged reputation.

Constantinople is the setting of Massinger's *Emperor of the East* (1631), during the reign of the emperor Theodosius the Younger, or Theodosius II (408–50). His eldest sister, Pulcheria, heavily influenced him and pushed him toward Eastern Christianity. Pulcheria was the primary driving power behind the emperor and many of her views became official policy. Theodosius married the poet Aelia Eudocia, who in the play appears as the virgin Athenais, afterward the empress named Eudocia. Massinger has given a coloring of romance to historical characters and this tragicomedy is an attractive hybrid very much because of the romantic aura invested in the city in which the play is set. The fascination of the ancient Eastern city of Christianity blends with the exotic and captivating stories about the Ottoman other in the English audiences' imagination. On the other hand, Western European Renaissance theories blend with this Eastern atmosphere: there are a commercial barter in Constantinople, a theory of the body politic expressed by the emperor, and Renaissance medical theories of Paracelsus, along with those of Galen and Hippocrates. This mixture of beliefs and customs emerges from the conglomerate aspect of early modern drama, which borrowed from and influenced the mentalities of the time, but also from the historical fact that the English had a considerable contact with the Turks and other peoples of the Ottoman Empire. Moreover, it is a fact that there were many Muslims and Turks in England, mainly in London. As Nabil Matar points out, "Renaissance Britons were far more likely to meet or have met a Muslim than . . . an [American] Indian."[26] There is a great deal of evidence to suggest that the attractions of the Levant in general were such that many Englishmen chose to remain in the area and even converted to Islam.[27]

References to Turkey and Turkish customs in early modern drama are numerous and they generally yield political rather than geographic connotations. The term applied not only to the area around the city of Constantinople, but to all the countries under the dominion of the Osmanli Turks. In a narrow sense, the term related to Asia Minor only, and the focus was the capital city of Constantinople. In the broader sense, it included in the sixteenth century Asia Minor, Syria, Egypt, North Africa, Greece and the Balkan provinces, and even a part of Hungary, namely, the Romanian province of Transylvania. Many plays dramatize events in the Turkish Empire, and this setting gives them the appropriate aura of exoticism and outlandishness that would incite the audiences' curiosity. Marlowe's *Tamburlaine the Great* features the sultan Bajazet I, Kyd's *Solyman and Perseda* refers to sultan Suleyman I, and Fulke Grenville's *Mustapha* deals with the reign of the same sultan. Carlell's *Osmond the Great Turk* professes to deal with the reign of the sultan Osman but is quite unhistorical. In addition, the Turks appear in many of the plays chiefly as pirates who carry off one of the characters into slavery or as fighters against Malta, Rhodes, Venice, and other Italian cities.

References to Christians captured by the Turks and sold into slavery or forced to serve in their galleys are numerous. However, these references appear in jest in comedies, where the interplay between spurious identity and pretense is the source of the plot. In Jonson's *Volpone,* in act 2, scene I, Sir Politic Would-Be and Peregrine continue a discussion about travels, amazing eccentricities, and incredible prodigies. When Mosca and Nano enter disguised, they shift the topic to Italian mountebanks, who have fame as impostors. At this point, Volpone enters disguised as a quack doctor and delivers a remarkable speech. He says that he is not one of those impostor *ciarlitani,* who would speak of "their travels, and of their tedious captivity in the Turk's galleys, when, indeed, were the truth known, they were the Christian's galleys" (2.2.60–63),[28] where they had been sent for pilfering. In fact, Volpone seems to speak from personal experience, but the scene describes an apparently tragic situation in comic terms, emphasizing the character's deceit. Dekker's *The Honest Whore* gives another biased opinion about the Turks' alleged viciousness. In his rage against women, because he believed his beloved Infelice was dead, Count Hippolito speaks disparagingly of Bellafont, the chaste or "honest whore." He considers women like her to be "crueler than the Turks," because the latter "sell Christians only, you sell yourselves away" (2.1.431).[29] This kind of ethical indictment would appear normal for a society in which loose women, Muslim foreigners (both Turks and Moors), and all sorts of outcasts were invested with negative moral traits.

References to the eastern European country of Russia, or Muscovy, in early modern drama are frequent and they cover several areas, from descriptions of position and climate and historical allusions to Russian national character, dress, customs and practices, or trade and commerce. Naturally, references to the country's cold climate, with long winter nights, were mostly used to suggest coldness of character or even frigidity or infertility in women of loose morals. In Webster's *The Duchess of Malfi,* the grieving Duchess says she could curse the stars, "And those three smiling seasons of the year / Into a Russian winter" (4.1),[30] and in *The White Devil,* Monticello defines the bareness of "whores" to Vittoria as "cold Russian winters" (3.1).[31] In Jonson's *Volpone,* the protagonist tries to lure Celia by describing various manifestations of their fictitious lovemaking in the disguise of women from many nationalities, among which "the cold Russian (3.6);"[32] thus, Volpone transfers the characteristics of the climate to the women of the country. A tedious story could also be as long as a Russian winter, as the impatient Angelo in *Measure for Measure* says of Pompey's long tale (2.1.122–23). The inconvenience of the Russian cold climate is extrapolated to its people, and thus cultural stereotypes gathered from travel narratives about the unpleasantness encountered during travels in Russia are transferred to the inhabitants and their national history as represented in English drama.

Examining the representations of Muscovy and Russia in early modern travel texts, ethnographies, or "histories," Marshall Poe observes that these accounts describe a barbarous nation of "people born to slavery," and these texts reflect "the collective sense of difference that the travelers felt when they passed over the Muscovite frontier."[33] Early modern drama was ready to take over these cultural typecasts and create an image of wintry climate and barbarous people. In *Selimus,* in order to impress his generals with his power, Selim reviews his victories over Eastern European kings, of Poland and Hungary, but also announces that "Basilius, / The mightie Emperour of Russia, / Sends in his troupes of slave-born Muscouites" (540). This Russian emperor is Basil, who reigned from 1505 to 1533, while Selim's date is 1512–20. The dramatic purpose of Selim's boasting is to impress his interlocutors with the extension of his power, but the underlying notion of the Russians as a people of slaves ruled by a despot is present in many instances in early modern plays. Similarly, in *The Duchess of Malfi,* when Antonio advises the Duchess to bear with strength the trials of ill fortune, the Duchess replies in anger: "Must I, like to a slave-born Russian, / Account it praise to suffer tyranny?" (3.5.75–76). In a parallel image, Ferdinand, pretending to be mad, says he is studying the art of patience that would enable him to drive six snails from Milan to Moscow (5.2.45–48, p. 481), implying a very long journey. It seems that early modern playwrights, influenced by ethnographic accounts of travelers in the far eastern Russia, took over the image of the Russian people as oppressed, bearing their servitude in silence, a nation of slaves under a tyrannical ruler.

The scene of Beaumont and Fletcher's *Loyal Subject* is laid in Moscow during a war with the Tartars, but the date of the action is otherwise indeterminate. An explanation for this play's setting might be the fact that Fletcher's uncle, Giles Fletcher, was a diplomat and the author of a book on Russia. However, the idea of an extreme test of a subject's loyalty under outrageous royal misbehavior goes next to the more subtle suggestion of Muscovy as a country of raging wars and tyrannical kings. Besides the wildness of the people, Russia was famous for its wild beasts, especially the bears, which were imported into England for the bear baitings in London. There are references to the "Russian bear" in Shakespeare's *Henry V,* where Orleans, during a conversation on horses, women, and mastiffs, calls the English "foolish curs, that run winking into the mouth of a Russian bear" (3.7.129–30). This reference to bear baiting is consistent with the animal imagery of the passage and conveys the idea of rude savageness but also contempt, from the perspective of the supposedly more civilized French, who look down on English popular sports. In *Macbeth,* the king defies Banquo's ghost and dares it to approach in the most fearsome form, like "the rugged Russian bear" (3.4.99) or "th'Hyrcan tiger" (100). The animal imagery involving ferocious creatures supposedly inhabiting the wild eastern parts of Europe is meant to exorcize the demons of Macbeth's own mind by mocking the ghost's impending menace. However, in English consciousness, the Russian territory remains a place breeding fierce wild animals and savage people.

Next to the Eastern European country of Russia, names of ancient peoples and places were used to conjure up images of foreign distant savagery. The Cimmerians were ancient equestrian nomads who, according to Herodotus, originally inhabited the region north of the Caucasus and the Black Sea, in what is now Russia and Ukraine, in the eighth and seventh centuries BC. Although the Cimmerians of historical record only appear on the stage of world history for a brief time, numerous Celtic and Germanic peoples have traditions of being descended from the Cimmerians or Scythians, and some of their ethnic names seem to bear out this belief (e.g., *Cymru, Cwmry,* or *Cumbria*). In early modern drama, references to this ancient people were used to summon connotations of darkness, mist (relating to their northern country), and savageness of the people, in contexts of plots drawing on classical history. In *Tamburlaine, Part 1,* the betrayed Agydas visualizes Tamburlaine's wrath and wish for revenge through the image of "an army of Cimmerian clouds" (3.3.77), suggesting menacing fury associated with a land of clouds and mists. In a similar style and in the same play, Bajazet describes to Zabina the force of Tamburlaine's fortune, which is believed to be stronger than "Cimmerian Styx or Destiny" (5.2.171), meant to suggest the gloom and the richness of the underworld. Both examples illuminate the evocative force of a geographic location and a mythical population, whose historical veracity was less important than the compelling images of darkness and savageness these references could intimate.

The Amazons' image is connected with a savage race of female warriors usually located in the neighborhood of Caucasus on the Thermodon, but the word is often used in early modern drama for a woman who acts independent. Thus, in Beaumont and Fletcher's *The Woman's Prize; or the Tamer Tam'd,* Bianca and Livia, the two liberated females, propose "to seek out a land / Where like a race of noble Amazons / We'll root ourselves, and to our endless glory / Live and despise all men" (2.2).[34] Beaumont and Fletcher's comedy *The Sea Voyage* is set in an island where certain Portuguese ladies have fled for refuge from the French and have decided "thus shaped like Amazons, to end our lives" (5.4);[35] when confronting robbers they seek revenge but are finally reunited with their families. In Beaumont and Fletcher's *The Woman Hater,* Gondarino the misogynist meditates on the fate of men in the presence of women: "The much-praised Amazons / Knowing their own infirmities so well, / Made of themselves a people, and what men / They take amongst them they condemn to die; / Perceiving that their folly made them fit / To live no longer, that would willingly / Come in the worthless presence of a woman" (2.1).[36] The twisted interpretations of the Amazon figures from classical mythology bear the mark of each play's dramatic purpose. However, the cultural afterlife of this myth in early modern drama still preserved images of savageness, barbarity, and violence, which are connected with a distant land around the Caspian Sea, inhabited by warrior women.

The Scythians were a nomadic tribe who wandered over the region to the north of the Black Sea, which constitutes the steppes of southern Russia, but their home had no definite boundaries. The last traces of the Scythians disappeared around 100 BC, but the name continued to be applied in a vague way to the tribes of central Russia and Asia. Timur or Tamburlaine is often described as a Scythian and so he is in Marlowe's eponymous play. The Scythians were expert archers, but the plays insist mostly on their barbarity. In *The Second Part of Tamburlaine,* Olympia, the wife of the captain of Balsera, knows that, after her husband's death, she and her son will become the conqueror's slaves and calls for death, fearing that "those barbarous Scythians full of cruelty / And Moors in whom was never pity found / Will hew us piecemeal" (3.4.3430–32) In Field's *A Woman is a Weathercock,* the jilted young Scudmore confronts the lady Belafront and her wedding party; he insists on the inconstancy of women and accuses Sir John Worldly of dishonesty, implying that he has no conscience and should import some from "wild Virginia / Black Afric, or the shaggy Scythia" (2.1).[37] In the early seventeenth century, these regions were reputedly savage and their inhabitants were thought to lack any sign of European civility. Western European ladies are more likely to enjoy this attribute, as it appears from Glapthorne's *Albertus Wallenstein,* where Frederick, Wallenstein's son, praises the graces of Emilia, daughter of Saxon-Weimar. Frederick says, "She bears a spell about her that would charm / A Scythian's native fierceness into softness" (2.2).[38] Whether from ancient or early modern sources, references to Eastern European nations summoned images of foreignness and incivility to early modern audiences. English playwrights took over many such undigested stories about the less known parts of the Continent.

Early modern plays have numerous references to Eastern European countries and peoples from texts of various periods, and they often show contradictory positions that often defy reducing interpretations. Positing the intertextual "overlap" of early modern drama with texts, events, and individuals, Douglas Bruster examines "the patchwork of early modern plays" and defines *quotation* as "a thick description of the text's place in a complex cultural milieu."[39] However, as I argue, these plays and their authors could not avoid a certain stereotypic tendency in their manipulations of foreignness, probably because they thought this was what their audiences wanted to see and hear. Sometimes authors romanticized strange foreign places and populations with exotic names, in accordance with their dramatic purpose, but many times they offered the image of barbarous nations at the margins of Western Europe, whose customs were uncivilized just because they were different. On the other hand, the wish to enrich their plots with ever increasing attracting stories made writers include many references to foreign Eastern European locations, which led to the collapse of distinctions between the foreign and the familiar. This contradictory practice illuminates a time of transformation and a culture in transition, which took over the exotic and strange and adapted it to local circumstances. Such a seasoned mix was meant to attract the audiences in a dynamic game of intertextuality and succeeded.

Audiences enjoyed these exotic stories and, although bringing Goths and Scythians into Rome or London, for example, seemed somewhat inadequate, the foreign Eastern European others were part of the play's ethnographic allegory, which offered variety and incited the audience's curiosity. Generally speaking, these Eastern European aliens were bearers of national, imperial, familial, and social violence. However, their presence provided a mirroring perspective, so much appreciated in Renaissance iconography, which made the viewer look different by reflection. Referring to the place signifiers on the English Renaissance stage, Henry Turner observes that locations have primarily a symbolic rather than realist function. Turner defines his *topographic approach* to theatrical representation as "those moments in which the physical features of a location are designated as descriptively or flatly as possible and the connotative charge recedes relative to the signifier's denotative aspect."[40] In addition, as Russell West observes, "Discussions of the theatre were couched in a spatial language which assumed that performance space was social space."[41] Whether these locations were spaces of exchange (foreign trade with Eastern European countries), spaces of social mobility (comparative class structure), or geographic spaces suggestive of a particular ethnography, there was a permanent shift in early modern drama between the familiar and the foreign within a specific spatial signifying practice: the theater.

6

Romances and Theatrical Geography

SHAKESPEARE CAN BE INSCRIBED IN THE CATEGORY OF AUTHORS WHO USE the attributes of the theatrical potential to condense space and geography and to visualize for the audiences, on the unique expanse of the stage, a multitude of regions of the Earth through shifts of locale and many geographic allusions. In doing so, according to Jonson, these authors manage to exceed the audience's expectations and their limited possibility of comprehending space; this allows them to travel vicariously. Moreover, Shakespeare's demythologized physical geography and ethnography create stimulating contrasts and point to inherent contradictions extant in his contemporary England by showing other nations and spaces.

In focusing on *Pericles* as a possible marker of Jacobean history and claim of imperial domination, Bradin Cormack offers a topical reading that involves Shakespeare's play in the contemporary discourses of power and locality. Evidencing the play's "awkwardly virtuosic fracturing of dramatic action and national boundaries,"[1] Cormack places *Pericles* in the context of the Jacobean use of the sea in service of empire and of contemporary chorography. He argues that *Pericles* dramatizes the impact of legal jurisdiction on the integrity of sovereign authority and the status of national identity beyond national boundaries. As the author says, "in the story of Pericles Shakespeare represents the extension of authority across international distance, the agent of that extension being the sovereign himself, cast by the contingencies of romantic tragicomedy into other jurisdictions and, crucially, onto the sea."[2] Cormack explains the dispersion of the dramatic action across countries and the Mediterranean as signifying the political use of the sea in the service of empire. It is possible, therefore, to admit that the Jacobeans' consideration of the Mediterranean and the more distant seas as marginal waters could have dramatic potential and be theatrically enabling. When viewed from the inside of the British shores, these extraneous spaces might seem distant and marginal, apt to be appropriated for political purposes or discourses of empowerment. When seen from the restricted space of Shakespeare's theater, however, the margins become shifting and variously signifying centers, and subtle or obvious questions are raised regarding the legitimacy of drawing boundaries or confiscating all chances to progress in the name of political advancement.

Documenting the importance of maps in the fashioning of early modernity, Richard Helgerson compares the representation of the world in Jean de Gourmont's Fool's Cap Map (1575) to the ironic mode of Shakespeare's geography. "Like the Fool's Cap Map," Helgerson writes, "Shakespeare's plays work to expose the folly of the world at the same time that they embrace its heady disruptive modernity."[3] Since the image of the Fool Cap's map is an illustration on the dust jacket of *The Norton Shakespeare,* it is appropriate to address the issue of the complementary correlation between drama and the perplexing representations of geographic space in Shakespeare's time. In a period when the refractory representations of selfhood and its integration into space were regarded as the only valid way of intersecting a volatile reality, the ironic mode seemed to be an acceptable form of progress. The injunction on the frontispiece of the illustration is the Latin "Nosce te ipsum" (Know yourself) and the implication is that, by being placed outside the world of fools and observing the mad globe go round, one can reach at least some degree of self-knowledge. Other Latin inscriptions on the Fool's Cap, among them "Who does not have asses' ears?" and "The number of fools is infinite" evoke an Erasmian vision of universal folly, not far from the Shakespearean manipulation of irony in his drama. Moreover, this global image serves as well to suggest the exceptional capacity of this theater to set the mirror up to nature and induce self-knowledge in most viewers and readers, which explains the astonishing worldwide success of Shakespeare's drama.

This chapter parallels the Shakespearean plays belonging to a particular genre with their relevance from the point of view of a specific geography. This method raises a subsidiary question: Does genre affect Shakespeare's dramatization of a certain kind of geographic space? Do the comedies yield a different perspective on stage space and on the presentation of the countries of Europe than the tragedies? John Gillies suggests that theater and cartography are "dialogically related,"[4] and the representation of the Shakespearean other is significantly indebted to these conventional representations of space. Peter Holland stresses the ambiguity of the Shakespearean countries, where place leads to a kind of indeterminacy that is imaginatively potent, both here and there, now and then.[5] The organization of this study suggests that some Shakespearean plays are more geographically oriented than others are. The classical tragedies, dramatizing the irregularities of space and locality connected with power in the Roman world, display an explicit geography that is comparable to the importance attached to ethical issues in tragedy. Such is the significance of geography in some romantic comedies, especially those set in a composite ancient–early modern–Hellenistic world. Much of the initial conflict in these comedies depends on displacement and loss, and the disposition of space has an important role in the definition of the comic closure. In most of Shakespeare's great tragedies, however, ethical problems make the rules, and correlation with space and geography is only incidental and less significant. The romances, on the other hand, borrow the structure of the ancient mythical-historical-geographical narratives of wonder, compelling the audiences to follow the order of the theatrical voyage and to develop an interest in the vague topographic coordinates of that particular imaginary travel during the making of the dramatic fiction.

If the literate part of the Elizabethan public learned to trace unknown regions through the mediation of cartographic materials and travel narratives, for a large majority of people such spaces did not exit at all, except for the dramatic negotiations to be seen at the Globe. There was an "umbilical" relationship, in Simon Palfrey's coinage, between the political constructs of legitimacy in the romances and the "mouldy" tales on which they drew: "Translating into romance's always-creative engagement with beginnings, one finds myth interlacing with history, fantasy transforming allegorical satire. . . . Accordingly, Shakespeare enjoys the mode's sometimes extravagant liberties, but always ballasts any flightiness with classical or contemporary contextualization. In *Pericles,* ancient Athens and Jacobean London underlie the story's oceanic itinerance; *Cymbeline* filters Roman and British mytographies; *The Winter's Tale* reworks Ovid and secular analogy; while *The Tempest*'s multiple utopias juggle Virgilian, Ovidian, and various topical New World discourses."[6] Similarly, Boika Sokolova explains the inconsistency of the romance mode in terms of ideological mediation: "the antiquated, far-off flavour of the romances, so much deplored by critics and variously explained as the consequence of old age, generic specificity, or the change of theatrical taste, can also be seen as an expression of ideology which posited certain social beliefs as 'true,' and pitted them against the others which seemed questionable or downright objectionable."[7] In addition to the ideological and topical dimensions that translate the vague romance mode into the definite form of Shakespeare's theater, an understanding of topography and stage space may be equally relevant for the bizarre dynamics of the romances. This particular theater generates, at once, an act of *knowing* and *doing* within the concrete confines of the spectacle.

In order to set boundaries to their empire and to claim to have reached those that were marked out, the ancient Romans needed a certain perception of geographical space, of its dimensions, and of the area they occupied. The necessities of conquest and government require an understanding of the physical space that one hopes to dominate. There was a similar attempt to map the cosmos, to stabilize it, in the period of Tudor and Stuart England. As Arthur F. Kinney observes, the complex semiological system released through the abundance of maps, atlases, and chorographies had, in fact, destabilized the cosmos, had "unmapped" it.[8] The large assortment of diagrams and visual semiotic codes canceled any notion of fixed eternal truth, or the idea that there was a prevailing image of the universe in the Renaissance. Instead, a composite picture of differing images was formed, none convincingly authoritative. The playwright, therefore, assumed the license to create his own spatial narrative. How do topographical descriptions and place-names function in Shakespeare's romances? Just what is the geographic component, and how does it operate? These are questions critics have tried to answer ever since Ben Jonson's famous commentary on the inaccuracy related to the coast of Bohemia, and in more recent studies. This chapter examines the dialectic of the romances between dramatic texts and the geographic and physical spaces they negotiate and shows the way they lead to the charting of a different topology of the imaginary. My suggestion is that in exploring how identity is constructed and reconstructed through space, Shakespeare models space in a pattern of concentric circles, the center of which is the body on stage. We witness the subversion of space and its transformation into a presupposed conceptual landscape. The play becomes a virtual hypertext, and the audience is invited to find the atopical in each specific case of referential topography. In this way, the dramatist is able to distance the story and to convey a continual reminder that each play is, after all, only a play, reinforcing the duality of the play world and the real world.

Real places were described by travelers and adventurers, codified by cartographers, and systematically explained by geographers. Drama is a different way to talk about space by personifying it and doing something about it. Such personifications are both a form of knowledge and potent speech acts. They deal with "knowing" and "doing" simultaneously. What we know about Bohemia, Sicilia, eastern Mediterranean locations, or a desert island somewhere between Tunis and Naples is irreversibly modified by the concrete contact with a Shakespeare play, be it *The Winter's Tale, Pericles,* or *The Tempest.* Doing implies movement, and the Latin prefix *trans-*, signifying "across, beyond, through," indicates a transaction, negotiation, performance. I notice three directions of spatial progress inscribed in the dynamics of the Shakespearean spectacle in the romances: transmutation, in its concrete form of banishment; *translation,* or the representation of space through travel and shifting spatial references; and *transgression,* the dissolution of the ethical space. To many people, Pericles's peregrination is an unusual form of self-banishment. So is Thaisa's monastic retreat in the improbable pagan-Christian space of Ephesus. Being born at sea, Marina belongs to nowhere, but she is a virtuous exile in the morally corrupted world of Mytilene on the island of Lesbos. In *Cymbeline,* Posthumus is the play's principal wanderer. He is banished to an implausible Renaissance Rome, and the two lost princes are innocent exiles taken secretly away from their father by Belarius, a banished lord. Imogen is temporarily and unwittingly banished to Wales by her husband's misguided rage. In *The Winter's Tale,* the audiences are confronted with faultless Perdita's banishment because of her father's insane passion, with Camillo's enforced exile to Bohemia, and Hermione's retreat in the secret seclusion of her quarters. Nothing more can be said about Prospero's expulsion from Milan and its sociopolitical implications, the banishment of books, the alienation of the shipwrecked, or Caliban's social ostracism as a slave. From my perspective of the negotiations of space in the romances, these erratic displacements and spatial transmutations through exclusion and estrangement contribute to the special dynamics involved in this genre.

Translation is a different method of dramatizing space in the romances. The multiple and often-discordant shifts of locale in *Pericles,* as in the other romances, account for a potent energy that centers on the stage and involves various geographical regions. In *Cymbeline,* there is permanent motion in space and in time. The play's casual anachronisms are an ingenious form of putting to good dramatic use the need for a constant dynamic of *translation* in both space and time. Travel is effected between ancient Britain and Renaissance Rome, or between "Lud's town" (3.1.32) and Milford Haven. Giacomo is an Italian Machiavellian personality. A definitely Renaissance Frenchman attests that he met Posthumus in Orléans (1.4.29), while the Britons expect the Roman troops to move on them from ancient Gallia (3.5.24). These techniques of spatiotemporal ambivalence and discrepancy create a general confusion. They produce a bizarre and active notion of space and time, adequate to the romances' indefiniteness. *The Winter's Tale* shifts from Sicilia to Bohemia, in a disturbance of temporal deficits and anatopical surface features. These incongruities have often been explained as a privilege of representation within certain genres.[9] *The Tempest* makes progress horizontally, through narrative space, between Prospero's island and Milan, Naples, and Tunis, but mostly in the vertical intensity and inconsistency of psychological amplitude. Space and geography act as symbolic triggers of mental animation in this play's diverse dramatic topography. These theatrical techniques of rapid progress in time and space create only apparent confusion. In fact, they help the audience produce their own mental geography, in close relation to the theater they see.

A third spatial coordinate, which potentially defines the dynamics of the stage world in the romances, can be termed as *transgression*. Moral codes signify differently in the ambivalent brothel space in *Pericles*, where the Pander, the Bawd, and Boult are no better or worse than their clients of various nationalities, a Transylvanian, a Spaniard, and a Frenchman, or the governor Lysimachus. The revelations of incest at the court of Antiochus and the strange gamble of marriage and death riding on a riddle's answer make the play's ethical movement go distressingly haywire. Gower's placid interventions in the order of moral judgment only extend the discrepancy between the slow-moving distancing narrative of the chorus and the dynamic multiple moral violations in this play. Giacomo's amorality in *Cymbeline*, as well as the Queen's needless wickedness and Cloten's fury, generate the direction of moral transgression on stage, building an actual space of evil. Similarly, Leontes' anomalous rage dominates the stage world in *The Winter's Tale*, imposing a fiery Sicilia on the audience, in contrast to an apparently pastoral Bohemia. What the audience will never know about *The Tempest* is whether Antonio clearly repents in the end, or his silence is merely a measure of the disproportionate depth of evil. The stage space opens amply in this play, generating a special dialectic of movement. It forces the audience to travel from an initial dislocation away from native places, as experienced by Prospero in his self-reflective narrative of exile, through various actual and mental geographies disclosed in the play, to the final deduction that ethics provides the only individual space that counts.

Pericles: Sociality of the Brothel

Theoretical work in the domain of cultural studies during the eighties emphasized the need for a complex reorganization of temporal and spatial relations, a reordering of space in accordance with the complex postmodern constructions of human geographies, life practices, global values, and discourses.[10] According to Clifford Geertz, "The world is a various place,"[11] and by confronting its actuality and difference, one can barely hope to access a fragment of its complexity. Foucault's "heterotopias"[12]—heterogeneous spaces of sites and relations—include, in a convergence of socially created spatiality, the theater and the garden, the museum and the library, the brothel and the prison. This interpretation of space and time juxtaposes in a single real place several socially produced spaces of imagination: "The brothel is in fact a place, and an architecture of pleasure . . . The men of the city meet at the brothel; they were tied to one another by the fact that the same women passed through their hands, that the same diseases and infections were communicated to them. There was a sociality of the brothel."[13] The Elizabethan theater seems to have been a similar space, a marketplace of interlocking social energies[14] and psychological tensions.

While sociohistorical criticism of Shakespeare's romances in the eighties and the nineties examined the representations of political power in Jacobean England, particularly the king and his family,[15] other recent studies have centered on an interpretive geography of Shakespeare's last plays.[16] The late sixteenth- and early seventeenth-century ideological constructions of Eastern European and eastern Mediterranean cultures saw them as liminal locations, outside the margins of the civilized world. The ambiguous *topoi* in *Pericles* and the vague Hellenistic atmosphere dramatize these places as part of a common "European" ancient and early modern world. This romance is a site of fluid interference of archaic and Elizabethan practices intersecting within the imaginary world of a far-traveled story, the Apollonius of Tyre narrative. The brothel space functions as an authentically shared social architecture of communal cultural paradigms; it is an Eastern and Western concurrence of mutual habits converging in the omnipresent and multiply rewritten narrative of loss and recovery. For reasons of brevity, I call the author of *Pericles* "Shakespeare" and I hope to encompass the entire vexing problem of authorship and text within these conventional limits. Whether Shakespeare revised an earlier play does not alter my analysis of the play's imaginative landscape in relation to the Apollonius story. However, since my argument focuses mainly on the topical references in the two brothel scenes, definitely considered to be by Shakespeare, probably my comments on these locations will illuminate indirectly the problem of authorship. All Apollonius narratives center on a brothel scene, yet only *Pericles* mentions the three European nations in connection to this place.

My focal point is mainly on the two brothel episodes in act 2, scenes 2 and 4 (the *Arden* edition), or scenes 16 and 19 (*The Norton Shakespeare*). In these scenes, the intriguing references to various European nationalities in the context of the discussion on venereal disease have a special importance for the play's topographical organization. The Pander reports on a "poor Transylvanian" (16.18), who is dead for having lain with one of the "poor three" (6) prostitutes left in the depleted Mytilene brothel. Boult gives an account of the lecherous and ludicrous "Spaniard" (16.87), whose mouth watered at the mere description of Marina's charms. The already diseased "French" Monsieur Veroles (16.90) gloats in expectation of seeing the young and beautiful Marina. In an anomalous model of distorted rhetoric, the Bawd tries to convince Marina of the "pleasure" (16.17) of alterity experienced in the brothel, where she is supposed to "taste gentlemen of all fashions' (16.69), and "have the difference of all complexions" (16.17). The cosmopolitan society of this particular establishment contains, in a loose democracy of the body, Eastern "barbarians" and "civilized" Western Europeans, all confounded in a mixture of interracial sexual liaisons. The "poor Transylvanian" is already dead in the play's time scheme, and his presence has an indirect effect for the audience's consideration. The report of his medical affliction, the venereal disease he had contracted at the brothel, telescopes the geographical reflections from a vague Hellenistic space of indeterminate location to a specific early modern chorography. This urbane milieu articulates the reductive Jacobean view of the other as alien and intruder with the play's clearly charted awareness of difference. The audiences might infer that at least some trade was on between Mytilene on the island of Lesbos and the region of Transylvania, which the unfortunate traveler at the brothel had left.

The authors of *The Shakespeare Name Dictionary* consider Shakespeare's reference to the "Transylvanian" as incidental. They argue that "in Shakespeare's England this would have been a remote and obscure place, so it is likely that Shakespeare is merely drawing on the common knowledge of Latin in which Transylvania means 'across the forest.'"[17] It is true that Ortelius's atlas mentions the Latin origin of the name of the province of Transylvania, but the embodied imagery of the stage offers at least a double, if not a multiple, version of the reference to this province existing now in modern Romania. Indeed, the author of *Pericles* plays on the audiences' expectations of liminality of this region, and its nice-sounding Latin and extravagant name. However, he places reports of this nonexistent personage in an eastern Mediterranean location, where they practice the world's oldest profession, in the company of two representatives of well-known Western European countries, the Spaniard and the Frenchman. This vicinity and the mutual venereal disease they suffer from are meant to question the audiences' expectations of vulgarity and crudeness from the representatives of a distant Eastern European region. The poor Transylvanian is, after all, human, like any other member of the Western European countries. The stage space includes the Transylvanian in the European community of nations. Concurrently, the reference suggests the intensive trade existing between the eastern Mediterranean area and this particular province surrounded by the Carpathians and their forests. As evident from the geographical texts of the period, Transylvania exported much of its overabundance of cattle, corn, minerals, and honey through the Black Sea, to Constantinople and farther south, to the Greek cities and islands in the Mediterranean.

The particular reference to the three white male Europeans, a Transylvanian, a Spaniard and a Frenchman, formerly lodged or expected to stay at the brothel on the island of Lesbos, integrates the Western paradigms of race, sex, and travel within the common space of the brothel, the marketplace, the theater, and a geography of illusion. All national stereotypes of virtues and vices converge within the socially conditioned space of love as commodity, an artificially constructed site of self-delusion and grotesque reality, as specified in Boult's explicit remark: "Well, if we had of every nation a traveler, we should lodge them all with this sign" (99–100). According to the pimp's figurative logic, his verbal description of Marina, the image of an image, simultaneously expands geographically to include all the nations (of Europe) and contracts into the iconic representation of a social space: the brothel, the theater, or the printing house. The Pander informs his coworkers that "Mytilene is full of gallants" (16.3) and the cynical discourse revolves around the value of money (16.4) represented by sexuality at market time (16.4). The Bawd, Pander, and Boult elaborate on "trade" (16.9), "credit" (16.26), "estate" (16.28), and sex as "commodity" (16.26; 27), which implies "wages" (16.27), marketing value, "warrant" (16.51), and bargaining, while they eagerly express their wish to "prosper" (16.10) financially and the invitation to "search the market" (16.3; 14; 20; 82).

This economic banter suggestive of international trade is curiously blended with echoes of "conscience" (16.9; 18), the profession's standing with "the gods" (16.30), or the "mystery" of religious "calling" (16.33). Boult is invited to describe the attractive colors of Marina's seductiveness, and the pimp perceives his portrayal as theatrical representation, with himself as the author and the actor of an original performance and the philanderers of Mytilene as his audience: "Performance shall follow" (16.55). After he has "drawn her picture with [his] voice" (16.83), Boult is sure that a Spaniard and a Frenchman will be lured presently to their multinational Mediterranean Greek, Jacobean English, and Western European place of artificially constructed illusion and make-believe pleasure. The arbitrary sign of the brothel outlines a cosmopolitan site of encounter between past and present, history and geography, in the global representation of a common European and Mediterranean space incorporating shared weaknesses, vicissitudes, and fears. The political and moral ambiguity surrounding Mytilene throughout the play alludes to an antagonistic place of self-represented reality and harsh deception that deserves no closure.

Pericles is a particular representation of the Shakespearean "theatre of wonder,"[18] and it relies specifically on Apollonius's "mouldy tale" to reconstruct collectively a narrative concerned with tale making and remaking within a shared theatrical space that creates the telescoping illusion of an entire globe. The brothel space articulates, in the audience's imagination, the horizontal geographic expansion of Europe and the Mediterranean with the vertical antiquity of the tale. Shakespeare may have been aware of the temporal and geographic extension of the Apollonius saga from other sources besides Gower and Twine, or the popular Medieval Latin *Gesta Romanorum.* The author of *Pericles* is likely to have come across the 1578 Falckenburgk version of the story, printed in London at Richard Graphei.[19] It is a poem in Latin hexameters dedicated to Queen Elizabeth, the earl of Leicester, Lord Burghley, and others. Apart from the fact that, in the initial dedicatory verses to the queen, the author mentions the hero's "mille periclis," this version combines the traditional story of Apollonius with the parts of the Jewish-Syrian struggle related in the two Books of Maccabees, identifying the incestuous king as Antiochus IV Epiphanes. The final justification of the poem is particularly interesting. Here, the author adds a brief biography of Apollonius and explains that he reconstructed the story from manuscript fragments, "from an ancient exemplar," in both Greek and Latin. He saw this special copy of the story during a military expedition in Hungary.

Average Elizabethans or Jacobeans would know that Transylvania, now in Romania, was at that time an independent principality neighboring the kingdom of Hungary. If they did not know, they would probably hear about it, or check in one of the English versions of Ortelius' *Theatrum Orbis Terrarum* (1606). They could read there about "Transsylvania, Wallachia and Moldavia."[20] The 1606 edition of Ortelius's atlas is also interesting because it presents aspects of contemporary and ancient geography, the "Peregrinations of St. Paul," maps of the Roman Empire and the Mediterranean, with the Greek islands (Cyprus, Rhodes, and Lesbos) in detailed framed presentations. History blends with geography in the graphic presentation of "The Voyage of Alexander the Great." Finally, visual and literary discourses coalesce in "The Voyage and Navigation of Aeneas, especially gathered out of the renowned poet Virgil: with some other matters perteining to that historie collected out of others."[21] The poetry of traveling and the spatial geographic dimension of poetry are absorbed in a disconcerting correspondence of texts and images. Moreover, a monumental perspective picture of "Daphne, or the pleasant Suburbs of Antiochia in Syria" is offered to the curious eye. The 1610 English edition of Ortelius's atlas describes the Transylvanians in favorable colors, mentioning that they are a brave people fighting against the Turks. The inhabitants of this region are favored by the topographical characteristics of their country, surrounded by the Carpathians on three sides.

According to most Elizabethan and Jacobean historians and geographers, at that time Transylvania acted as a barrier for the civilized world against the menacing Turks, an ambivalent space of intermingling Western and Eastern cultures where margins and center converged for the accomplishment of a common anti-Ottoman goal. There is a consensus among Renaissance scholars regarding the Elizabethan and early Jacobean anxieties toward the "Turk," who was perceived as the alien other invading the supposedly civilized Christian world.[22] As Constance C. Relihan observes, "The liminal cultures in which *Pericles* occurs, cultures which simultaneously belong to Classical Greek and New Testament traditions—the sources of Western civilization; and to the infidel, anti-Christian Ottoman Empire—the location of that which is perceived as the non-Western Other, both promote and defeat English identification with the events of the play."[23] The ambivalent setting and action in this play, as noted by many critics, originate in the classical narratives of wonder. Thus, geographical and political ambiguity in *Pericles* paraphrases the technique of classical authors to leave blanks in their narratives about distant places, in order to attract the readers'/audiences' attention. The stage space, on the other hand, magnifies, condenses, and visualizes these vague locations in a way only early modern cartography could in Shakespeare's time. If there is a Jacobean English analogue in *Pericles,* it may be explored through the cultural, geographic, and linguistic allusions that go beyond the domestic political constructions of early Jacobean rule. The alleged outsiders of the Western European world, such as the Transylvanian, have a special place on Shakespeare's stage, beside other more privileged nations.

By mentioning the three European ethnic groups associated in the adversities of pleasure and suffering within the socially empowered sign of a brothel, placed in a suggestive Eastern Mediterranean location, the author of *Pericles* dramatizes the ambiguity of a cultural space balanced between two colliding worlds. The now-corrupt classical Greek culture, in a debased state of submission to the former "barbarians," encounters the Western liberal spirit in the emblem of a long-lost yet multiply rewritten tale, in which the undeserved adversities of fortune play an important part. Shakespeare's apparently random reference to a "Transylvanian" might conjure the image of a traveler from an uncertain Eastern and bizarre land, placed in the same location and in direct relation to the familiar Western Europeans, the Spaniard and the Frenchman. The "poor Transylvanian" is already dead, he atoned for his sexual transgressions, and an attentive actor may introduce a glimmer of pity in the Pander's otherwise cynical discourse. Boult's derogatory version of the diseased Spaniard and Frenchman, on the other hand, offers large scope for irony. Theatrical productions may enhance the Transylvanian's convenient and significant absence in a variety of ways. In the 2002 RSC production of *Pericles* in Stratford-upon-Avon, directed by Adrian Noble,[24] for example, the image of the Transylvanian's death was summoned through the powerful suggestion of a rough wooden coffin being lowered into the pit during the Transylvanian's grim funeral. In this production, the dumb show addressed the international issue from the direction of the macabre but cathartic image of death on stage.

The Jacobean audience must have been aware of at least a few of the many variants of the Apollonius story, if only from the onomastic allusions in the Apocrypha, *The Geneva Bible.*[25] Pericles' *mille pericles* and alterations of fortune paraphrase the cultural and geographical adventures of Apollonius's antique story: an original lost Greek manuscript, supposedly rendered into Latin; translated into many vernaculars, including English, French, and Spanish, printed in Transylvania; and translated into medieval Greek. This story is like a palimpsest, an inscription that testifies to the fragility of all cultural negotiations. Shakespeare must have been aware, at least in part, of the antiquity and geographic extension of the story. The specific ethnic allusions include this theatrical representation (the first extant dramatization in a long succession of prose and verse narratives) in an authentically shared European and Mediterranean textual geography, a new form of *Theatrum Orbis Terrarum,* celebrating the centrality of Europe in the formation of modern nationhood or, according to Ortelius, "This our Europe . . . honourable throughout all the world. . . . And although it be in compass lesser then the other, yet for the worthinesse of the people it is preferred before all other partes of the world, & euer hath bin by all auncient writers, hauing both for the Empier of the Macedonians, and mightynesse of the Romaines bin moste renowned."[26] Gower's choric presence in this amalgam of interconnected perspectives acknowledges the Apollonius story as a medium of dynamic exchange between past and present. He links *Pericles*' dramatic appropriation to a long narrative tradition and creates a telescoping effect of a story within a story within a story, amplifying ad infinitum the arbitrariness of an allegedly authenticated poetic discourse. The *mise-en-abyme* effect produces an imaginary historical geography best suited for the dramatic representation grounded as it is in the visual and the imaginary.

Other place-names referred to or suggested in *Pericles* may be seen as abstractions in a symbolic landscape, but when they are considered in a concrete geographic reference, they outline an authentic Mediterranean territory. Antioch, Tyre, Tarsus, Troy,[27] Ephesus, the islands of Lesbos and Cyprus,[28] Pentapolis, even the equivocal homelands of the contestants in the uncertain tournament scene (Sparta, Macedon, Athens, Corinth): all these places define a common site of Hellenistic and Renaissance culture. What was formerly a paragon of civilization and learning is currently "corrupted" by the Turkish military invasion, as it is, in the play, by incest, famine, disease, envy, ambition, political duplicity, lechery. Even the "mind" (19.20) and the language are perverted, as the owner of the brothel suggests and the metaphor of the riddle implies. Linda McJannet makes the case of a likely location of Shakespeare's Pentapolis, out of the seven candidates of this name known in the ancient world. McJannet argues that this location is more geographically consistent with the play's detail that the ship was driven by a north wind toward Ephesus.[29] In this geographical context, McJannet names the city of Tomis, the place of Ovid's exile, as the Pentapolis in *Pericles,* because Tomis was one of the five Greek colonies on the western side of the Black Sea. As a modern inhabitant of this ancient city, now named Constanta (Romania), I would very much like to subscribe to this suggestion, all the more so as McJannet quotes Ortelius's map of the Black Sea in support of her argument. However, in the play's vague geographical situation, the question of the exact location of Pentapolis becomes irrelevant. What the audiences know from this explicit early modern geographical romance, sustaining vague Hellenistic undertones, is that some extravagant tales happened in far-out places. The reality of the location is less important than the imaginary force of the dramatic evidence.

The Mediterranean Sea as a geographic space of imagination and illusion making is very much present in Pericles' voyages, in Marina's name, and, it appears, in the second brothel scene, in a grotesquely distorted way, by Lysimachus's callous declaration that Marina's beauty "would serve after a long voyage at sea" (19.45). This particular geographic space, the scene of transaction for most of ancient and Renaissance history, is a commonly shared expanse of mirage and reality that can take shape only in the audience's imagination, as Gower repeatedly points out (10.53–8; 18.2–4;

21.13–5). The Mediterranean is the central sea where most of the Judeo-Christian stories were played out. The Romans called it *Mare Internum,* or sometimes self-sufficiently *Mare nostrum.* The Mediterranean was not called by its present name, which means "in the middle of the land" or "at the center of the Earth," until the third century A.D. in the works of the geographer Caius Julius Solinus. The key scenes of parting and reunion take place at sea, as in the long-voyaged Apollonius saga. Shakespeare's dramatic rendering of the source tale replicates it with such narrative accuracy that one wonders whether this is not a subtle way of indicating the cloudy zones that lie beyond, before, and between text(s) and author(s). Particular spaces and geographical ambiguities may confuse the issue even more, but they can also indicate significant landmarks and a starting point for one of the many possible readings. Instead of being seen as representative of what is alien to Western culture, the English Jacobean brothel space, the vague eastern Mediterranean exotic geography, and the representation of ethnic groups in *Pericles* outline areas of association in difference and identification through dislocation.

The Winter's Tale: Graphic Images of Europe

The opening scenes of *The Winter's Tale* place together royalty from three different regions in Europe: Leontes, king of Sicily; his wife, Hermione, daughter of the emperor of Russia; and Polixenes, king of Bohemia. This basic triad of geographical regions, as well as the oblique references to Delphos (Apollo's Oracle, at 5.2.6)[30] and Italy (through the Italian master Julio Romano, at 5.2.6), map out a familiar real-life itinerary intersecting the Shakespearean anomalous, yet self-consistent, representations of geographic space. The presence of anachronistic and anatopical exterior features and the diptych structure of a wintry and metallic-cold Sicilia and an idyllic and summery-green Bohemia in the sheep-shearing scene have been observed by many critics.[31] Shakespeare's reversal of settings as to the chief source, Robert Greene's prose romance *Pandosto* (1588), has been variously interpreted. Certain critics maintain that these anomalies suggest that the play should be understood as "timeless."[32] The play's structural peculiarities have often been explained as a characteristic of the romance genre.[33] Other critics see these "mistakes" as intentional and alert us to the presence of a

Shakespearean topical agenda of some kind.[34] In Greene, the jealous protagonist, Pandosto, is king of Bohemia and his childhood friend rules in Sicilia. This reversal of the kingdoms' geographic position has been seen as "the local enactment of the annual drama of the winter solstice."[35]

The much-debated haphazard topographical references in *The Winter's Tale* are part of a theatrical geography of wonder[36] that can be traced back to ancient and Elizabethan written constructions of a common European space. The presence of Time as Chorus, connecting the split temporal and spatial relations in the play's configuration, indicates Shakespeare's confidence in the power of speech to conjure the geographical muse. This is a muse of the eye according to Ortelius, who states that "the knowledge of geography is the eye of history."[37] The Shakespearean locations in this play visualize graphically and condense spatially a large number of European places in successive and consistent images drawing on the audiences' cultural expectations. At the same time, however, these European spaces provide a cultural contrast and are part of a topographic triangulation that, while excluding England, makes it a stable point of social and political contrast visible from the outside of the action on stage. Thus, the graphic sign provided by the three main western, central, and eastern European locations in the play, Bohemia, Sicilia, and Russia, suggest analogous points of contact with an allegedly more stable Jacobean England.

Early modern geographical accounts draw extensively on classical sources. One of these is that of the Latin geographer Pomponius Mela. According to him, Sicily was long ago part of the Continent, but the violence of volcanic eruptions tore it apart from mainland Italy. Drawing on mythological accounts, Mela depicts terrifying images of the Sea of Sicily: "It is frightful, violent, and renowned for the savage names of Scylla and Charibdis. Scylla is a rock, Charibdis the sea. Both are deadly to those who are driven unto them."[38] The legend goes that being placed between Scylla and Charibdis epitomizes a hopeless and extreme situation of indecision, when one must choose the lesser evil, at a drastic decisional cost. The image of dangerous psychological turbulence and confusion ending in apparent disaster evokes the violent state of mind distinctive for the sovereign of Sicilia, Leontes. His exclusionary and peremptory discourse attempts to assert an apex of linguistic and political absolutism from an abyss of increasing psychological disintegration. The Scylla and Charibdis geographic metaphor of inner conflict can be applied to the dramatization of private discord surging from the mind of Shakespeare's Sicilian royal character. Strange and turbulent Mediterranean waters can only produce images of inexplicable psychological disturbance and may be easily connected with Leontes' sudden and unaccountable jealousy, which surges like a force of nature, engulfing all reasonable faculties.

In Mela's ancient description of distant icy waters, in northern Europe lies the Baltic Sea, or the Codanus Bay. He mentions the populations living in these places: "On the bay are the Cimbri and the Teutoni; farther on, the farthest people of Germany, the *Hermiones*."[39] In this ancient geographic text, the Hermiones are a northern tribe who live at the extreme limit of the civilized world, in a land known mostly by report and contradictory tales. However, Mela locates a town called Hermiona on the coast of the Peloponesos, in the Saronic Gulf, near the towns of Epidaurus and Troezene,[40] in the very center of the classical civilized world. The ambiguous connotations derived from the origin of Hermione's name can be interpreted as a suggestive disclosure regarding the relativity of cultural inferences derived from geographic position. By presenting the benign and victimized Hermione as a possible crossbreed of north and south, barbaric and civilized, the play questions established assumptions about such cultural labels. While her Eastern European Russian ancestry is a fact of the play's dramatic present, the classical toponymic allusions inherent in Hermione's name suggest an atemporal space emerging from the dramatic action. All these ancient sites could relate to *The Winter's Tale,* insofar as the play's anachronous spatiotemporal setting is at once classical and Jacobean, southern and northern, eastern and western, civilized and barbarian. Since so many characters' names in the play are taken from North's Plutarch, it seems reasonable to assume that Shakespeare may have consulted other classical sources that would provide him with some information about the ancients' knowledge of geography.

Edward Sugden's *Topographical Dictionary* mentions that "the island of Sirens, from where Odysseus escaped by filling his ears with wax was somewhere near Sicily, if not Sicily itself."[41] The classical paradigm of the mermaid's song as illusion and the implications of irrationality coincide with Leontes' suspiciousness. Besides, in citing Thomas Heywood, Sugden comments on the dramatist's reference to "that monstrous beast of Cicily called Chimera."[42] According to Sugden, although the legendary home of the chimera was Lycia, the existence of the volcano Etna in Sicily may have transferred the image of the horrible illusion-making monster in the region of the triangular island of Sicily. Whatever the case and the allusions to ancient myth, the play's indefinite location in space and time is rendered more equivocal through the reversal and confusion of familiar classical references to the island of Sicily. As Michele Marrapodi points out, "Changing the cold Bohemia into Sicilia, Shakespeare rejects the convention of the latter as only an Arcadian country, the stereotyped and monothematic island which Greene inherited from the pastoral tradition."[43] This geographical shift transforms Shakespeare's Sicilia in "a land overloaded with ambiguous, contrasting, and polysemous connotations."[44] Moreover, the graphic representation of the island of Sicily as the image of the triangle may be one of the multiple visualizations produced for the audience, with the specific purpose of drawing their attention to a geographic space having so complex connotations, both ancient and contemporary.

The 1610 edition of Ortelius's atlas lists the commonly known facts about "Sicilia." As Ortelius does, both Shakespeare and Greene use the Italian name of the island, instead of the English name *Sicily*. The geographical text refers to the island's position in the Mediterranean, the three regions it is divided into, the important cities, the fertile land, the famous Mount Etna, and the formerly dangerous Scylla and Charibdis, considered less harmful now than they had been in ancient times. The conventional geographic information about Sicilia is spiced with an interesting episode that introduces the fascination of the pregnant body, conception, and childbirth, lending a dramatic aura to the relatively arid topical discourse: "There is a plaine of spacious place, where Constanza Normanna was delivered by Frederyck the second, under a pavilion, and would so bee delivered and not in any house because it should not be said that her chyld bearing was uncertaine, or by stelth, and this she did for that she was past the ordinary yeares of conception."[45] This perplexing fragment seems to be paraphrased dramatically, in a curiously reversed mirror image, by Hermione's confined delivery in prison, Leontes' twisted suspicion about the baby's conception, and the troubling image of public spectacle versus private life that acquired almost incredible connotations in the early modern period.

Early modern syncretic cosmography relied on complex interwoven discourses rooted in classical history and geography, geometry, astronomy, and music. For example, the frontispiece of William

Cuningham's *Cosmographical Glasse* (1559) shows that his study is governed by Mercury; inspired by the muses Arithmetica, Geometria, Astronomia, and Musica; drawing on the writings of ancient historiographers and geographers. The preface sets forth the utility of cosmography for other fields of knowledge, including Poetry: "because of the names of Regions, Cities, Townes, waters, fluddes, mountains, ceremonies, people and monsters, which every Poet do commenlye introduce in all theyr writinges."[46] Cuningham's eloquent presentation, as a dialogue between Spoud and Philo, emphasizes the dynamic and didactic function of his cosmographic discourse. In an attempt to define the domain of his discipline, Philo states "geographie is the imitation and description of the face and the picture of the earth," while "Chorographie . . . showeth the parts of the earth, divided in themselves."[47] An analogy borrowed from the visual arts sets forth the descriptive and interpretive nature of these monographs: "And in this respect, . . . of Cosmographie, as if a painter should set forth the eye, or eare of man, and not the whole body, so that chorographie consisteth rather in describing the qualitie and figure, then the things, and quantitie of anythinge."[48]

Qualitatively comparing and contrasting "Among the infinite doings of the world" (1.2.253), true and false knowledge, the reliability of reports and tales, are some issues debated in *The Winter's Tale*. The two monarchs are often referred to paradigmatically by the name of their respective countries: Leontes is "Sicilia" and Polixenes represents "Bohemia." The synthetic and descriptive quality of the topographical discourse comes into focus through this synecdoche. The opening conversation between two representative courtiers, Archidamus, a lord of Bohemia, and Camillo, a lord of Sicilia, dialogically introduces the argument. Archidamus observes "the great difference between our Bohemia and your Sicilia" (1.1.4) and the two lords consider intercultural issues of entertainment, hospitality, friendship, love, progeny, and even matters of life and death, in a contrastive manner. The chorographic distinction is highlighted by the image of the two kings' youthful friendship, when they could shake hands metaphorically "from the ends of opposite winds" (1.1.30–31). The formal language that the two courtiers use in describing these happenings and places is similar to the episode reporting the final family reunion off-stage (5.2.1–112), and it has the effect of telescoping the events into the blurred region of arbitrary report and recorded experience. Moreover, the visualization of the two countries as distant spaces makes a mental representation possible and even necessary. By mapping the spatial coordinates of the two countries in their minds, the audiences can function in a particular cognitive mode, which permits them to gain control over the world of the play. In synthesizing cultural and geographical information, they are able to navigate successfully through both physical and mental space.

Cuningham's *Cosmography* specifically describes "Bohemie" as a landlocked region, offering it as an example for the geographic notion of "continent," "which is not parted by Seas à sounder, but is continually in length, so that you may go from one part unto another without navigation."[49] All the geographical texts of the time are precise as to Bohemia's continental location, and Shakespeare was most probably aware of it. The issue of whether he inadvertently or intentionally attributed to his Bohemia a seacoast seems irrelevant, all the more so as Greene's *Pandosto* refers to "the coast of Bohemia"[50] as a safe place of landing for the young fugitives, Dorastus and Fawnia, after a tempest at sea. Theatrical conventions of the time required tempests and shipwrecks as the common apparatus of romance, and the audience would not be very suspicious about geographical inaccuracies. They would be more attentive to astrological and cosmological analogies, for example. Cuningham presents "regions and cities subject to the signes of Planets" and he mentions "Italy, Sicilie . . . Boheme . . . under Leo and the Sunne."[51] The name *Leontes,* invented by Shakespeare and nonexistent in either Greene or Plutarch, might carry highly relevant zodiacal connotations in the geotopographical world of the play. Sugden maintains that "Shakespeare had the authority of his author for giving Bohemia a seacoast, and did not trouble to inquire further."[52] From this point of view, the geography of the play is just as indefinite as the historical reference related to this Central European country, since there is no king of Bohemia whose name even distantly resembles either *Pandosto* or *Polixenes.*

The play's heterogeneous geographic tangentiality suggests antithetical and indeterminate visible images connected to Bohemia. One shows a space containing "deserts" (3.3.2), with frozen and tempestuous seas, which is famed for its wild beasts (3.2.12–13). The apparition of the bear on stage, as confirmed by the famous stage direction, further visualizes the savageness of the landscape. These connotations of Bohemia as a harsh country are part of the impressions of two Sicilians, Antigonus and the Mariner, when they land for the first time on this shore. Since they are foreigners, their knowledge of this place is based on reports and hearsay, as it must have been for many of Shakespeare's contemporaries. However, their expectations are fatally confirmed by Antigonus's death, caused by one of these famed wild beasts. A different image of Bohemia appears in the idyllic pastoral of the sheep-shearing scene. All menace is gone here, because it is the natives of this country who perform the merriment and the fertility rites. Florizel wants Perdita to "apprehend / Nothing but jollity" (4.4.24–25), and the only vague reference to beasts in this scene is the domesticated classical allusion to the gods metamorphosed into animals for the love of mortal females. The mention of Jupiter's transformation into a bull to carry off Europa might convey unstable geographical connotations, reminding the audience that the country of Bohemia is in Europe. When viewed from the tangible perspective of everyday life, however, real places cease to be only what other people's reports make of them. Thus, Shakespeare gives his audiences an inside corporeal view of Bohemia, a country they knew from indirect accounts, but that very few had ventured to visit.

It is interesting, however, how the early modern connotations of the alleged crudeness of the inhabitants of Bohemia and the stereotypical constructions of barbarity and wildness are constructed dramatically to have a stronger impact on the audiences than the particular geographical or historical accuracy about this country. Francis Griffin Stokes notes the term *Bohemian* as meaning both "a native of Bohemia" and "a gypsy, or vagabond, since the gypsies were thought to have come to Western Europe from, or through, Bohemia."[53] The Autolycus episode can be seen in a different light when the image of the vagabond gypsies, living in an untamed and distant land, appeals to the cultural geography of early modern audiences. Western Europeans considered the gypsies to be rogues, vagabonds, and pickpockets, and Autolycus's actions and declarations only strengthen this assumption. After stealing the Clown's purse, and doing a great deal of pilfering at the sheep shearing, Autolycus ends in helping Florizel and Perdita; this makes him a more agreeable character in the end. However, his disdain of honesty as a philosophy of life and the tendency to cheat everyone link him with the common Western European conception about the gypsies. Even in modern times, the cultural stereotype related to the gypsies from Eastern Europe is one according to which they are a race of people who practice begging, cheating, and stealing, because they frequently do so in Western countries. Early modern audiences must have been aware of such connotations, and Shakespeare's many-sided presentation of Bohemia plays on the period's antiquated cultural clichés. Notwithstanding, at the theater, the geographical region can also be viewed from the inside of the country's borders, not only from the cultural constructs deriving from the way other people's reports presented it.

In George Abbot's popular geographical treatise (1599) the reader finds out that "Bohemia is a kingdome in the middle of Germanie, which is compassed rounde with a mightie wood, called *Silva Hicinia.*"[54] Abbot enlarges upon the political situation of the region in his time, when "Germania" was ruled by the "Emperor of Germanie," elected by seven Princes. However, Abbot notes the autocratic political situation in his time: "There is not that free libertie of choosing the Emperour out of any countrie, as was heretofore. But the election is tied within one hundred yeares, unto the house of Austria, and at this day of them, the king of Boheme is Emperour."[55] Although the political authority rests with a democratically elected emperor, the Princes are considered as "absolute gouernors in their dominions. So that they haue libertie of religion, they do make lawes, they do raise souldiers, they do stampe money with their owne coyne as absolute princes."[56] In Shakespeare, the king of Sicilia displays an extremely authoritarian attitude, close to "tyranny" (3.2.31). He causes a princely guest to flee, banishes a daughter, convicts his queen under the appearance of a fair trial, attempts to control language, and ultimately dismisses the classical epitome of divine foreknowledge of the Delphi Oracle. Shakespeare's ruler of Bohemia, on the other hand, shows almost no sign of authority: he fears to confront the irrationally jealous Leontes and does not have control over his own family. Polixenes attempts to supervise his son's personal life through the ambivalent form of disguise, avoiding responsibility, and conducts veiled discussions with Perdita on the social outrage that lies in the prospect of a prince's marrying a peasant.

In Ortelius's 1603 edition of the atlas, Polixenes' Bohemia is described as a rich country, populated by Germans and Slavs, governed by a king aided by lords and barons:

> Bohemia is all rounde about environed by the forest and the hills of Hercinia, enveloping the same like Amphitheatre. . . . The aire is colde, but the grounde exceedinge goode for cattel and corne. . . . The cheapnesse of victuailles is the cause that this countrie is inhabited as it is, for therein

> are compted above thirty thousand villages, and little lesse than eight hundred cities, townes and castles, some belonging to the crovvne of Bohemia, and other some unto private Lords and Barons. Amongst the reste we vvill onlye speake of Prage, the metropolitan of the kingdome, and wherein for the moste parte th'Emperour holds his courte . . . they are greatlye geuen to drunknesse, pride and Pompe, as well the men as vvomen. They are of stature high, and of gallant carriage.[57]

This description puts in focus the comparative discussion between the two lords of Bohemia and Sicilia. Archidamus, a lord of Bohemia, speaks "in the freedom of [his] knowledge" (1.1.11) about the comparatively lesser "entertainment" (8) they can offer the king of Sicilia on his future expected visit and of the "sleepy drinks" (13) they would give their guest. The slippery paradoxes are confusing again. A country renowned for indulging in frolic and joyful pleasure, such as Bohemia appears to be from the texts of the period, is reported to lack such delights by a courtier who repeatedly insists on the truthfulness of his report. However, the pastoral merriment in the sheep-shearing scene is compatible with Ortelius's chorographic description of this country and its inhabitants.

In the 1610 edition of the atlas, the interested reader finds out about the location of Bohemia and the wild beasts living in its woods, including the bears: "This kingdome, lying in *Germany*, is compassed about with hilles and woods. . . . In wheat and barley the country is very fruitful, beasts both wild and tame it nourishes in great abundance, among the wyld beastes are store of Beares, Red-deere, and Ouroxen."[58] There has been considerable scholarly discussion regarding the episode of Antigonus's being devoured by a bear on the coast of Bohemia.[59] The episode does not exist in the source text and it is introduced by Shakespeare in order to justify the shepherd's and his son's reports on Perdita's discovery. In addition to the historical and cultural critical interpretations, it is safe to assume that the bear episode may simply be related to the audience's vague knowledge of the wild beasts of Bohemia, gathered from geography books or from reports on these popular written texts. Actually, the entire plot plays on reported events, things, and places never seen and only imagined, and a time-space-event continuum generally connected to fairy tales.

Abbot's political and chorographic description of Sicilia defines the geological configuration of the island; comments upon its prosperity in ancient times, when it was considered the granary of Rome;

and inscribes contemporary realities of subjection: "This countrie is now also under the king of Spaine."[60] In the play's world, a country that was in Shakespeare's time under Spanish rule has a despotic monarch in the person of Leontes, while a more malleable Polixenes governs the Renaissance absolutist Habsburg-ruled Bohemia. The reversal of historical facts and cultural assumptions plays on the common notion that things in drama are never what they seem to be, or what they are in real life. Moreover, this device is part of the complex series of reversals and dislocations extant in the play, which generate a sense of the never-never-land of the romances, but, at the same time, places these inadequacies and dissolution uncomfortably close to the English shores and to home. Abbot's chorographic description of Sicilia accounts for the island's triangular shape: "The figure of this Cuntrie, is Triquetra, or triangle three-square."[61] The inevitable love triangle describing the suspected relationship at Leontes' court parallels the icon of a real-life Sicily and the deformed mental image conjured by its king's infected imagination. A geometric symbol paraphrases an illusory psychological representation formed in the mind of a fictitious character. This analogy can raise serious questions about the limits of the knowable reality, and it does so with very few words and much of the geographic paraphernalia.

The figure of the triangle is inscribed geographically in the play's larger symbolic iconography through the position of Hermione's country of origin, Russia (3.2.119). This is another powerful monarchy placed at the easternmost end of Europe. Abbot gives an extensive account of this northern and cold country: "On the East side of Sweden beginneth the dominion of the Emperor of Russia . . . , which is a great, and mightie Monarchie . . . The gouernor there, calleth himselfe Emperour of Russia, great Duke of Muscovia . . . The passage by sea into this country . . . was first discovered by the English.[62] . . . The Empire is at this day, one of the greatest dominions of the world: both for the compasse of grounde, and for multitude of men: saving that it lieth far North, and so yeeldeth no pleasure or good trafique, with many other of the best nations."[63] The imaginary line connecting the southwestern island of Sicily, the northwestern Bohemia, and northeastern Russia indicates a large topographical triangle crosscutting Europe, which looms over the smaller triangle of the island of Sicily. The play's fictitious love triangle Leontes-Hermione-Polixenes, as well as the subtler and equally fictitious (and incestuous) love triangle Leontes-Perdita-Florizel (barely suggested at 5.1.222–27) create telescoping perspectives connecting the real world represented by maps and the play world delineated on stage.

An interesting reference about Russia in Ortelius's text incorporates syncretic territorial, economic, political data, and sociocultural elements, customs, and traditions that are faintly discernible in Shakespeare's complex dramatic and narrative configuration. Ortelius describes the geographic situation of the vast country of Russia; its neighbors, waters and climate; its wealth and wildlife; the cities ruled by the emperor, probably Ivan the Terrible, and the people's religion. Then, the monograph addresses an issue of jurisprudence: "Their lawes are very plaine according to an ancient simplicitie, no advocates are admitted, but every man to tell his owne tale for himself."[64] The passage of Hermione's trial, with some similarities to this report about the Russian habits, appears in *Pandosto,* but the echoes of the queen's eloquent self-defense are read differently in the context of her Russian ancestry: "The testimony on my part no other / But what comes from myself" (3.2.24–26). The queen's justification summons the argument of numberless and humble actions of truthfulness and probity. She pledges her moral integrity and declares that her ethical status cannot be rendered in mellifluous words, nor recorded by history (3.2.35). However, this humble enactment of honest conduct can "be play'd to take spectators" (3.2.37), because the theater has the capacity to capture and render visible these unique and unassuming decisive moments in life. History, mainly concerned with generalities, tends to overlook such individual accomplishments. In order to reinforce the absurdity of Leontes' self-delusion, Hermione's persuasive discourse is ineffectual, as is that of her advocate, Paulina, who tries to soften the king's heart with the presence of his baby daughter. Innocent life does not appeal to the irrational king of Sicilia; nor does the ambiguous answer of Apollo's Oracle. Only the brutal spectacle of death makes Leontes reconsider his intolerant position.

The chorographic annotations in Shakespeare's dramatic context associate reversed general geographical and cultural knowledge of Sicilia, Bohemia, and Russia and recall a colorful picture of an ancient–and–early modern Eastern and Western Europe. Shakespeare requires from his audience progressive steps of the imagination, in order to recreate a new-fashioned world of the play from their conflated knowledge of the places described in the popular atlases of the period. This innovative process involves a visual representation of geography and local culture, like the common *cartes à figures* published in city atlases, which depicted local inhabitants in their native costumes on the margins of the perspective maps of their cities. *The Winter's Tale* maps out a vivid world similar to early modern chorographies of European countries. The play's directness and materiality are realized through the pictorial mutation of reference, and the subtly graphic significance of Shakespeare's locations. Moreover, the multicolored costumes of shepherds and shepherdesses in the sheep-shearing scene attract the audience's attention and give an inside glimpse of certain European locations, from the perspective of their inhabitants. Shakespeare recreates geography and spaces and introduces topographical changes of his own; he enriches an already overabundant iconography of early modern European territory with new theatrical connotations.

Cymbeline: Contrasting Nationhood

Analyzing the staging of Italy by English Renaissance dramatists, A. J. Hoenselaars argues for a reconsideration of clichés or stereotypes that tend to underpin the national identity construct. In his view, these plays can be read as an exploration of the energies involved in the formation of the early modern sense of nationhood, and the references to Italian topography, climate, and national character provided the alternative image of a nation with its own identity construct. "Turning to Italy for their stage locations, the dramatists frequently placed that nation in an explicitly international context. The most effective means of establishing a desired sense of topographical distance, and an initial identity-alterity co-ordinate, was to have the play begin in an English setting, and by means of what Leech terms the 'framing' effect, to develop the Italian location as an extension."[65] The anachronous and atopical shift of locale in *Cymbeline,* from ancient Britain to Renaissance Rome[66] in the wager scene, plays on this device of dramatizing alterity by a special kind of triangulation in space and time. Through the imaginary reproduction of different places and different time frames, the audiences are likely to create a mental map invoking images of British insularity versus the rest of Europe. In defining the early configuration of British nationhood, which includes the stamina of Celtic derivation and the Roman civilizing factor, the play works to construct a complex narrative about national origins.

The Folio text stage direction to 1.4, set in Filario's home in Rome, announces: "[A table brought out, with a banquet upon it.] Enter Filario, Giacomo, a Frenchman, a Dutchman, and a Spaniard." Two of these representatives of Western European nationalities never speak and are remnants from the source, but the cosmopolitan note of this scene is very clear. It invites audiences to ponder on the existing nations of early modern Europe, as they knew them from atlases or geography books. Posthumus's reference to yet another European national ("a German one" 2.5.16) to add to the French, Dutch, Spaniards, and Italians makes of these Roman scenes early modern variants of a twenty-first-century European Union (EU) member states reunion or, as Robert Smallwood puts it, a "Renaissance version of the Strasbourg parliament."[67] In this important assembly of nations, expected to orchestrate a global European entente, Filario refers to Posthumus as "the Briton" (1.4.23). Despite the scene's casual anachronisms and the early modern nations gathered at the roundtable of a Renaissance Europe, Filario does not call Posthumus "the Englishman." Actually, the hero's national identity is as ambiguous as the reference to him, because he is the son of Sicilius, an oddly Roman name for a British fighter, in an age that had barely yet encountered Roman culture. Sicilius received a second Roman name, because of his service in the Roman wars, being called *Leonatus* (lion-born). Moreover, according to Filario's account, Sicilius had been a fellow soldier with him, and the Roman Filario owed him his life. Taken under the Briton Cymbeline's protection, Posthumus in disguise fights with the Britons but is then taken prisoner as a Roman soldier. The borders of national and personal identities in this play are perforated on various sides, to allow for questions about the mutable nature of the relative national and political frontiers.

The anonymous Frenchman declares he has met Posthumus on a previous visit to Orléans; that makes Posthumus a special kind of intermediary between Britain and continental Europe. The discussion between the Frenchman and Posthumus reveals that the Briton was involved in a duel in France, on account of a confrontation concerning the superiority in virtue of British ladies as compared to the French ones. This dialogue foreshadows the actual wager between Posthumus and Giacomo, where the confrontation regarding British and Italian ladies' virtue is brought into question. Generalizations and conventionalized ideas about women belonging to three nationalities are the main order of this stereotypical discourse, which narrates the duel between a Frenchman and Posthumus or presents the wager between an Italian and the Briton. The play negotiates among geographic territories, identities, and mental landscapes in an erratic manner. However, all the nations present at this multinational spectacle of conviviality are Western European.

The uncertain and shifting national or personal identities display a theatrical mode aimed at defining the porous boundaries of genders, nations, religions, and philosophies. At the shared feast including many principal members of the European community, the expectation might be one of a general entente, as should be the case with the urbane residents of civilized nations, whether from classical Rome or Renaissance Italy. However, the friendly conference results in division and misunderstanding. The wager is an absurd form of competition with no visibly creative end. It is a tug of war in which contention means showing the adversary that the strength is at the winning end. Whatever the means of confrontation, whether a duel or a wager, the pulling tension must not be maintained long, and the winner proves his superiority at the loser's expense. Although the wager scene draws on the source, it is easy for the playwright to make it a motive for exposing disruptive practices and unjustified cultural demarcations. In any case, the feast is a visible location where various nations could meet convivially, a socializing place satisfying the needs of the body, just like the brothel space in *Pericles,* with less licentious but similar hedonistic connotations.

This *tableau vivant* of nations at the banquet in *Cymbeline* is a visual representation comparable to a scene depicted in John Florio's *Second Fruites,* an exuberant collection of recreational material and cultural modes, rendered in the theatrical form of dialogue in an Italian setting. During a discussion over dinner of three friends, Thomas, Iohn, Henry, and Piccinino, a servant, the company considers congenially the best ways of spending the time. One of the suggestions is going to see a play. In this context of feasting, entertainment, and leisure, the following dialogue emerges:

G: And then after dinner we will goe see a playe.
H: The playes that they playe in England, are not right comedies.
T: Yet they do nothing else but playe every daye.
H: Yea, but they are neither right comedies, nor right tragedies.
G: How would you name them then?
H: Representations of histories without any decorum.[68]

The notion of appropriateness, propriety, or decorum was indeed not widely observed in English Renaissance drama until later in the seventeenth century. However, this manifest carelessness for the matching of style to content appears as beneficial when it comes to theatrical representations of spaces and locations contrasting those inhabited by the British.

Historical anachronisms, spatiotemporal disruptions, and frequent shifts of action signify only a seeming disregard of accuracy. In fact, these detectable signs of negligence outline a pattern of theatrical comparisons and contrasts. The wager scene, set in a refined Italianate Renaissance cosmopolitan milieu, is expected to generate common understanding and congenial amiability. The resulting action is in total opposition to this superficial expectation of amiable discourse between nations: a Frenchman starts a conversation whose contesting argument sets an Italian (Giacomo) against a British princess, ending in many misfortunes for the young couple. All this happens under the auspices of a Maecenas-like Roman personage, Filario, who opposes vaguely and feebly the idea of the wager (1.5.130). Moreover, the other Western European participants in this confrontation have nothing to say. They are passive attendants in an international game of cards, merely visual representatives of European nations, like the decorative *cartes-à-figures* on the sides of atlases. This play indeed lacks all decorum in its representation of geography and history, be it classical Roman,[69] ancient British, or early modern. It is as if Shakespeare would self-ironically play according to other nations' critical opinion about the theater in England, while his drama orchestrates in polyphonic harmony the common national stereotypes attributed by the British to other nations of Europe.

In *Cymbeline,* the spatial representations circumscribe Britain's insularity in relation to the wider space of Western Europe. The island was often described as being part of the world, yet not part of it, because of its watery separation from the Continent. The concept goes back to a line in Virgil's *Eclogues* 1.67 (which Holinshed quotes), but is also in Florus, Claudian, and Horace. It provided the British with a conception of their own place in the world, which to this day affects even the negotiations within the European Union. Jean E. Howard discusses Imogen's metaphorical presentation (3.4.136–39) of the world as a huge book ("volume"), and Britain as a detached page, seeming "as of it but not in't" (3.4.138). Imogen's visual metaphor of Britain is "in a great pool a swan's nest"

(3.4.139). Howard explains that the play negotiates a vision of England suited to the Stuart moment and considers that "Britain remains the special seat of grace and beauty. But it is also connected to something larger than itself. There are other pages in the volume to which, even if detached, Britain belongs."[70] This metaphorical presentation of Britain's insularity, and its concomitant existence as part of the community of European nations, is concordant with the play's ambivalent negotiation of the issue of nationhood and political relations. However, the graphic image of the swan's nest suggests a complex visualization of a spatial and cultural relation involving Britain and the rest of Europe.

While the image of the book conveys an abstract representation of the British Isles, like an atlas, where the island is depicted graphically according to a certain geographic order, the synecdoche of the swan's nest denotes a real and mythical space of beauty and isolation. The image draws together the cosmos and the nation, comprehended in a visual representation accompanied by a mythological allusion. The myth is of Jupiter's union, in the form of a swan, with Leda, the Spartan princess. This theatrical image suggests the visual condensation of a map with mythological figures populating the seas, for example, Drayton's map of Cornwall in *Poly-Olbion* (1612). Here, as Arthur F. Kinney remarks, "The ships offshore are outnumbered by mermaids and Neptunes, three of whom ride dolphins."[71] Mythical personages populating the ocean and condensed images of an island amid a watery expanse begin to float free of their specific landscapes and seascapes, into the zone of the audience's imagination. Expressing her wish to leave her native island, in an attempted self-exile that would obscure her British identity, Imogen announces her awareness of the existence of other nations living outside Britain. However, she agrees to take Pisanio's advice of going to Milford Haven in disguise to meet Lucius, the Roman ambassador. Wales is as far as "other place" (3.5.142) means for both Imogen and Pisanio. Although the Anglo-Saxons called the Welsh *wealas,* "the foreigners," Wales is still a part of the British Isles. Actually, Britain's swan, Imogen, never leaves her insular swan's nest, although she professes to acknowledge the geographic extension of a larger Europe.

National identity is very strongly defined by linguistic criteria, and the muddle of languages and etymologies in *Cymbeline* attests to the importance of a common language in the process of nation formation. Apart from the much-debated theme of the origin and spelling of *Iachimo/Giacomo* and *Imogen/Innogen,* other names in the play suggest that Britain and Rome, and their languages, are in a state of flux, even at times flowing one into the other. The Britons, represented by Posthumus; his father; Guiderius; Arviragus; and Cornelius, all have Roman names. Guiderius is known as Polydore in the Welsh wilderness, while Imogen has a Latin-derived name, *Fidele,* in her disguise. In the same way, the banished lord Belarius has a composite name containing the root *air* (fine air), similar to the Soothsayer's revelation about the British princess as being "mollis aer" or Filario as "loving air." Actually, many Britons' names have Latin or Italian roots, which might imply, not necessarily the massive Latin influence on the English language, but the fact that Latin was the lingua franca in ancient Europe, just as it was in the Renaissance period. The European concert of nations and their languages was formed from the complex interpenetration of local idioms and Latin, to a larger or smaller extent. As the word went in the Renaissance, Latin was the language of knowledge and learning, of civility and tolerance. When transplanting Latin and Italian-sounding names into ancient Britain, Shakespeare does not diminish the importance of the British nation as to its Continental counterparts. Moreover, the British have their special place in the desired harmony of nations, as the Soothsayer *Philharmonus* (friend of harmony) reveals through the final emblematic image of the imperial Roman eagle.

In the erratic national and geographic context of *Cymbeline,* a southeastern European space has its special notification. It is a region whence the allegedly terse nations of "the Pannonians and the Dalmatians" (3.2.71) have raised their armies against the Romans and resisted Caesar's assaults. The Pannonians were tribes inhabiting that section of modern Hungary west of the Danube. The Dalmatians were tribes inhabiting the territory of modern Serbia and Bosnia. They were indeed fighting Rome in the time of the emperor Augustus. Caesar felt he needed to have the broad Danube as Rome's boundary to the north, to protect the civilization of the empire from the "barbaric" Dacian populations inhabiting the north of the lower river and the region around the Carpathians. To reach the Danube, Augustus had to institute a naked war of aggression against the independent tribes that lived on the south of that river, in the territory of modern-day Bulgaria. This province was called Moesia Inferior in those times. By 9 BC, the Roman legions had reached the Danube all along the line, and the river became the boundary of the empire, which would remain reasonably intact for four centuries. In the British king's discussion with the Roman ambassador, Cymbeline is fully aware of the resistance of the independent tribes of the Pannonians and the Dalmatians against the Romans. He calls their resistance "a precedent" (3.2.72) and implies that, by not emulating them, the British might be seen as lacking in spirit. However, Cymbeline's argument takes a conciliatory tone, after the ardent patriotic and anti-Roman speeches declared by the queen and Cloten. The Briton's final word is a "Welcome" (3.2.82) pronounced in an ambiguous mode.

Through the reference to the Southeast European peoples of the Pannonians and the Dalmatians, considered barbaric by the Romans, who wanted to impose their own civilizing code on all of Europe, Shakespeare effects a geographic triangulation including Britain, Rome, and the regions south of the Danube. The Romans considered the regions north and south of the Danube as being inhabited by barbaric peoples, just as they thought about the ancient Britons that they were incapable of adopting domesticated manners. However, these Eastern European nations did not have the same image of themselves. As did some Britons presented in the play, the supposedly savage nations of Eastern Europe saw the Roman aggression as an infringement upon their national and cultural identity. As some Britons, they were prepared to fight in order to maintain this independence. However, Cymbeline's ambiguous attitude as to opposing direct resistance to the emperor shows an implicit recognition of Rome as a civilizing factor. The British king tells the Roman ambassador that his subjects would not endure the "yoke" (3.5.5) of submission to the Romans, which meant paying tribute to them.

Cymbeline's position as a king does not allow him to go against his subjects' wishes, so he must comply with the idea of war. Cymbeline's final peacemaking decision, after all, shows the inconsistent boundaries of conflicts. According to Marjorie Garber, "This is a play that tackles, and to a large extent solves, an intriguing set of problems about the relationship between political stories and psychological stories, between the state or polity and the subject, and between the political fiction and the dream."[72] Moreover, it is a play dealing with geographic and cultural oppositions from a unifying perspective. The absurdity of the wager as a form of personal competition, presented earlier, foreshadows the disastrous consequences of war, as a drastic form of national competition. As in a tug of war, one party's success is only apparent, because it means the other party's defeat. If, instead, the two opponents could learn to maintain the *tension* involved in the competition for the benefit of both sides, the results would yield victory for all parties. By provoking a geographic triangulation including the Romans, the British, and the Eastern European tribes represented by the Pannonians and the Dalmatians, Shakespeare shows his audience a map of Europe that, although seen from the British perspective, includes all nations in a special kind of geography of tolerance and mutual understanding.

The Tempest: Real and Imaginary Places

The geography of *The Tempest* has a twofold theatrical representation: the location of the island is vague and erratic, yielding various perceptions in accordance with each character's cultural and psychological horizon, while various characters' narratives in the play outline a real space of Italy, North Africa, and the Mediterranean. These real places have a correspondent in the images induced in the audiences' minds by the atlases and chorographies of Italian locations. Prospero's island has an indefinite location. However, this is the actual encased space where all real events in the play happen. In this sense, it is similar to the Jacobean stage, where the play progressed between two and six in the afternoon. In a distinctive order, we have the kingdom of Naples, the dukedom of Milan, and Tunis. These places are essential in the dramatic development of the plot structure, but they exist in the play only through the *narratives* about them. In this special theatrical arrangement, we see how a totally fictional space, represented by the island, which has no correspondent in the real world (despite the critics' attempts to locate it in the Mediterranean or the Bermudas), is the material enclosed space of the theater where the audience are sitting. It is also the real expanse of Britain, another island in the middle of the ocean, where that particular theater was placed.

The tangible geographic territories of Naples, Milan, and Tunis, however, are brought on stage through the medium of narrative, just as they are in the early modern atlases or the classical descriptions. There are two superimposed planes, the real and the imaginary, where an imaginary space is tangibly real, while the real places, which have a certain topical ring for the audiences, are fictionalized through their intersection with the dramatic narrative. As in the geographical accounts about Naples, Milan, and Tunis, the audiences receive their information about these places through an intermediary, a character who narrates an episode. However, unlike these geographical texts, the audience at the theater can actually see people from these countries interact in a fictional area that is also their material space. Thus, fictional and geographic spaces become the discursive sum total of coexisting texts that intersect in the world of the theater, where they acquire an undefined structural sufficiency pertaining to the romance genre and a definite stage corporeality deriving from the play's performative potential. This is how Shakespeare's theater becomes a means of negotiating both physical and cognitive space in the romances, and especially in *The Tempest.*

George Abbot's geography divides the Earth into "either Ilandes, which are those which are wholly compassed by the sea, as Britannia, Sicilia, Corsica, or the Continent."[73] This clear division between land and sea, and the land within the sea being described in the ocean section, is derived from the ancients' geographic recognition that the ocean occupies a large amount of the Earth's surface, and it must be given proper importance. In the poetic range of signification, the sea is connected with myth, imagination, and the general representation of a vast expanse that can modify experience to the point of blurring or annihilating any borders with reality. When the human mind suffers a sea change, it can transform reality into something rich and strange. This new form of representation can grow into something of high constancy, both strange and admirable, or it may easily take a bush for a bear. Prospero's island in the middle of the sea is a placeless notion that can trigger a comparable image-making process. All of the characters perceive the island differently, according to their psychological amplitude. The island's nonmateriality shows in the fact that the shipwreck has no effects on their bodies, and their clothes are as intact as when they wore them at the wedding in Tunis. Instead, their minds are caught in an indeterminate image-making process of creation, or in nightmarish visions. The audiences see it all happening within the restricted stage space. Some of them can even visualize the fact that they are sitting on the theater-island within the circle of the city, in a larger enclosed space of the British isle, which is only a part of the great world, as they know it.

Many Jacobeans know from Abbot's geographical report that the dukedom of Milan has a long and controversial history of illicit occupation and shifting government. As Abbot notes, "In this Lumbardy, standeth also the Dukedome of Milaine, a most rich and pleasant thing, which sometime had beene gouerned by a Duke of their owne: but of late hath beene possessed by the Spaniard, and sometime by the French, and it is now in the gouernment and possession of the King of Spaine."[74] The real place of Milan is known for unstable rule. So is the kingdom of Naples. According to Abbot's assorted geographic, classical, and historical report, Naples used to be ruled by a local king, until "Ioane Queen of Naples" gave the kingdom as a gift to the kings of Argon. The same queen revoked her former grant and left the kingdom by will to the House of Anjou in France. Since then, the Kingdom of Naples had been governed either by the French or by the Spanish, and at the end of the sixteenth century it was under Spanish rule. In the interference between what is real and only imagined, the audiences can see that everything is unstable. Perceptions of an imaginary island are unreliable. Moreover, the coordinates of government, politics, and history fluctuate incredibly in an administratively fragile and divided Italy existing in the real world. In the first half of the sixteenth century, the Kingdom of Naples was a focus of dispute between France ad Spain. In this labile geopolitical context, it is expected that Antonio usurped his brother's dukedom of Milan, or the king of Naples took part in a political conspiracy. What is common to both Naples and Milan, in Abbot's description, is the fact that both places are perceived as rich and pleasant, therefore desirable. From the British perspective, the climate and fertility of these locations in Italy make them alluring, despite the political instability.

Echoes of political insecurity connected to the dukedom of Milan and the Kingdom of Naples also come to early modern readers from the direction of the 1610 edition of Ortelius's atlas. About "The Dukedome of Milan" Ortelius writes, "The citie of *Milan* is the chief of all citties of this duchie, & hath bene even the balle of fortune to be tossed & transposed to & from so many commaunders . . . & scarsly is their any one towne or cittie to bee found, where the memorie of warr either at it or neere about it doth not yet remaine."[75] Apart from the recitals of war and destruction, Ortelius writes about the natural abundance of the place, the region's rich hydrographic system, the beautiful buildings and churches of the city, and its citizens' excellence in all arts and sciences. Prospero's love and promotion of the liberal arts in Milan might not be as exceptional and symbolic as has been considered so far. Taking into account the popular geographic reports about the dukedom of Milan and its people, to English eyes, the duke of Milan could be just another inhabitant of this exceptional city, a city that is renowned for its greatness and learning.

Ortelius combines similar antagonistic facts in his report about "The Kingdome of Naples." The kingdom is famed for a history of political instability, but it is also admired for its natural resources. The pleasant surroundings of the city of Naples have gained it the name of "an imitation of *Paradise.*"[76] However, the country's productivity and its favorable geographic position have made it the desired fruit of many world powers. The geographer's rhetoric insists on the hegemonic shifts concerning Naples along the centuries, emphasizing the vulnerability of the city and its multiple changes of fortune: "If we look into the histories of former ages we shal not see any knowne kingdome in the world, that hath seemed more unfortunate then this, having beene as it were the very butte whereat fortune hath shot her sharpest-hedded arrowes, heer have the *Romaines,* the *Gothes,* the *Longobards,* the *Greeks,* the *Saracins,* the *Normannes,* the *Frenchmen* & *Spagniards,* at severall tymes, had their several domination."[77] Topographic and climatic reports about the fertility of the Naples region merge with the territory's troubled history. Changes of fortune are common to this nation, and the audiences can see them happen in the play world. Prospero calls "bountiful Fortune" his dear lady and admits to Miranda that he had to act in accordance with an astrological plan of favorable fortune (1.2.178–84). In instigating Sebastian to plot against his brother for the elusive possession of a distant Kingdom of Naples, the pragmatic Antonio entices Sebastian to action by warning him that he lets his fortunes sleep (2.1.211). The other would-be conspirator, Stephano, concludes the play's *fortuna labilis* theme in a drunken parody of political intrigue saying, "All is but fortune" (5.1.257). All these people are from Milan and Naples, which are famed for their rulers' frequent changes of fortune, and the recurrent shifts of power in their government.

The island the audiences see in *The Tempest* has all the appealing characteristics of the pleasant regions of Italy, as they know it from geographic reports, or from the description of some characters such as Gonzalo, but they also see it as being governed by an absolute ruler. This monarch-magician imposes his will on the elements and his world but yields his power to the omnipotent audience in the end. Naples and Milan are real locations in Italy, famous for shifting government and political instability, but they appear to the audience mainly in Prospero's narrative, who is also lord of discourse.

He manipulates language, thought, and meaning, people and their destinies, in the fashion of the absolute rulers of the world. The audiences hear more about the politics in these Italian countries from Ferdinand, who identifies himself with Naples (1.2.437), or in Alonzo's reference to his son as the heir of Naples and Milan (2.1.108). Sebastian's pragmatic allusion to the large number of widows existing in Milan and Naples (2.1.128) as a result of fratricidal wars and Antonio's insidious remark on the kingdom's doubtful lineage after the heir's supposed death (2.1.242) offer a realistic picture of the domestic wars in these countries. Gonzalo's final summarizing of the story gives an afterlife to the play, by announcing that the lineage of the wronged duke of Milan will be kings of Naples (5.1.205–6). Thus, the audiences hear about Naples and Milan from several characters, natives of these places. These views meet their expectations about political instability in Naples and Milan, as gathered from geographical treatises of the period. However, only the imaginary space of the island accumulates the collective anticipation of Naples and Milan as being rich and pleasant Italian spaces of wonder, which is also a British idealized perspective of these Italian regions, influenced by geographic texts.

One of the many changes of fortune that had disturbed the Kingdom of Naples along its troubled history was, according to Ortelius's atlas, the invasion of the "Saracins." The Saracens were Moors or Berbers who lived in North Africa and who made several incursions into southern Spain and Italy. Ortelius defines the country of Barbarie as containing four kingdoms, Marocco, Fez, Telesine, and Tunis. These North African locations and the warlike inhabitants of the coast of Barbary might elicit explanations about Claribel's political marriage to the king of Tunis. An interesting perception of cultural attributes and particularities of language in Ortelius's presentation of Barbarie is the particular etymology he finds for this name. "The inhabitants are of a dullish colour," he writes, "& are called Barbarians of the woord *Barbara* which in the *Arabec* tongue signifieth grumbling; because their speech soundeth in the eares of the Arabians as no perfect or clearly pronounced speech, but as a kynde of grumbling."[78] Problems with language, cognition, and speech do exist with many characters in *The Tempest.* Caliban's speech must have sounded like some kind of grumbling to Prospero's European ears, so he felt the need to teach him language. Trinculo and Stephano's drunken babble might seem gibberish to Caliban's perception. Ariel could also make sounds that were perceived differently by various characters in the play. As Ian Smith writes about language as a cultural sign in early modern England, "Through a network of linguistic evolutions within various textual and rhetorical performances, the nation-subject and its excluded other—the "barbarian," the foreigner and stranger—are produced as racialized."[79] To Shakespeare's audiences, the North African location of the kingdom of Tunis summoned images of alterity involving alien desert territories and dangerous pirate ships lurking at high seas. People in those remote locations were speaking unintelligible languages, which made communication difficult. However, in the play, Tunis is merely an imaginary space that can offer the geographic range for a necessary triangulation with the Italian cities of Naples and Milan.

Tunis is the third place of geographic triangulation in *The Tempest.* According to Abbot, the kingdom of Tunis, together with Fez and Marocco, was part of the larger region called Barbary. The ancient name of the region of Barbary was *Mauritania,* and the connection with Dido and Carthage[80] occurs through the classical reference to the Punic Wars. Early modern readers were used to finding insertions of classical history in contemporary geographical accounts. Abbot relates that in the eastern part of the region containing the kingdom of Tunis stands the "Citie of Carthage, supposed to be built by Dido."[81] Abbot continues with a long report of the causes and sections of the Punic Wars, the conflict between Carthage and Rome for the supremacy over the western Mediterranean region, and concludes with the contemporary situation of the area: "This whole countrey at this day is called the kingdome of *Tunis,* the king whereof, is a kinde of Stipendiary unto the great Turke. The people that inhabit there are generally Sarazens, and do professe Mohammed."[82] As in many geographic texts of the early modern period, Abbot collates contemporary facts with classical fictions, thus producing an indeterminate amalgam that could only confuse the reader.

The religious rift between Christian Europe to the north and Islamic North Africa to the south is brought into focus in *The Tempest* through the ambivalent marriage of Alonzo's daughter. What made Claribel marry the king of Tunis is unclear. Probably it was a menacing invasion of the North African Saracens of Naples, because Sebastian reports that Claribel was torn between unwillingness to marry and a desire to obey her father, whereas Alonso was "kneel'd to" (2.1.124), or forced to accept this marriage. The spiritual and geographic space that counts in this play is strategically ambivalent, allowing for multiple national, racial, and religious ramifications. Sebastian perceives Claribel's marriage as a loss to "our Europe" (2.1.120), in favor of "an African" (2.1.121), an outsider. Christian Europe is set against Islamic Mauritania, yet this marriage is not seen as a harmonious union, but as a forced alliance to prevent further conflicts. Moreover, attendance at Claribel's nuptials is occasion for another loss, in Alonzo's view, since he thinks this voyage caused his son to be lost at sea. Tunis, the third point of Shakespeare's geographic triangulation implying real spaces detectable on a map, has disruptive connotations of adversity, loss, and suffering. Moreover, echoes of the Spanish anti-Moorish resistance, completed in the time of the Catholic Spanish kings Ferdinand and Isabel of Castile, keep the religious Islam-Christianity tension very much alive in the play. However, all the pressure elements and potential conflicts are dissolved and annihilated on the special magic island of the theater, where nothing is but what is not.

Geographical narratives and dramatizations of space in the romances follow a convoluted trajectory that aligns them, in general terms, with the diagrammatic practice of map drawing, or the composite early modern geographical texts. As in maps, the condensation of space in the romances is remarkable. Various coordinating lines, mainly triangular projections, define psychological, ethical, or political evolution, and the graphic image is similar to that of a Mercator projection, or the scientific method of obtaining latitude and longitude with the help of a sextant. Similarly, anachronisms, displacements of space and time, and unlikely events recall the early modern reiteration of ancient geographical texts, which are compiled mélanges of historical or geographical fact and extravagant fiction. In appropriating the heterogeneous method of these texts, Shakespeare attracts the audiences' attention and makes them visualize spaces they had never seen before. Once their curiosity is aroused, as in the ancient narratives of wonder, the playwright questions issues of language, national identity, race, the ubiquity of ethical values, psychology, and religion by immersing the audiences directly in a certain particular location. With the symbolically condensed dramatic means of early modern theater, Shakespeare allows nations and individuals to speak each in their own corporeal language, from their personal perspective. Moreover, the global view of the theater makes each individual or nation a part of the European and world commonwealth. The blurred geographic regions in the romances and the indefinite time markers stress the relativity of history, political power, and conventional borders. What remains is a far-reaching image of the people, with their problems and possible solutions to them.

Early modern geographical accounts, as did ancient works, saw the European regions outside their well-known world, especially the Eastern European countries, as menacing locations seething with barbarous peoples and practices. Shakespeare's anomalous geography, however, makes the audiences see these places directly from the interior, from their populations' perspectives. Thus, purportedly alien spaces are humanized by individualization, and what used to be a vaguely frightening "elsewhere," summoning startling images of barbarity, becomes the "here" and "now" of dramatic action. Stephen Greenblatt traces the early modern narratives about the New World and observes how "porous" cultural boundaries could be in early modern Europe. He argues that plays, as do narratives of the New World, play on wonder[83] as powerful triggers of connective meanings and allusions. I would add that this method was borrowed from the classical narratives, which filled the gaps of less known territories with confabulations about these places. Similarly, the Shakespearean allusions to Eastern European regions, especially those existing in the romances, trigger associations with an alien world whose coordinates are differently and tangibly redrawn on the stage. However, Shakespeare uses these references not merely as geographic, ethnographic, or anthropological exotic resources to replicate or adorn his source tales and reconfigure the plots: his drama is an enactment that is altering and replacing earlier authorities in the here and now of performance, and this gives these plays a disturbingly potential actuality, observed by all the critics who posit Shakespeare as our contemporary.

It becomes clear, therefore, that the Shakespearean allusions to Eastern European politics and spaces can have a significant resonance for the various contemporary productions of Shakespeare's plays emerging in these particular locations, including present-day Romania. Jonathan Hart discusses early modern European interpretation of the New World and asks a significant question: "Can the strangeness of other cultures or the past be understood through interpretation, or is difference or change such that the gap in understanding and communication from culture to culture or across time is insurmountable or at least ever-widening?"[84] One particular Eastern European appropriation of Shakespeare in Romania shows that the difference of past and foreign admits no impediment in communication. Given the multiplicity of performance potential, contemporary Romanian directors have adapted Shakespeare to signify differently according to their political or artistic agenda. They have reinvented Shakespeare according to an almost chameleonic principle of perpetual metamorphosis, which is exactly what Shakespeare did when he dealt with the extraneous locations in Eastern Europe and elsewhere.

Conclusions: Eastern European Liminal Locality

There can be no comparison in point of frequency and symbolic consideration between the less recurrent and usually invalidating allusions to the Eastern European area under discussion in this study and the several Italies of political, religious, philosophical, geographic, and topographical discourses produced by the Elizabethans and Jacobeans. As concerns Italy, each text drew upon its own traditions, each with its own commonplaces available for often-contradictory constructions of this other place. However, this is not exactly the case with the space of the more remote and less appreciated eastern part of Europe, about which many different discourses conveyed the same idea of social or political instability and disregarded liminality. Classical geographers and travel writers owed this fatal preconception to insufficient knowledge of these spaces, derived from the difficulty of travel in those remote areas and the writers' tendency to rely on hearsay or noncorroborated one-sided reports. In addition, the method and the structural design of their narrative account allowed for the exclusion or marginal notification of these regions in the classical texts. When the allusions to these spaces find their way into Shakespeare's classical plays, however, they take the form of an interesting dramatic conflation between classical authority and contemporary expectation, plus their inherent subversion and negation. Since Shakespeare was the cultural product of his own time, there are few, or next to no, direct references to the Balkan and the Black Sea area in his plays, especially those drawing on the classics. However, the school-induced authority of the classical writers was present, so Shakespeare could not escape replaying *their* allusions to these spaces.

Filtered through the classical lens, which could be adeptly used by authors, contemporary audiences, critics, and later interpreters of all times and manners, the remote Eastern European locations acquired an interestingly ambivalent function. The classical topical allusions could be used directly as a means of comparison or contrast with Shakespeare's contemporary England, and in this way the spaces under consideration attained a metasymbolic function. They exited the geographic and illustrative context of their location and became potent theatrical signifiers for conveying certain emotions. When rage needed visualization on stage, the stormy and icy Pontic Sea was summoned. When terror and the horrible image of a body torn to pieces were needed to emphasize atrocity, the image of Medea having her brother's body cut into parts and thrown off the coast of the Black Sea was readily invoked. In some of these dramatic situations, the dialectic tension of contrast was between an Eastern and remote space of cruelty and crime as opposed to the Western expectation of harmony and civility. In other dramatic instances, however, Shakespeare used his audience's preconceived assumptions of liminality and savageness about these spaces and their inhabitants to subvert and even annihilate the self-confident image of an urbane and complaisant Western world. He adduced contrastive references and showed characters belonging to the presumably civilized Western Europe displaying features traditionally ascribed to the reviled Thracian or Scythian others.

The Eastern European spaces were not the only projection screen for Elizabethan fantasies of otherness, but, as could other places, they could offer an interesting subject of comparison, in a Plutarch-like manner. Besides, seeing other people and other locations through the filtering and often-diminishing classical lens, the effect was one of self-complacent and benign acceptance of revered classical authority, without the harsh notes of opprobrium or reproof. This self-satisfied attitude, which implied a sense of security derived from the varied reception of classical texts, was not elicited only of Shakespeare's and his contemporaries' audiences. It is a recorded fact that most geographers and travel writers of the late sixteenth century, and well into the seventeenth, adopted indiscriminately the information deriving from the classical texts about the remote areas of Europe, Asia, and Africa. While pretending to deliver a "most true and authentic report" of travels, or an otherwise coherent and logically sustained account of the places of eastern and southern Europe, Elizabethan and Jacobean writers and geographers merely refurbished some classical reports about these places. Most of these countries were under Ottoman occupation at that time, but the issues of race and reviling of the menacing "Turk" were camouflaged, I believe, by the writers' urgency to render their accounts through the filtering lens of a gracious classical authority. Only in the latter part of the seventeenth century did the scientific spirit of research and confirmed evidence progress enough to allow writers to refer to the space of easternmost Europe and the Black Sea in terms of hard-fact reality.

Notes

Introduction

1. John Gillies, *Shakespeare and the Geography of Difference* (Cambridge: Cambridge University Press, 1994), 9.

2. Krystyna Kujawinska-Courtney, "Shakespeare's Geography of the World," *Acta Universitatis Lodziensis* 66 (1980): 43–62, esp. 56–61.

3. John Gillies, "Introduction: Elizabethan Drama and the Cartographizations of Space," *Playing the Globe: Genre and Geography in English Renaissance Drama,* edited by John Gillies and Virginia Mason Vaughan (Madison, NJ: Fairleigh Dickinson University Press, 1998), 19.

4. Christopher Dawson, *The Making of Europe: An Introduction to the History of European Unity* (Washington, DC: Catholic University of America Press, 2002), 69.

5. Gillies, *Shakespeare and the Geography of Difference,* 4.

6. S. Schoenbaum, *Shakespeare's Lives* (Oxford: Oxford University Press, 1993), 36.

Chapter 1. Ancient Fables

1. See Alessandro Serpieri et al., *Nel laboratorio di Shakespeare: Dalle fonti ai drammi* (Parma: Pratiche Editrice, 1988).

2. Louise George Clubb, "Intertextualities: Some Questions," in *The Italian World of English Renaissance Drama: Cultural Exchanges and Intertextuality,* ed. Michele Marrapodi and A. J. Hoenselaars, 179–89 (Newark: University of Delaware Press, 1998), 179.

3. For works exploring Shakespeare's use of classical writings see John Artos, "Shakespeare and the Ancient World," *Michigan Quarterly Review* 10 (1971): 149–63; Lydia Baumbach, "Shakespeare and the Classics," *Acta Classica* 28 (1985): 77–86; Charles and Michelle Martindale, *Shakespeare and the Uses of Antiquity: An Introductory Essay* (London: Routledge, 1990); Robert S. Miola, "Reading the Classics," *A Companion to Shakespeare,* ed. David Scott Kastan, Blackwell Companions to Literature and Culture 3 (Oxford: Blackwell, 1999), 72–85; Sarah Annes Brown, " 'There Is No End but Addition': The Later Reception of Shakespeare's Classicism," *Shakespeare and the Classics,* ed. Charles Martindale and A. B. Taylor, 277–93 (Cambridge: Cambridge University Press, 2004).

4. The problem was debated amicably on the SHAKSPER electronic conference, especially the matters regarding whether he could read Italian and French; see for example the posting on February 3, 2003, SHK 14.0176. Archived at http://

www.shaksper.net/archives/2003/0175.html. However, I subscribe to the common positing about Shakespeare's classical education.

5. Russ McDonald, *The Bedford Companion to Shakespeare*, 2nd ed. (Boston: Bedford/St. Martin's, 2001), 149.

6. Robert S. Miola, *Shakespeare's Reading* (Oxford: Oxford University Press, 2000), 158.

7. Henry Stephen. *A World of Wonders: or An Introduction to a treatise touching the conformitie of ancient and modern wonders: or A Preparative treatise to the Apologie for Herodotus* (London: Imprinted for Iohn Norton, 1607), 1–2. The author is the French printer Henri Estienne (died in 1598), Henricus Stephanus, or, as translated into English, Henry Stephen. The second edition is published in 1608 in Edinburgh. The book is a satire on the author's age and Catholicism by comparing it to the credulity of Herodotus's histories. Its anti-Catholic stance would have been favorably received in Scotland and England of the time. Estienne was from a long line of scholar-printers who moved around Europe as the climate of toleration waxed and waned.

8. Ibid., 17.

9. Isabel Rivers, *Classical and Christian Ideas in English Renaissance Poetry*, 2nd ed. (London: Routledge, 1994), 2.

10. Thomas Wylson, *The three Orations of Demosthenes chiefe Orator among the Grecians, in favor of the Olynthians, a people in Thracia, now called Romania: Englished out of the Greeke By Thomas Wylson* (London: Henrie Denham, 1570), STC 6578, sig. Bj. I have used the copy in the Phorzheimer Library collection, Austin, TX. Thomas Wylson was Elizabeth's Secretary of State and an admirer of Demosthenes, whom he translated from Greek. Apart from its political significance, Wylson's translation is notable as the earliest English version of Demosthenes and attains a high level of scholarship.

11. Claude Nicolet, *Space, Geography, and Politics in the Early Roman Empire* (Ann Arbor: University of Michigan Press, 1991), 58.

12. In the fifth century BC, the Greek word *historia* still meant "research."

13. F. E. Romer, Introduction to *Pomponius Mela's Description of the World* (Ann Arbor: University of Michigan Press, 1998), 11.

14. Gordon Braden includes a discussion of the influence of Arthur Golding's translation of Ovid's *Metamorphoses* on *As You Like It* and *A Midsummer Night's Dream* in *The Classics and English Renaissance Poetry: Three Case Studies*, Yale Studies in English 187 (New Haven: Yale University Press, 1978).

15. I have used the facsimile edition of the 1587 version, *The Excellent and Pleasant Worke Collectanea Rerum Memorabilium of Caius Julius Solinus: Translated from Latin (1587) by Arthur Golding*, ed. Harry R. Warfel (Gainesville, FL: Scholars' Facsimiles Reprints, 1955). There are two other English versions issued in the same year: STC 22896 and STC 22896.5.

16. George Kish, introduction to *The Excellent & Pleasante Worke Collectanea Rerum Memorabilium of Caius Julius Solinus. Translated from Latin (1587) by Arthur Golding*, ed. Harry R. Warfel (Gainesville, FL: Scholars' Facsimiles Reprints, 1955), 3.

17. Solinus, "Epistula Dedicatoria," *The Excellent & Pleasante Worke*, sig. B.ii.

18. Dacia is the ancient name of the European region corresponding roughly to modern Romania (including Transylvania). Before the Christian era, the Greeks called its inhabitants Getae, while the Romans called them Daci. Trajan invaded

Dacia in AD 102 and again in 105 and thus it became a Roman province. In the third century AD, the Goths invaded the region, and Aurelian was obliged to concede Dacia.

19. Mary B. Campbell, *The Witnesses and the Other World: Exotic European Travel Writing, 400–1600* (Ithaca, NY: Cornell University Press, 1988), 53.

20. Churchyard translated three books of Ovid's *Tristia* (1572) and began a translation of Pliny, which he destroyed. For an account of translations of Ovid see Lee T. Pearcy, *The Mediated Muse: English Translations of Ovid 1560–1700* (Hamden, CT. Archon Books, 1984), xviii.

21. When ancient Greeks first entered the Black Sea, about the sixth century BC, the most appropriate name they found for the sea was *Pontos Axenos,* i.e., literally "inhospitable, hostile sea." However, after a while, getting to know the sea better, they changed the name for *Pontos Euxinos,* i.e., "kindly, hospitable sea."

22. Ister was the ancient name of the river Danube, which forms most of the southern border between modern-day Bulgaria and Romania.

23. Pliny, *The Historie of the World. Commonly called, The Naturall Historie of C. Plinius Secundus.* Translated into English by Philemon Holland, Doctor in Physic, vol. 3. bk. 26, *Moesia* (London: Adam Islip, 1601), 71. STC.20029.

24. Russ McDonald, *Bedford Companion to Shakespeare,* 146.

25. All my references to the Shakespeare text are keyed to *The Norton Shakespeare,* ed. Stephen Greenblatt, Walter Cohen, Jean E. Howard, and Katharine Eisaman Maus (New York: Norton, 1997).

26. Heather James, in "Shakespeare's Learned Heroines in Ovid's Schoolroom," *Shakespeare and the Classics,* ed. Charles Martindale and A. B. Taylor, 66–85 (Cambridge: Cambridge University Press, 2004), argues that Shakespeare's learned heroines of the comedies—Hermia, Portia, Rosalind, and Viola—quote and adapt the works by Ovid in order to attain for themselves the expressive liberties Ovid takes with social conventions.

27. John W. Velz, "Portia and the Ovidian Grotesque," *The Merchant of Venice: New Critical Essays,* Shakespeare Criticism 26, ed. John W Mahon and Ellen Macleod Mahon, 179–86 (New York: Routledge, 2002), 181.

28. Ibid., 185.

29. Isabella Wheater, "Aristotelian Wealth and the Sea of Love: Shakespeare's Synthesis of Greek Philosophy and Roman Poetry in *The Merchant of Venice,*" *Review of English Studies* 43 (1992): 467–87; *Review of English Studies* 44 (1993): 16–36, esp. 16.

30. Wheater, *Review of English Studies* 44, 23–24.

31. Ibid., 19.

32. Ibid., 36.

33. According to Apollonius of Rhodes, *Argo* was the name of the ship built by Argos for the Argonauts' expedition. Apollonius of Rhodes, *Apollonius Rhodius: Argonautica,* ed. and trans. R. C. Seaton (Cambridge, MA: Harvard University Press, 1912), 1:4.

34. Alessandro Serpieri, "Contratti d'amore e di morte in *The Merchant of Venice,*" The Merchant of Venice *dal testo alla scena,* ed. Mariangela Tempera, 9–21 (Bologna: Editrice CLUEB, 1994), 10.

35. *Scythian* is a vague term for the Iranian-origin peoples who ranged across the Eurasian steppes during the first millennium BCE. We do not know the specific

names of the tribes involved, but it is a scholarly convention to refer to them collectively and loosely as "Scythian."

36. William Lithgow was a well known Scottish traveler of the seventeenth century, who seems to have attracted very little general notice prior to the publication of his travels in 1614.

37. William Lithgow, *A Discourse of a Peregrination in Europe, Asia, and Affricke* (London, 1614) (Amsterdam: Da Capo Press, Theatrum Orbis Terrarum, 1971), sig.H2.

38. William Biddulph, *Travels into Africa, Asia, and to the Black Sea* (Amsterdam: Da Capo Press, Theatrum Orbis Terrarum, 1968), 34.

39. Solinus, *The Excellent & Pleasante Worke,* sig. Oi.

40. Herodotus, *The Histories,* trans. Robin Waterfield, Introduction and notes by Carolyn Dewald, Oxford's World Classics (Oxford: Oxford University Press, 1998), 4:239. One early modern copy of Herodotus is *The Famous Hystory of Herodotus. Deuided into nine bookes* (London: T. Marshe, 1584), STC 13224. The translation is attributed to Barnabie Rich.

41. Herodotus, *The Famous Hystory of Herodotus,* tr. Barnabie Rich (London: Thomas Marshe, 1584), 1:224–22r, STC13224.

42. Katharine Eisaman Maus, introduction to *Titus Andronicus: The Norton Shakespeare,* ed. Stephen Greenblatt, Walter Cohen, Jean E. Howard, Katharine Eisaman Maus (New York: Norton, 1997), 373.

43. Id.

44. *As You Like It,* 3.3.5. The analogy is meant as a pun on *Goths* and *goats,* but this does not dismiss the fact that Shakespeare knew of Ovid's exile at Tomis.

45. Lucian Boia, *Romania: Borderland of Europe* (London: Reaktion Books, 2001), 43.

46. Herodotus, *The Histories,* 4:255.

47. Clifford J. Ronan, "An Ovidian 'Farthest Greece' in *Errors, Titus,* and *Pericles,*" *Discoveries: South-Central Renaissance Conference News and Notes* 19, no. 1 (2002): 3–4.

48. The present-day city of Constanta (Romania).

49. I have used the microfilm copy of the first English translation of Salustius, *The Two most Notable Histories which remaine unmained to Posterity: The Conspiracie of CATELINE, undertaken against the gouernment of the Senate of Rome, and the Warre which Iugurth* (London: Iohn Jaggard, 1608), STC 21625. Other editions of Sallustius are 1520, 1557, 1595, 1573 (Latin, two editions: STC 21622.4, 21622.6); 1569 (Latin, STC 216222.2); 1620; 1629; 1639.

50. Salustius, *Conspiracie of Cateline* (1608), 16.

51. The version of the English translation from Pliny I have used is a 1634 reprint of the 1601 translation by Philemon Holland. Pliny's *Natural History* was so popular in the early modern period that it was translated twice. The first translation was out of French, *A Summarie of the antiquities and wonders of the worlde, out of the sixteene first books of Plinie.* Tr. oute of the French by P. de Changy (H. Denham for T. Hackett, [1566]) (STC 20031). This translation was reprinted in 1585 (STC 20032) and 1587 (STC 20033). Philemon Holland's translation was entitled *Caius Plinius Secundus. The [xylographic] historie of the world.* Tr. P. Holland (London: A. Islip, 1601) (STC 20029). Three subsequent issues of this translation were in 1611 (STC 20029.5), 1634 (STC 20030), 1635 (STC 20030a).

52. *Pliny's Natural History: A Selection from Philemon Holland's Translation,* ed. J. Newsome (Oxford: Clarendon Press, 1964), 43.

53. Christopher Baker, "Ovid, Othello, and the Pontic Scythians," *A Search for Meaning: Critical Essays on Early Modern Literature,* ed. Paula Harms Payne, 61–80 (New York: Lang, 2004).

54. Jerry Brotton, "Tragedy and Geography," *A Companion to Shakespeare's Works,* ed. Richard Dutton and Jean E. Howard, Blackwell Companions to Literature and Culture, 1: 219–40 (Malden: Blackwell, 2003).

55. For the Pomponius Mela text, I have used a modern English translation: *Pomponius Mela's Description of the World,* ed. and tr. F. E. Romer (Ann Arbor: University of Michigan Press, 1998). The London editions were *The Worke of P. Mela: The Cosmographer, concerninge the situation of the world.* Tr. A Golding (London: J. Charlewood for T. Hacket, 1585); STC 17785; *The rare & singular worke of P. Mela. Whereunto is added, that of J. Solinus Polyhistor.* (London: J. Charlewood for T. Hacket, 1590), STC 17786.

56. Mela, *Pomponius Mela's Description,* 1.97:62.

57. Herodotus, *The Histories,* 4:259.

58. Ibid., 5:304.

59. Solinus, *The Excellent & Pleasante Worke,* ch. 14, K.iii.

60. I have used the microfilm copy of the 1595 edition of *The Lives of the Noble Grecians and Romanes* (London: Richard Field for Thomas Wight, 1595), STC 20067.5. There were twenty-eight editions of Plutarch's *Lives* (in Latin and English) in the period 1513–1631.

61. Plutarch. *The Lives of the Noble Grecians and Romans,* translated by Thomas North (London: Richard Field for Thomas Wight, 1595), 179. STC20067.5.

62. Plutarch, "Life of Theseus," 1H.

63. Harold F. Brooks, ed., *A Midsummer Night's Dream,* Arden edition (London: Routledge, 1993), 135.

64. Ibid., 129.

65. Hyrcania was an ancient name for the area south and southeast of the Caspian Sea.

66. Mela, *Pomponius Mela's Description,* 113.

67. Jeanne Addison Roberts, *The Shakespearean Wild: Geography, Genus, and Gender* (Lincoln: University of Nebraska Press, 1991), 6.

Chapter 2. Stage Maps

1. Gordon Braden explores how the Platonic theory of the tripartite soul underlies the lives of Brutus, Mark Antony, and Coriolanus and suggests that Shakespeare intuitively develops these particular characterizations to a greater extent than in North's translation; see "Plutarch, Shakespeare, and the Alpha Males," in *Shakespeare and the Classics,* ed. Charles Martindale and A. B. Taylor, 188–205 (Cambridge: Cambridge University Press, 2004).

2. David Daniell, ed., *Julius Caesar,* Arden edition, 3rd series (Walton-on-Thames, Surrey: Thomas Nelson, International Thomson Publishing, 1998), 88.

3. John Mulryan, in "Tradition and the Individual Talent: Shakespeare's and Jonson's Appropriation of the Classics," *Ben Jonson Journal* 10 (2003): 117–37, com-

pares Shakespeare's and Ben Jonson's uses of classical models in both comedy and tragedy and shows that Shakespeare's use of Plutarch in *Julius Caesar* expresses the tension that exists between language and thought in classical history and rhetoric.

4. Lesley B. Cormack, "Britannia Rules the Waves? Images of Empire in Elizabethan England," in *Literature, Mapping and the Politics of Space in Early Modern Britain,* ed. Andrew Gordon and Bernhard Klein (Cambridge: Cambridge University Press, 2001), 45.

5. Bill Delaney, "Shakespeare's *Julius Caesar,*" *Explicator* 60 (2001–2): 122–24.

6. Daniell, notes 168–87, 171, p. 262 and appendix, p. 344.

7. See Ion Horatiu Crisan, *Burebista and His Time,* trans. Sanda Mihailescu (Bucharest: Bibliotheca Historica Romaniae, 1978), 241–49. Crisan mentions the paucity of sources regarding Burebista's death, so that it is a modern deduction that Burebista was assassinated, on the grounds that so dominant a ruler could not have lived after being overthrown. The date is thought, not unanimously, to be 44. The connection of his overthrow to Roman designs, to tribal tensions, to some aristocrats opposing the extent of Burebista's power, to class struggle, etc., can only be conjectured.

8. Gillies, *Shakespeare and the Geography of Difference,* 10.

9. John Michael Archer, *Old Worlds: Egypt, Southwest Asia, India, and Russia in Early Modern English Writing* (Stanford: Stanford University Press, 2001), 24.

10. Ibid., 61.

11. Geraldo U. de Sousa, *Shakespeare's Cross-Cultural Encounters* (London: Macmillan, 1999), 2–3 and 129–58.

12. Emily C. Bartels, *Spectacles of Strangeness: Imperialism, Alienation, and Marlowe* (Philadelphia: University of Pennsylvania Press, 1993), 5.

13. John Wilders, ed., *Antony and Cleopatra.* Arden edition, 3rd series (London: Routledge, 1995), 20.

14. Jean-Marie Maguin, in "A Note on Shakespeare's Handling of Time and Space Data in *Antony and Cleopatra,*" *Cahiers élisabéthains* 13 (1978): 61–67, gives a "synoptic table" on time, space, and action in the play and argues that it displays the characteristics of a complex puzzle in time and space.

15. David Bevington, ed., *Antony and Cleopatra,* New Cambridge Shakespeare (Cambridge: Cambridge University Press, 1992), 5–7.

16. Wilders, ed., *Antony and Cleopatra,* note to 3.6, 186–87.

17. Walter Cohen, "The Undiscovered Country: Shakespeare and Mercantile Geography," *Marxist Shakespeare,* ed. Jean E. Howard and Scott Cutler Shershow, 128–58 (London: Routledge, 2001), 154.

18. Peter Holland, "Staging Europe in Shakespeare," in *Shifting the Scene: Shakespeare in European Culture,* ed. Ladina Bezzda Lambert and Balz Eugler, 21–40 (Newark: University of Delaware Press, 2004), 28.

Chapter 3. Early Modern Chorographies

1. Caterina Albano, "Visible Bodies: Cartography and Anatomy," in *Literature, Mapping, and the Politics of Space in Early Modern Britain,* ed. Andrew Gordon and Bernhard Klein, 91 (Cambridge: Cambridge University Press, 2001).

2. Matthew Dimmock, *New Turkes: Dramatizing Islam and the Ottomans in Early Modern England* (Aldershot: Ashgate, 2005).

3. For studies drawing on early modern anxieties regarding the Ottomans, especially focusing on *Othello,* see Bindu Malieckal, "'Bondslaves and Pagans Shall Our Statesmen Be:' Moors, Turks, and Venetians in *Othello,*" *Shakespeare Yearbook* 10 (1999): 162–89; Patricia Parker, "Barbers and Barbary: Early Modern Cultural Semantics," *Renaissance Drama* 33 (2004): 201–44; Daniel J. Vitkus, "Turning Turk in *Othello:* The Conversion and Damnation of the Moor," *Shakespeare Quarterly* 48 (1997): 145–76; this study is incorporated with revisions in *Turning Turk: English Theater and the Multicultural Mediterranean, 1570–1630,* Early Modern Cultural Studies (New York: Palgrave Macmillan, 2003).

4. George Abbot, *A Briefe Description of the Whole Worlde* (Amsterdam: Da Capo Press, Theatrum Orbis Terrarum, 1970), sig. Avi.

5. Kenneth Fincham, "Abbot, George (1562–1633)," *Oxford Dictionary of National Biography,* ed. H. C. G. Matthew and Brian Harrison (Oxford: Oxford University Press, 2004). http://www.oxforddnb.com/view/article/4.

6. William H. Sherman, "Stirrings and Searchings (1500–1720)," *The Cambridge Companion to Travel Writing,* ed. Peter Hulme and Tim Youngs, 17–36 (Cambridge: Cambridge University Press, 2002), 19.

7. Claire M. Howard, *English Travellers of the Renaissance* (New York: John Lane, 1914), x.

8. Thomas Blundeville, "To the Reader," *A Briefe Description of Universal Mappes and Cardes* (Amsterdam: Da Capo Press, Theatrum Orbis Terrarum, 1972), sig. A3v.

9. Gillies, *Shakespeare and the Geography of Difference,* 35.

10. Thomas Docherty, *After Theory: Postmodern Theory* (Edinburgh: Edinburgh University Press, 1996), 45.

11. Arthur Hopton, *Speculum Topographicum: or the Topographicall Glasse* (London: N.O. for Simon Waterson, 1611), STC 13783.

12. Andrea Cambino, *Commentaries* (Amsterdam: Da Capo Press, Theatrum Orbis Terrarum, 1970), 31.

13. Modern-day city of Feodosiya, Ukraine.

14. *Newes from diuers countries* (London: Valentine Sims, 1597), STC 18504.5.

15. Sigismund Bathory (1572–1613) was prince of Transylvania, Moldavia, and Wallachia, and nephew of the Polish king, Stephan Bathory. In the 1593–1602 war between Austria and the Turks, the prince of Transylvania took the side of the German emperor Rudolf II. Bathory made efforts to unite with the Habsburgs for a grand assault on the weakening Ottoman power.

16. For an account of Edward Webbe and other English travelers see Sara Warneke, "Educational Travelers: Popular Imagery and Public Criticism in Early Modern England," *Journal of Popular Culture* 28, no. 3 (1994): 71–94.

17. Edward Webbe, *The rare and most wonderful things* (London: William Wright, 1590; Amsterdam: Da Capo Press, Theatrum Orbis Terrarum, 1973), sig. B. STC 25152.

18. Daniel Goffman, *The Ottoman Empire and Early Modern Europe* (Cambridge: Cambridge University Press, 2002), 14–15.

19. This is the first English edition of the very popular description of Turkey by Nicolas de Nicolay.

20. Nicolas de Nicolay, *The Navigations, peregrinations and voyages* (Amsterdam and New York: Da Capo Press, Theatrum Orbis Terrarum, 1968), sig. q2r.

21. This is the earliest edition known. In the same year, there was another edition and then six subsequent editions in 1600, 1605 (enlarged), 1608, 1617, 1620, and 1623.

22. George Abbot, *A Briefe Description of the Whole Worlde* (Amsterdam: Da Capo Press, Theatrum Orbis Terrarum, 1970), sig. Aiij.

23. Richard Hakluyt, The Second Volume of *The Principal Navigations, Voyages, Traffiques and Discoveries of the English Nation.* (London: George Bishop, Ralph Newberie, and Robert Barker, 1599), 290. STC 1262a.

24. Fynes Moryson, *An Itinerary Containing His Ten Yeeres Travell through the Twelve Dominions of Germany, Bohmerland, Sweitzerland, Netherland, Denmarke, Poland, Italy, Turky, France, England, Scotland & Ireland,* vol. 2 (Glasgow: James MacLehose and Sons, 1907), 495.

25. For studies including references to Giovanni Botero's influence on early modern European diplomacy and economy see Robert Markley, "Riches, Power, Trade and Religion: The Far East and the English Imagination, 1600–1720," *Renaissance Studies* 17 (2003): 433–55; Paul Slack, "Measuring the National Wealth in Seventeenth-Century England," *Economic History Review* 57, no. 4 (2005): 607–35.

26. Giovanni Botero, *The Travellers Breviat* (Amsterdam: Da Capo Press, Theatrum Orbis Terrarum, 1969), 39.

27. Sultan Achmed, *Letters from the Great Turke* (Amsterdam: Da Capo Press, Theatrum Orbis Terrarum, 1971), B2.

28. Edward Topsell, *The Historie of Serpents* (Amsterdam: Da Capo Press, Theatrum Orbis Terrarum, 1973), 201.

29. Sir Thomas Palmer, *An Essay of the means how to make our Travailles into forraine countries the more profitable and honourable* (London: Imprinted by H. L(ownes) for Matthew Lownes, 1606), STC 19156.

30. Sir Thomas Palmer, *An Essay of the means how to make our Travailles into forraine countries the more profitable* (Amsterdam: Da Capo Press, Theatrum Orbis Terrarum, 1972), 60–61.

31. Daniel Vitkus, "Adventuring Heroes in the Mediterranean: Mapping the Boundaries of Anglo-Islamic Exchange on the Early Modern Stage," *Journal of Medieval and Early Modern Studies* 37 (Winter 2007): 75–95, esp. 92.

32. For an examination of the accuracy of the Elizabethans' and Jacobeans' knowledge regarding the Orient, which includes the Shirley brothers and their exploits, see Louis Wann, "The Oriental in Elizabethan Drama," *Modern Philology* 7 (January 1915): 423–47.

33. Anthony Nixon, *The Three English Brothers* (Amsterdam: Da Capo Press, Theatrum Orbis Terrarum, 1970), sig. K3.

34. Biddulph, *Travels,* 16.

35. Ibid., 81.

36. Abraham Ortelius, *His Epitome of the Theatre of the Worlde* (London: James Shawe, 1603), 92. STC 18856.

37. Ioannes Dubravius (1486–1553) from Pilsen, Bohemia, was a Czech poet who wrote *Theriobulia* (1520), epic poetry after Aesopic fables. He also wrote about pisciculture in *De piscinis* (1547). Later he became bishop of Olmütz and wrote *Historiae regni Boiemiae de rebus memoria* (Prosznitz 1552), a history of Bohemia.

38. Abraham Ortelius, *Theatrum Orbis Terrarum. The theatre of the whole world,* folio edition (London: J. Norton 1606), 60.

39. Antonio Bonfinius (late fifteenth century) was an Italian by birth who resided at the Hungarian court of Mathias Corvinus. *His Rerum Ungaricarum decades tres, nunc demum industria* was published by Martinus Brenneri Bistricensis Transylvani in Basel in 1543 and 1568. He is known as the Hungarian Livius.

40. Abraham A. Ortelius, *Ortelius his Epitome of the Theater of the worlde: Now lately renewed and augmented by M. Coignet* (London: J. Norton, 1610), 1B. STC 18857.

41. George Sandys, *A Relation of a Journey began an. Dom. 1610. Containing a description of the Turkish Empire* (Amsterdam: Da Capo Press, Theatrum Orbis Terrarum, 1973), 1–2.

42. Lithgow, *Discourse of a Peregrination,* sig. H3.

43. Joseph Hall, *Quo Vadis? A Just Censure of Travell* (Amsterdam: Walter J. Johnson, Theatrum Orbis Terrarum, 1975), 31.

44. Fynes Moryson, *An Itinerary written by F. Moryson* (London: John Beale, 1617; Amsterdam: Theatrum Orbis Terrarum, 1973), 119.

45. John Hagthorpe, *Englands Exchequer or a Discourse of the Sea and Navigation* (Amsterdam: Walter J. Johnson, Theatrum Orbis Terrarum, 1974), 18.

46. Peter Heylyn, *Microcosmos, a little description of the great world,* The fifth edition (Oxford: Printed by Will. Turner, 1631). STC 13279.5. The first edition of this popular geographical book was in 1621, followed by seven subsequent editions (1625, 1627, 1629, 1631, 1633, 1636, and 1639).

47. Lewes Roberts, *The Marchants Mapp of Commerce* (Amsterdam, Norwood, NJ: Walter J. Johnson, Theatrum Orbis Terrarum, 1974), 123, sig. M2.

48. Julia Briggs, *This Stage-Play World: Texts and Contexts, 1580–1625* (Oxford: Oxford University Press, 1997), 299.

49. Thomas Docherty, *After Theory: Postmodern Theory,* 45.

Chapter 4. Early Modern Drama

1. Ben Jonson, *Every Man Out of His Humour,* in *The Works of Ben Jonson,* ed. W. Gifford, vol. 2 (London: W Bulmer & Co, 1816), 23–24.

2. In a note to this passage, the editor W. Gifford observes, "Against this passage, Theobald had written, in the margin of his copy, *a flurt on Shakespeare.* This jealousy of our great poet, commenced under such respectable auspices, has since become epidemical, and infected almost all his critics. The charge, in the present case, is too absurd for serious notice, or indeed for any notice at all" (W. Gifford, ed., *Every Man Out of His Humour, The Works of Ben Jonson,* 2:23n4).

3. David Farley-Hills, "Jonson, Shakespeare, and the Italian Theorists," *Journal of Anglo-Italian Studies* 6 (2001): 35–42.

4. Robert Weimann, "Bifold Authority in Shakespeare's Theatre," in *Shakespeare in Performance,* ed. Robert Shaughnessy, New Casebook Series, 78–99 (London: Macmillan, 2000), 91.

5. Ibid.

6. For studies on Shakespeare's Western European locales see A. J. Hoenselaars, "Italy Staged in English Renaissance Drama," *Shakespeare's Italy: Functions of Italian Locations in Renaissance Drama,* ed. Michele Marrapodi, A. J. Hoenselaars, Marcello Cappuzzo, and Lino Falzon Santucci, 30–48 (Manchester: Manchester University Press, 1993); "Mapping Shakespeare's Europe," *Reclamations of Shakespeare,* ed. A. J.

Hoenselaars, DQR Studies in Literature 15, 223–48 (Amsterdam: Rodopi, 1994); "Shakespeare, Foreigners, and National Ideologies," *Shakespeare: Varied Perspectives,* ed. Vikram Chopra, New World Literature Series 90, 11–33 (Delhi: B. R., 1996); Patricia, Dorval, ed., *Shakespeare et la France,* Société Française Shakespeare, Actes du Congrès de 2000 (Paris: Société Française Shakespeare, 2001); Felicia Hardison Londré, "Elizabethan Views of the 'Other': French, Spanish, and Russians in *Love's Labour's Lost,*" *Elizabethan Review* 3, no. 1 (1995): 3–20.

7. Christopher Marlowe, *The Jew of Malta* (London: I. B. for Nicholas Vavasour, 1633), *A Select Collection of Old Plays,* ed. Isaac Reed and Octavius Gilchrist, vol. 8 (London: Septimus Prowett, 1825), act 1, p. 257.

8. Ben Jonson, *Every Man in His Humour,* in *The Works of Ben Jonson,* ed. W. Gifford, introduction by Octavius Gilchrist, vol. 1 (London: W Bulmer & Co, 1816), II, 2, p. 54. The editor's note to this text adds some interesting information: "In the French version of this play, we are told that this and what follows is an account of the campaigns really made by Jonson! It's a pity that the editors stopped here: a life of Jonson, on the authority of quarter-master Brainworm, would have been a great curiosity" (54n2).

9. For studies on Shakespeare's possible implication in *Locrine*'s authorship or revision, see C. F. Tucker Brooke, ed., *The Shakespeare Apocrypha* (Oxford: Clarendon Press, 1908); Terence P. Logan and Denzell S. Smith eds., *The Predecessors of Shakespeare: A Survey and Bibliography of Recent Studies in English Renaissance Drama* (Lincoln: University of Nebraska Press, 1973), 258–72.

10. Homer, *The Odyssey,* translated by George Chapman (London: R. Field for Nathaniel Butler, 1615), book 10, p. 144. STC 13637.

11. Ovid, *The Fifteen Books of Ovid's Metamorphoses,* translated by Arthur Golding (London: William Seres, 1567), book 15, p. 197. STC 18956.

12. George Peele or Robert Greene, *The Tragedy of Locrine,* ed. Ronald B. McKerrow (London: Malone Society Reprints, 1908), 1.2.142–44, sig. B.

13. Abraham Ortelius, *Theatrum Orbis Terrarum* (1606), 92.

14. Fynes Moryson, *Itinerary,* 104–5.

15. Christopher Marlowe, *The Second Part of the Bloody Conquests of the Mighty Tamburlaine,* in *The Works of Christopher Marlowe,* ed. C. F. Tucker Brooke (Oxford: Clarendon Press, 1910), 1.1.2386–89, p. 77.

16. Jeff Dailey, "Christian Underscoring in *Tamburlaine the Great, Part II,*" *Journal of Religion and Theatre* 4, no. 2 (2005): 146–59, esp. 149.

17. Martin Procházka, "Shakespeare's Illyria, Sicily, and Bohemia: Other Spaces, Other Times, or Other Economies?" *Litteraria Pragensia* 12, no. 23 (2002): 130–49.

18. Sara Hanna, "From Illyria to Elysium: Geographical Fantasy in *Twelfth Night,*" *Litteraria Pragensia* 12, no. 23 (2002): 21–45.

19. Ann Blake, "Location, Imagination, and Heterotopia in *Twelfth Night,*" *Litteraria Pragensia* 12, no. 23 (2002): 66–79.

20. Peter Milward, "The Religious Dimension of Shakespeare's Illyria," *Litteraria Pragensia* 12, no. 23 (2002): 59–65.

21. Cicero, *Marcus Tullius Ciceroes three bookes of duties to Marcus his sonne,* translated by Nicholas Grimalde (London: Richard Tottell, 1556), book 2, p. 78r. STC 5281.

22. Richard S. Ide, "Shakespeare and the Pirates," *Iowa State Journal of Research* 58 (1984): 311–18.

23. Anon., *Misogonus, Six Anonymous Plays,* Early English Dramatists, second series, ed. John Stephen Farmer (London: Early English Drama Society, 1906), 205, 213.

24. Beaumont and Fletcher, *The Prophetess,* in *The Dramatic Works of Ben Jonson and Beaumont and Fletcher,* ed. George Colman, vol. 3 (London: John Stockdale, 1811), p. 367.

25. James R. Simon, "'Perplex'd beyond Self-Explication:' *Cymbeline* and Early Modern/Postmodern Europe," *Shakespeare in the New Europe,* ed. Michael Hattaway, Boika Sokolova, and Derek Roper, 294–309 (Sheffield: Sheffield Academic Press, 1994).

26. Erica Sheen, "The Pannonians and the Dalmatians: Reading for a European History in *Cymbeline,*" *Shakespeare in the New Europe,* ed. Michael Hattaway, Boika Sokolova, and Derek Roper, 310–20 (Sheffield: Sheffield Academic Press, 1994).

27. Anon., *The Tragedy of Nero* (1623), in *The Tragedy of Nero and Other Plays,* ed. Herbert P. Horne, Havelock Ellis, Arthur Symons, and Wilson Verity, Mermaid Series (London: T. Fisher Unwin and Charles Scribner's Sons, 1904).

28. Thomas Middleton and T. Dekkar, *The Roaring Girl or Moll Cutpurse* (London: Thomas Archer, 1611), in *A Select Collection of Old Plays,* ed. Isaac Reed and Octavius Gilchrist, vol. 6 (London: Septimus Prowett, 1825), 87.

29. Daniel J. Vitkus, ed., Introduction to *Three Turk Plays from Early Modern England: Selimus, a Christian Turned Turk, and the Renegado* (New York: Columbia University Press, 2000), 3.

30. Robert Greene, *The Tragical Reign of Selimus* (1594), gen. ed. W. W. Greg, ed. W. Bang, Malone Society Reprints (London: Charles Wittingham & Co, Chiswick Press, 1908), sig. C2.

31. Christopher Marlowe, *The Second Part of Tamburlaine,* 1.1.2334, p. 76.

32. Glapthorne, *Albertus Wallenstein* (1634–38), in *The Old English Drama: A Selection of Plays from the Old English Dramatists,* vol. 2 (London: Hurst, Robinson & Co., 1825), 12.

33. John Webster, *The White Devil or Vittoria Corrombona,* in *Six Plays by Contemporaries of Shakespeare,* ed. C. B. Wheeler (London: H. Milford, Oxford University Press, 1915), 53.

34. Péter Dávidházi, "Camel, Weasel, Whale: The Cloud-Scene in *Hamlet* as a Hungarian Parable," *Shifting the Scene: Shakespeare in European Culture,* ed. Ladina Bezzola Lambert and Balz Engler, 95–110 (Newark: University of Delaware Press, 2004).

35. Katharine Eisaman Maus, ed., "Additional Passage," in *The Norton Shakespeare.* Based on the Oxford Edition, ed. Stephen Greenblatt et al. (London and New York: Norton, 1997), 2087.

36. Anon., *The Merry Devil of Edmonton,* in *A Select Collection of Old English Plays: Originally Published by Robert Dodsley in 1744,* ed. W. Carew Hazlitt, vol. 10 (London: Reeves and Turner, 1874), 227.

37. Ibid., 244.

38. Brewer, *Lingua,* in *A Select Collection of Old English Plays: Originally Published by Robert Dodsley in 1744,* ed. W. Carew Hazlitt, vol. 9 (London: Reeves and Turner, 1874), 364.

39. Philip Massinger, *The City Madam,* in *Specimens of English Dramatic Poets Who Lived about the Time of Shakespeare,* ed. Charles Lamb (London: Taylor and Francis, 1854), 359.

40. Philip Massinger, *The Picture,* in *A Select Collection of Old Plays,* ed. R. Dodsley, vol. 8 (London: Pall Mall, 1744), 321.

41. William Rowley, *A Match at Midnight, A Pleasant Comedie* (London: Aug. Mathewes for William Sheares, 1633), in *A Select Collection of Old Plays,* ed. Isaac Reed and Octavius Gilchrist, vol. 7 (London: Septimus Prowett, 1825), 331.

42. Robert Greene, *The Tragical Reign of Selimus* (1594).

43. Thomas Kyd, *Soliman and Perseda,* in *A Select Collection of Old English Plays: Originally Published by Robert Dodsley in 1744,* ed. W. Carew Hazlitt, vol. 5 (London: Reeves and Turner, 1874), 285.

44. John Webster, *The White Devil or Vittoria Corrombona,* 138.

45. Ibid., 169.

46. Anon., *Wily Beguiled,* in *A Select Collection of Old English Plays: Originally Published by Robert Dodsley in 1744,* ed. W. Carew Hazlitt, vol. 9 (London: Reeves and Turner, 1874), 285.

47. Francis Beaumont and John Fletcher, *The Knight of the Burning Pestle,* in *Six Plays by Contemporaries of Shakespeare,* ed. C. B. Wheeler (London: H. Milford, Oxford University Press, 1915), 268.

48. R. J. W. Evans, Review of "*Relatiile politice ale Angliei cu Moldova, Tara Româneasca si Transilvania în secolele XVI–XVIII* by L. Demeny and P. Cernovodeanu," *English Historical Review* 91, no. 360 (July 1976): 640–41.

49. R. Hakluyt, *The Principal Navigations, Voyages, Trafiques and Discoveries of the English Nation,* vol. 3 (London: Everyman, 1907), 51–53. See also P. Wittek, "The Turkish Documents in Hakluyt," *Bulletin of the Institute for Historical Research* 19 (1942–43): 121–38.

50. Ibid., 64–72.

51. Nicolae Iorga, *A History of Anglo-Romanian Relations* (Bucharest: Societatea anglo-română, 1931), 17.

52. Marcu Beza, *Vechi legaturi cu Anglia,* Academia Românа, Memoriile sectiunii literare, series 3, tome 8 (Bucharest: Monitorul Oficial si Imprimeriile Statului, 1938), 34. See also Maria Mociorniţa, "Romanian-English Cultural Relations in the 16th and 17th Centuries," *English Literature and Civilization: The Renaissance and the Restoration Period,* ed. Ioan Aurel Preda (Bucharest: Editura Didactica si Pedagogica, 1983), 188–92.

53. Ben Jonson, *Epicoene, or The Silent Woman,* ed. Aurelia Henry, Yale Studies in English 31, gen. ed. Albert S. Cook (New York: Henry Holt, 1906), 100.

54. Aurelia Henry, the editor of Ben Jonson's *Epicoene,* remarks in note 27 to the passage mentioning the prince of Moldavia: "What princely representative of this far-off land had ever come to London, I am unable to discover" (ibid., 258).

55. Russell West, *Spatial Representations and the Jacobean Stage: From Shakespeare to Webster* (New York: Palgrave Macmillan, 2002), 173.

56. Philip Massinger, *The Roman Actor,* in *The Dramatic Works of Massinger and Ford,* Introduction by Heartly Coleridge (London: Edward Moxon, 1840), 145.

57. George Peele or Robert Greene, *The Tragedy of Locrine,* 2.2.464–66, sig. C2.

58. Ben Jonson, *The Masque of Queens Celebrated in the House of Fame* (London: N. Okes for R. Bonian and H. Wally, 1609), sig. D3r. STC 14788.

59. Hughes and others, *The Misfortunes of Arthur,* in *A Select Collection of Old English Plays: Originally Published by Robert Dodsley in 1744,* ed. W. Carew Hazlitt, vol. 4 (London: Reeves and Turner, 1874), 318.

60. Anon., *The Return from Parnassus,* in *A Select Collection of Old English Plays: Originally Published by Robert Dodsley in 1744,* ed. W. Carew Hazlitt, vol. 9 (London: Reeves and Turner, 1874), 140.

61. Ben Jonson, *The Speeches at Prince Henry's Barriers,* in *The Works of Ben Jonson,* ed. Francis Cunningham and William Gifford (London: Bickers and Son, 1875), p. 151.

62. James Shirley, *The Lady of Pleasure,* in *The Dramatic Works and Poems of James Shirley,* ed. William Gifford and Alexander Dyce, vol. 4 (London: John Murray, 1833), 27–28.

63. James Shirley, *Honoria and Mammon,* in *The Dramatic Works and Poems of James Shirley,* ed. William Gifford and Alexander Dyce, vol. 6 (London: John Murray, 1833), 7.

64. James Shirley, *The Humorous Courtier,* in *The Dramatic Works and Poems of James Shirley,* ed. William Gifford and Alexander Dyce, vol. 4 (London: John Murray, 1833), 553.

65. Guy Halsall, ed., *Humour, History and Politics in Late Antiquity and the Early Middle Ages* (Cambridge: Cambridge University Press, 2002), 29.

66. Francis Beaumont and John Fletcher, *Wit without Money,* in *The Works of Beaumont and Fletcher,* introduction by George Darley, vol. 1 (London: Edward Moxon, 1840), 197.

67. Francis Beaumont and John Fletcher, *Philaster,* in *Elizabethan Drama,* ed. W. Eliot, vol. 2 (New York: P. F. Collier & Son, 1910), 706.

68. Julia Briggs, *This Stage-Play World,* 254.

Chapter 5. Eastern European Geography

1. Christopher Marlowe, *The Two Tragicall Discourses of Mighty Tamburlaine, the Scythian Shepherd,* in *The Works of Christopher Marlowe,* ed. C. F. Tucker Brooke (Oxford: Clarendon Press, 1910), 3.1.942–44, p. 34.

2. George Chapman, *The Tragedy of Bussy D'Ambois,* in *Old Plays; Being a Continuation of Dodsley's Collection,* ed. Charles Wentworth Dilke, vol. 3 (London: Rodwell and Martin, 1816), 328.

3. Ibid., 239. For a discussion of this scene see Allan H. Gilbert, "Chapman's Fortune with Winged Hands," *Modern Language Notes* 52, no. 3 (March 1937): 190–92.

4. Thomas Kyd, *Cornelia,* in *A Select Collection of Old English Plays. Originally Published by Robert Dodsley in 1744,* ed. W. Carew Hazlitt, vol. 4 (London: Reeves and Turner, 1874), 230.

5. Ibid.

6. Jasper Fisher, *Fuimus Troes, The True Trojans* (1633), in *A Select Collection of Old Plays,* ed. Isaac Reed and Octavius Gilchrist, vol. 7 (London: Septimus Prowett, 1825), 385.

7. Ibid., 410.

8. Robert Greene, *The First Part of the Most Tyrannical Tragedie and Raigne of Selimus* (1594), scene 3, 519, sig. C2.

9. Robert Greene, *The Comicall Historie of Alphonsus King of Aragon* (1599), in *The*

Plays and Poems of Robert Greene, ed. J. Churton Collins, vol. 1 (Oxford: Clarendon Press, 1905), 3.2.779–935, pp. 102–6.

10. Thomas Kyd, *Soliman and Perseda,* 318.

11. Ibid., 343.

12. Ibid., 363.

13. Christopher Marlowe, *Tamburlaine, Part 1,* in *The Chief Elizabethan Dramatists Excluding Shakespeare,* ed. William Allan Neilson (Boston: Houghton Mifflin, 1911), 66.

14. Philip Massinger, *The Renegado,* in *The Dramatic Works of Massinger and Ford,* introduction by Heartly Coleridge (London: Edward Moxon, 1840), 113.

15. Attributed to Fletcher and Philip Massinger (1619), according to the chronology in *The Cambridge History of Early Modern English Literature,* ed. David Lowenstein and Janel Mueller (Cambridge: Cambridge University Press, 2002), 859.

16. Francis Beaumont and John Fletcher, *The Double Marriage,* in *The Dramatic Works of Ben Jonson, and Beaumont and Fletcher,* ed. Peter Walley and George Collman, vol. 3 (London: John Stockdale, 1811), 520.

17. Claire McEachern, "Literature and National Identity," in *The Cambridge History of Early Modern English Literature,* ed. David Loewenstein and Janel Mueller (Cambridge: Cambridge University Press, 2002), 464.

18. John Fletcher and Philip Massinger, *The Knight of Malta,* in *The Dramatic Works of Ben Jonson, and Beaumont and Fletcher,* ed. Peter Walley and George Collman, vol. 3 (London: John Stockdale, 1811), 623.

19. Fynes Moryson, *Itinerary,* 421.

20. Thomas Heywood, *The Fair Maid of the West, Part 1,* in *The Dramatic Works of Thomas Heywood: With a Life of the Poet and Remarks on His Writings,* ed. J. Payne Collier, esq., vol. 1 (London: Shakespeare Society, 1850), 20.

21. Anon, *Hickscorner,* in *A select collection of old English plays: Originally Published by Robert Dodsley in 1744,* ed. W. Carew Hazlitt, vol. 1 (London: Reeves and Turner, 1874), 162.

22. Thomas Heywood, *If You Know Not Me You Know Nobody, Part* 2, in *Two Historical Plays on the Life and Reign of Queen Elizabeth by Thomas Heywood,* introduction and notes by J. Payne Collier, esq. (London: Shakespeare Society, 1851), 113.

23. In Fynes Moryson's *Itinerary* there is a passage describing the London Exchange; the author compares it to the Burse in Antwerp, Ancona (Italy), Hamburg (Germany), and the one in Constantinople, called Besensteine, where they also sell slaves. Fynes Moryson, *Itinerary,* 485–86.

24. Ben Jonson, *Everyman Out of His Humour,* 72.

25. Ben Jonson, *Epicoene, or the Silent Woman,* 44–45.

26. Nabil Matar, *Turks, Moors, and Englishmen in the Age of Discovery* (New York: Columbia University Press, 1999), 3.

27. Nabil Matar, *Islam in Britain, 1558–1685,* ch. 1 (Cambridge: Cambridge University Press, 1998).

28. Ben Jonson, *Volpone, or The Fox,* in *The Chief Elizabethan Dramatists Excluding Shakespeare,* ed. William Allan Neilson (Boston and New York: Houghton Mifflin, 1911), 295.

29. Thomas Dekker, *The Honest Whore,* in *The Chief Elizabethan Dramatists Excluding Shakespeare,* ed. William Allan Neilson (Boston and New York: Houghton Mifflin, 1911), 405.

30. John Webster, *The Duchess of Malfi*, in *Elizabethan Drama*, ed. Charles W. Eliot, vol. 2 (New York: P. F. Collier & Son, 1910), 780.

31. John Webster, *The Duchess of Malfi*, in *Six Plays by Contemporaries of Shakespeare*, ed. C. B. Wheeler (London: H. Milford, Oxford University Press, 1915), 128.

32. Ben Jonson, *Volpone; or The Fox*, 306.

33. Marshall Poe, *People Born to Slavery: Russia in Early Modern European Ethnography, 1476–1748* (Ithaca, Cornell University Press, 2001), 9.

34. Beaumont and Fletcher, *The Woman's Prize; or the Tamer Tam'd*, in *The Dramatic Works of Ben Jonson and Beaumont and Fletcher*, ed. Peter Whalley, vol. 4 (London: John Stockdale, 1811), 142.

35. Beaumont and Fletcher, *The Sea Voyage*, in *The Dramatic Works of Ben Jonson and Beaumont and Fletcher*, ed. Peter Whalley, vol. 4 (London: John Stockdale, 1811), 250.

36. Beaumont and Fletcher, *The Woman Hater*, in *The Dramatic Works of Ben Jonson and Beaumont and Fletcher*, ed. Peter Whalley, vol. 4 (London: John Stockdale, 1811), 481.

37. Nathaniel Field, *A Woman is a Weathercock*, in *The Tragedy of Nero and Other Plays*, ed. Herbert P. Horne, Havelock Ellis, Arthur Symons, and Wilson Verity, Mermaid Series (London: T. Fisher Unwin and Charles Scribner's Sons, 1904), 365.

38. Glapthorne, *Albertus Wallenstein*, in *The Old English Drama*, 25.

39. Douglas Bruster, *Quoting Shakespeare: Form and Culture in Early Modern Drama* (Lincoln: University of Nebraska Press, 2000), 4.

40. Henry S. Turner, *English Renaissance Stage: Geometry, Poetics, and the Practical Spatial Arts, 1580–1630* (Oxford: Oxford University Press, 2006), 165.

41. Russell West, *Spatial Representations and the Jacobean Stage*, 13.

Chapter 6. Romances

1. Bradin Cormack, "Marginal Waters: *Pericles* and the Idea of Jurisdiction," in Andrew Gordon and Bernhard Klein (eds.), *Literature, Mapping, and the Politics of Space in Early Modern Britain* (Cambridge: Cambridge University Press, 2001), 155–80, esp. 157.

2. Ibid.

3. Richard Helgerson, "The Folly of Maps and Modernity," *Literature, Mapping, and the Politics of Space in Early Modern Britain*, ed. Andrew Gordon and Bernhard Klein, 249 (Cambridge: Cambridge University Press, 2001).

4. Gillies, *Shakespeare and the Geography of Difference*, 70.

5. Peter Holland, "Staging Europe in Shakespeare," 40.

6. Simon Palfrey, *Late Shakespeare: A New World of Words* (Oxford: Clarendon Press, 1997), 15.

7. Boika Sokolova, *Shakespeare's Romances as Interrogative Text: Their Alienation Strategies and Ideology* (Lewiston, NY: Edwin Mellen Press, 1992), 2.

8. Arthur F. Kinney, "Imagining England: The Chorographical Glass," in *Soundings of Things Done: Essays in Early Modern Literature in Honor of S. K. Heiniger Jr. ed. Peter E. Medine and Joseph Wittreich* (Newark: University of Delaware Press, 1997), 182.

9. See Northrop Frye, *A Natural Perspective: The Development of Shakespearean Com-*

edy and Romance (New York: Columbia University Press, 1965); Charles Frey, *Shakespeare's Vast Romance: A Study of* The Winter's Tale (Columbia: University of Missouri Press, 1980), 114ff.; Howard Felperin, *Shakespearean Romance* (Princeton: Princeton University Press, 1972).

10. See Gaston Bachelard, *The Poetics of Space,* Maria Jolas tr. (Boston: Beacon Press, 1969); M. Berman, *"All That Is Solid Melts Into Air": The Experience of Modernity* (New York: Simon & Schuster, 1982); Michel Foucault, "Of Other Spaces," *Diacritics* 16 (1986): 22–27; Edward Soja, "History: Geography: Modernity," *Cultural Studies Reader,* ed. Simon During (London: Routledge, 1993), 135–50. For a discussion of "representational spaces" and "mapmindedness" in Shakespeare's England see John Gillies, "Introduction: Elizabethan Drama and the Cartographizations of Space," in *Playing the Globe: Genre and Geography in English Renaissance Drama,* 19–45, ed. John Gillies and Virginia Mason Vaughan (Madison, NJ: Fairleigh Dickinson University Press; London: Associated University Presses, 1998): 19–45; Andrew Gordon and Bernhard Klein, eds., *Literature, Mapping, and the Politics of Space in Early Modern Britain* (Cambridge: Cambridge University Press, 2001).

11. Clifford Geertz, *Local Knowledge: Further Essays in Interpretive Anthropology* (New York: Basic Books, 1983), 234.

12. Michel Foucault, "Space, Power, Knowledge," in *The Cultural Studies Reader,* ed. Simon During (London: Routledge, 1993), 168.

13. Ibid.

14. Any discussion of "the circulation of social energy" is, inevitably, indebted to Stephen Greenblatt's *Shakespearean Negotiations: The Circulation of Social Energy in Renaissance England* (Berkeley: University of California Press, 1988).

15. See David Bergeron, *Shakespeare's Romances and the Royal Family* (Lawrence: University Press of Kansas, 1985); Leonard Tannenhouse, *Power on Display: The Politics of Shakespeare's Genres* (New York: Methuen, 1986); Glynne Wickam, "From Tragedy to Tragicomedy: *King Lear* as a Prologue," *Shakespeare Survey* 2 (1973): 33–48. For a discussion of Shakespeare's plays and Jacobean political thought see Robin Headlam Wells, *Shakespeare: Politics and the State* (London: Macmillan, 1986); Alexander Leggatt, *Shakespeare's Political Drama: The History Plays and the Roman Plays* (New York: Routledge, 1988); Rebecca W. Bushnell, *Tragedies and Tyrants: Political Thought and Theater in the English Renaissance* (Ithaca, NY: Cornell University Press, 1990); Constance Jordan, *Shakespeare's Monarchies: Ruler and Subject in the Romances* (Ithaca: Cornell University Press, 1997), 35–67.

16. Constance C. Relihan, in "Liminal Geography: *Pericles* and the Politics of Place," *Philological Quarterly* 3 (1992): 281–99, considers that *Pericles* dramatizes "locations whose relations to Europe may be considered liminal," p. 281; John Gillies, in *Shakespeare and the Geography of Difference,* explores Shakespeare's geographic imagination in its intimate relationship with the "poetic" geographic tradition; the collection of essays edited by John Gillies and Virginia Mason Vaughan, *Playing the Globe,* nearly exhausts this topic.

17. Madison J. Davis and Daniel Frankforter, *The Shakespeare Name Dictionary* (New York: Garland, 1995), 488.

18. See T. G. Bishop, "*Pericles* or the Past as Fate and Miracle," in *Shakespeare and the Theatre of Wonder,* Cambridge Studies in Renaissance Literature and Culture 9 (Cambridge: Cambridge University Press, 1996), 93–124, particularly his comments on "etching—the enlargement or augmentation—of the story" (p. 109). Frederick

Kiefer, in *Writing on the Renaissance Stage: Written Words, Printed Pages, Metaphoric Books* (Newark: University of Delaware Press, 1996), considers the illustration on the title page of Wilkins's *Painful Adventures,* representing Gower beside an open book, as meaningful for "emphasizing the antiquity of events dramatized, the psychic distance separating past and present" (p. 211).

19. Jocob Falckenburgk, *Jacobi à Falckenburgk, Saxonis Brandenburgi: Britannia, siue de Apollonica humilitatis, virtutis, et honoris porta;* Londini. Typis Richardi Graphei. anno 1578 (STC 10674).

20. Ortelius 1606, 95.

21. Ibid., sig. xxxiij.

22. On the differences between the Greek and the barbarian in St. Paul's ethnopolitical theology see Julia Reinhard Lupton, "*Othello* Circumcised: Shakespeare and the Pauline Discourse of Nations," *Representations* 57 (Winter 1997): 73–89. In "Barbarian errors: Performing Race in Early Modern England," *Shakespeare Quarterly* 2 (1998): 168–86, Ian Smith makes an inquiry into the metalanguage of race and he points out that "barbarism . . . functions as a discursive site from which to examine racial formation in the period" (p. 170). This statement proves my point that geographic space in the romances functions as a discursive location questioning deep-seated orthodoxies.

23. Constance C. Relihan, "Liminal Geography: *Pericles* and the Politics of Place," 293.

24. The first performance of this production of *Pericles* was at the Roundhouse, London, June 28, 2002, and the first Stratford performance at the Royal Shakespeare Theatre was on August 12, 2002.

25. *The Geneva Bible. A Facsimile of the 1560 Edition* (Madison: University of Wisconsin Press, 1969): 450–74. *I and II Maccabees* mention Antiochus Epiphanes (p. 450); Apollonius, the governor of Coelesiria (p. 466); and Lysimachus, one in a series of corrupted governors and tyrants in a Seleucid-subjugated Jerusalem (p. 466). The biblical events unfold in a Mediterranean geography encompassing Tyrus, Tarsus, Ephesus, Egypt, the island of Lesbos (Mytilene).

26. Ortelius 1610, 2.

27. "The Trojan horse," (5.92); when Pericles enters Tarsus he compares his own ships with the Greeks' evil-bearing dissimulated gift to the Trojans.

28. The reference is to the "dove of Paphos" (15. Introd.32); Marina's exquisite skills and virtues make Philoten's pale by contrast. Paphos is a town sacred to Venus on the western side of Cyprus.

29. Linda McJannet, "Genre and Geography: The Eastern Mediterranean in *Pericles* and *The Comedy of Errors,*" in *Playing the Globe: Genre and Geography in English Renaissance Drama,* ed. John Gillies and Virginia Mason Vaughan (Madison, NJ: Farleigh Dickinson University Press, 1998), 91.

30. References to the play are keyed to *The Winter's Tale,* to *Arden* edition, ed. J. H. P. Pafford, 2nd edition (London: Routledge, 1991).

31. Ernest Schanzer, "The Structural Pattern of *The Winter's Tale,*" *Review of English Literature,* 52 (1964): 75; J.H.P. Pafford, Introduction to *Arden Shakespeare:* xxix–xxx; Michele Marrapodi, "'Of That Fatal country': Sicily and the Rhetoric of Topography in *The Winter's Tale,* in *Shakespeare's Italy: Functions of Italian Locations in Renaissance Drama,* ed. Michele Marrapodi et al., 213–28 (Manchester: Manchester University Press, 1997); Jean E. Howard, introduction to *The Winter's Tale, "The Norton Shakespeare:* 2875–76.

32. See, for example, Rosalie L. Colie, *Shakespeare's Living Art* (Princeton, NJ: Princeton University Press, 1974); Robert W. Uphaus, *Beyond Tragedy: Structure and Experience in Shakespeare's Romances* (Lexington: University Press of Kentucky, 1981); Joseph H. Summers, *Dreams of Love and Power: On Shakespeare's Plays* (Oxford: Clarendon Press, 1984); Robert Ornstein, *Shakespeare's Comedies: From Roman Farce to Romantic Majesty* (Newark: University of Delaware Press, 1986).

33. Northrop Frye, *A Natural Perspective: The Development of Shakespearean Comedy and Romance* (New York: Columbia University Press, 1965); Charles Frey, *Shakespeare's Vast Romance: A Study of* the Winter's Tale (Columbia: University of Missouri Press, 1980), 114ff; Howard Felperin, *Shakespearean Romance* (Princeton: Princeton University Press, 1972).

34. Leah S. Marcus, *Puzzling Shakespeare: Local Readings and Its Discontents* (Berkeley: University of California Press, 1988), 32–51.

35. Michael D. Bristol, "In Search of the Bear: Spatiotemporal Form and the Heterogeneity of Economies in *The Winter's Tale,*" *Shakespeare Quarterly* 42 1991): 156.

36. Richard L. Harp, in "*The Winter's Tale:* An 'Old Tale' Begetting Wonder," *Dalhousie Review* 58, no. 2 (Summer 1978): 295–308, links the Aristotelian notion of "wonder" as the incitement to philosophical inquiry with the way in which *The Winter's Tale* refers to the tradition of "old tales" as depicting improbable events.

37. Ortelius 1606, 1.

38. Mela, *Pomponius Mela's Description,* 3.2, 99.

39. Ibid., 3.32, 110.

40. Ibid., 2.49, 83.

41. Edward H. Sugden, *A Topographical Dictionary to the Works of Shakespeare and his Fellow Dramatists* (Manchester: Manchester University Press, 1925), 468.

42. Ibid.

43. Michele Marrapodi, "Sicily and the Rhetoric of Topography in *The Winter's Tale,* 214.

44. Ibid.

45. Ortelius 1610, 81.

46. William Cuningham, *The Cosmographical Glasse, Conteyning the Pleasant Principles of Cosmographie, Geographie, Hydrographie, or Navigation* (London: John Day, 1559), sig. A1.

47. Ibid., 6–7.

48. Ibid.

49. Ibid., 113.

50. J. H. P. Pafford, ed., Arden edition, 2nd ed. (London: Routledge, 1991), appendix 4, 217.

51. Cuningham, *Cosmographical Glasse,* 134.

52. Sugden, *Topographical Dictionary,* 66.

53. Francis Griffin, Stokes, *Who's Who in Shakespeare* (London: Studio Editions, 1993), 41.

54. Abbot, sig. Aiiij.

55. Ibid.

56. Ibid.

57. Ortelius 1603, 11.

58. Ortelius 1610, 53, sig. H5.

59. J. H. P. Pafford mentions that "a 'bear' episode was popular at this time" (*The Winter's Tale,* Arden edition, 69 n50). The problem of the bear has been addressed primarily as a question of theater history by Andrew Gurr, "The Bear, the Statue, and Hysteria in *The Winter's Tale,*" *Shakespeare Quarterly* 34 (1983): 420–25; Dale B. J. Randall, "'This Is the Chase': Or, the Further Pursuit of Shakespeare's Bear," *Shakespeare Jarbuch* 121 (1985): 89–95. François Laroque, in "Pagan Ritual, Christian Liturgy, and Folk Customs in *The Winter's Tale,*" *Cahiers Élisabéthains* 22 (1982): 25–33, identifies the symbol of the bear with the winter season, an image that seems to be pervasive throughout European folklore; Michael Bristol, in "In Search of the Bear," 161, connects the image of the bear with English Candlemas festivities.

60. Abbot, sig. D3.

61. Ibid.

62. Daryl W. Palmer, in "Jacobean Muscovites: Winter, Tyranny, and Knowledge in *The Winter's Tale,*" *Shakespeare Quarterly* 46 (Fall 1995): 323–39, documents the major points of contact between Shakespeare's *The Winter's Tale* and Jacobean wintry narratives of Muscovy.

63. Abbot, sig. Av.

64. Ortelius 1610, 98.

65. A. J. Hoenselaars, "Italy Staged in English Renaissance Drama," in *Shakespeare's Italy: Functions of Italian Locations in English Renaissance Drama,* ed. Michele Marrapodi, A. J. Hoenselaars, Marcello Capuzzo, and L. Falzon Santucci, 30–48 (Manchester: Manchester University Press, 1997), 31.

66. Further studies referring to Shakespeare's recreation of classical Rome include Paul A. Cantor, *Shakespeare's Rome: Republic and Empire* (Ithaca: Cornell University Press, 1976); Coppélia Kahn, *Roman Shakespeare. Warriors, Wounds and Women* (London: Routledge, 1997), who argues that, as is Romanness, the national identity is gendered masculine (pp. 160–70) and notices "the ambivalence inherent in Britain's emulation of Rome"(p. 164); Agostino Lombardo, "La Roma di Shakespeare," in *Studi romani* 42 (1994): 5–15; Robert S. Miola, *Shakespeare's Rome* (Cambridge: Cambridge University Press, 1983), who notices that "the play acknowledges the grandeur that was Rome, but suggests that such grandeur is past, superseded by that of a young nation, awakening to its strength and potential" (p. 207); Robert S. Miola, "Shakespeare's Valediction of Rome," *Roman Images.* Selected Papers from the English Institute, ed. Annabel Patterson (Baltimore: Johns Hopkins University Press, 1984), 51–62. See also Robert S. Miola, "Shakespeare's Ancient Rome: Difference and Identity," in *Cambridge Companion to Shakespeare's History Plays,* ed. Michael Hattaway, Cambridge Companions to Literature (Cambridge and New York: Cambridge University Press, 2002), 193–213.

67. Robert Smallwood, "'We Will Nothing Pay for Wearing Our Own Noses': Cosmopolitanism and Insularity in *Cymbeline,*" in *Shakespeare. Cosmopolitisme et insularité.* Actes du Congrès 1993, Societé Française Shakespeare, ed. M. T. Jones-Davies (Paris: Belles Lettres, 1994), 103. Smallwood analyzes the play's internationalism versus British insularity and argues that, in *Cymbeline,* Britishness is included in the cosmopolitan manifestation of nationhood in Europe.

68. John Florio, *Florio's Second Fruites, To which is annexed his Gar-dine of Recreation* (London: Printed by Thomas Orwin for Thomas Woodcock, 1591), 23. I have used the copy in the Carl H. Pforzheimer Library, Austin, Texas.

69. For a study on the integration of classical elements, especially the Ovidian myth, in the dramatic structure of *Cymbeline* see Carmine Di Base, "Ovid, Pettie, and the Mythic Foundation of *Cymbeline,*" *Cahiers Elisabéthains* 46 (1994): 59–70. For a study on the use of Plutarch in *Cymbeline* see Danielle Clarke, "*Cymbeline* and Plutarch," *Notes and Queries* 42 (1995): 329–31; Clarke suggests that Shakespeare's use of Plutarch's "Life of Antonius" in *Antony and Cleopatra* influences aspects of *Cymbeline,* especially Iachimo's description of Imogen's bedchamber and characterization of the queen.

70. Jean E. Howard, Introduction to *Cymbeline, The Norton Shakespeare,* ed. Stephen Greenblatt, Walter Cohen, Jean E. Howard, Katharine Eisaman Maus (New York: Norton, 1997): 2961. For an analysis of interlacing spatial and temporal levels in *Cymbeline* see Peter Holland, "Staging Europe in Shakespeare," 33.

71. Arthur F. Kinney, "Imagining England," 197.

72. Marjorie Garber, *Shakespeare After All* (New York: Pantheon Books, 2004), 804.

73. Abbot, sig. A2.

74. Abbot, sig. Aiv.

75. Ortelius 1610, 65, sig. K.

76. Ortelius 1610, 79.

77. Ibid.

78. Ortelius 1610, 109.

79. Ian Smith, "Barbarian Errors: Performing Race in Early Modern England," *Shakespeare Quarterly* 49 (1998): 173.

80. See Jerry Brotton "'This Tunis, Sir, Was Carthage': Contesting Colonialism in *The Tempest,*" in Ania Loomba and Martin Orkin eds. *Post-Colonial Shakespeares* New Accents (London: Routledge, 1998), 23–42. Brotton challenges recent postcolonialist readings of *The Tempest* and argues that the presence of a more definable Mediterranean geography suggests that *The Tempest* is a politically and geographically bifurcated play in the negotiation between its Mediterranean and Atlantic contexts.

81. Abbot, sig. Dc.

82. Ibid.

83. Stephen Greenblatt, *Marvelous Possessions: The Wonder of the New World* (Chicago: University of Chicago Press, 1991), 24–25.

84. Jonathan Hart, *Columbus, Shakespeare, and the Interpretation of the New World* (New York: Palgrave Macmillan, 2003), 1.

Bibliography

Anonymous. *Hickscorner*. In *A Select Collection of Old English Plays: Originally Published by Robert Dodsley in 1744,* edited by W. Carew Hazlitt. Vol. 1. London: Reeves and Turner, 1874.

———. *The Merry Devil of Edmonton*. In *A Select Collection of Old English Plays: Originally Published by Robert Dodsley in 1744,* edited by W. Carew Hazlitt. Vol. 10. London: Reeves and Turner, 1874.

———. *Misogonus*. In *Six anonymous plays*. Early English Dramatists, second series, edited by John Stephen Farmer. London: Early English Drama Society, 1906.

———. *The Return from Parnassus*. In *A Select Collection of Old English Plays: Originally Published by Robert Dodsley in 1744,* edited by W. Carew Hazlitt. Vol. 9. London: Reeves and Turner, 1874.

———. *The Tragedy of Nero* (1623). In *The Tragedy of Nero and Other Plays,* edited by Herbert P. Horne, Havelock Ellis, Arthur Symons, and Wilson Verity. The Mermaid Series. London and New York: T. Fisher Unwin and Charles Scribner's Sons, 1904.

———. *Wily Beguiled*. In *A Select Collection of Old English Plays: Originally Published by Robert Dodsley in 1744,* edited by W. Carew Hazlitt. Vol. 9. London: Reeves and Turner, 1874.

Abbot, George. *A Briefe Description of the Whole Worlde*. London 1599. Amsterdam: Theatrum Orbis Terrarum, 1970.

Achmed I, Sultan. *Letters from the Great Turke*. London, 1606. Amsterdam: Theatrum Orbis Terrarum, 1971.

Addison Roberts, Jeanne. *The Shakespearean Wild: Geography, Genus, and Gender*. Lincoln and London: University of Nebraska Press, 1991.

Albano, Caterina. "Visible bodies: cartography and anatomy." In *Literature, Mapping, and the Politics of Space in Early Modern Britain,* edited by Andrew Gordon and Bernhard Klein, 89–106. Cambridge: Cambridge University Press, 2001.

Apollonius of Rhodes. *Apollonius Rhodius: Argonautica,* edited and translated by R. C. Seaton. Cambridge MA: Harvard University Press, 1912.

Archer, John Michael. *Old Worlds: Egypt, Southwest Asia, India, and Russia in Early Modern English Writing*. Stanford, CA: Stanford University Press, 2001.

Artos, John. "Shakespeare and the Ancient World." *Michigan Quarterly Review* 10 (1971): 149–63.

Bachelard, Gaston. *The Poetics of Space*. Translated by Maria Jolas. Boston: Beacon Press, 1969.

Baker, Christopher. "Ovid, Othello, and the Pontic Scythians." In *A Search for Mean-*

ing: Critical Essays on Early Modern Literature, edited by Paula Harms Payne, 61–80. New York: Lang, 2004.

Bartels, Emily C. *Spectacles of Strangeness: Imperialism, Alienation, and Marlowe.* Philadelphia: University of Pennsylvania Press, 1993.

Baumbach, Lydia. "Shakespeare and the Classics." *Acta Classica* 28 (1985): 77–86.

Beaumont, Francis, and John Fletcher. *The Double Marriage.* In *The Dramatic Works of Ben Jonson, and Beaumont and Fletcher.* Edited by Peter Walley and George Collman. Vol. 3. London: John Stockdale, 1811.

———. *The Knight of the Burning Pestle.* In *Six Plays by Contemporaries of Shakespeare.* Edited by C. B. Wheeler. London: H. Milford, Oxford University Press, 1915.

———. *Philaster.* In *Elizabethan Drama.* Edited by W. Eliot. Vol. 2. New York: P.F. Collier & Son, 1910.

———. *The Prophetess.* In *The Dramatic Works of Ben Jonson and Beaumont and Fletcher.* Edited by George Colman. Vol. 3. London: John Stockdale, 1811.

———. *The Sea Voyage.* In *The Dramatic Works of Ben Jonson and Beaumont and Fletcher.* Edited by Peter Whalley. Vol. 4. London: John Stockdale, 1811.

———. *Wit without Money.* In *The Works of Beaumont and Fletcher,* Introduction by George Darley. Vol. 1. London: Edward Moxon, 1840.

———. *The Woman Hater.* In *The Dramatic Works of Ben Jonson and Beaumont and Fletcher.* Edited by Peter Whalley. Vol. 4. London: John Stockdale, 1811.

———. *The Woman's Prize; or the Tamer Tam'd.* In *The Dramatic Works of Ben Jonson and Beaumont and Fletcher.* Edited by Peter Whalley. Vol. 4. London: John Stockdale, 1811.

Berman, M. *"All That Is Solid Melts Into Air": The Experience of Modernity.* New York: Simon & Schuster, 1982.

Bergeron, David. *Shakespeare's Romances and the Royal Family.* Lawrence: University Press of Kansas, 1985.

Bevington, David, ed. *Antony and Cleopatra.* New Cambridge Shakespeare. Cambridge: Cambridge University Press, 1992.

Beza, Marcu. *Vechi legaturi cu Anglia.* Academia Romäna, Memoriile sectiunii literare. Series 3, Tome VIII. Bucharest: Monitorul Oficial si Imprimeriile Statului, 1938.

Biddulph, William. *Travels into Africa, Asia, and to the Black Sea.* London 1609. Amsterdam: Theatrum Orbis Terrarum, 1968.

Bishop, T. G. "*Pericles* or the Past as Fate and Miracle." In *Shakespeare and the Theatre of Wonder.* Cambridge Studies in Renaissance Literature and Culture 9. Cambridge: Cambridge University Press, 1996.

Blake, Ann. "Location, Imagination, and Heterotopia in *Twelfth Night.*" *Litteraria Pragensia* 12, no. 23 (2002): 66–79.

Blundeville, Thomas. *A Briefe Description of Universal Mappes and Cardes, and of Their Use.* Amsterdam: Theatrum Orbis Terrarum, 1972.

Boia, Lucian. *Romania: Borderland of Europe.* London: Reaktion Books, 2001.

Botero, Giovanni. *The Travelers Breviat.* Amsterdam: Theatrum Orbis Terrarum, 1969.

Braden, Gordon. *The Classics and English Renaissance Poetry: Three Case Studies.* Yale Studies in English 187. New Haven, CT: Yale University Press, 1978.

———."Plutarch, Shakespeare, and the Alpha Males." In *Shakespeare and the Classics,* edited by Charles Martindale and A. B. Taylor, 188–205. Cambridge and New York: Cambridge University Press, 2004.

Brewer. *Lingua.* In *A Select Collection of Old English Plays: Originally Published by Robert Dodsley in 1744,* edited by W. Carew Hazlitt. Vol. 9. London: Reeves and Turner, 1874.

Briggs, Julia. *This Stage-Play World. Texts and Contexts, 1580–1625.* Oxford: Oxford University Press, 1997.

Bristol, Michael D. "In Search of the Bear: Spatiotemporal Form and the Heterogeneity of Economies in *The Winter's Tale.*" *Shakespeare Quarterly* 42 (1991): 145–67.

Brooks, Harold F, ed. *A Midsummer Night's Dream.* Arden edition. London: Routledge, 1993.

Brotton, Jerry. "'This Tunis, Sir, Was Carthage': Contesting Colonialism in *The Tempest.*" In *Post-Colonial Shakespeare,* edited by Ania Loomba and Martin Orkin, 23–42. London and New York: Routledge, 1998.

———. "Tragedy and Geography." *A Companion to Shakespeare's Works,* edited by Richard Dutton and Jean E. Howard. Blackwell Companions to Literature and Culture, 1: 219–40. Malden, MA, and Oxford: Blackwell, 2003.

Brown, Sarah Annes. "'There Is No End but Addition': The Later Reception of Shakespeare's Classicism." In *Shakespeare and the Classics,* edited by Charles Martindale and A. B. Taylor, 277–93. Cambridge and New York: Cambridge University Press, 2004.

Bruster, Douglas. *Quoting Shakespeare: Form and Culture in Early Modern Drama.* Lincoln and London: University of Nebraska Press, 2000.

Bushnell, Rebecca W. *Tragedies and Tyrants: Political Thought and Theater in the English Renaissance.* Ithaca, NY: Cornell University Press, 1990.

Cambino, Andrewe. *Two Very Notable Commentaries . . . of the Turcks and Empire of the House of Ottomano.* Translated by John Shute. London 1562. Amsterdam: Theatrum Orbis Terrarum, 1970.

Campbell, Mary B. *The Witnesses and the Other World: Exotic European Travel Writing, 400–1600.* Ithaca, NY: Cornell University Press, 1988.

Cantor, Paul A. *Shakespeare's Rome: Republic and Empire.* Ithaca, NY: Cornell University Press, 1976.

Chapman, George. *The Tragedy of Bussy D'Ambois.* In *Old plays; Being a Continuation of Dodsley's Collection.* Edited by Charles Wentworth Dilke. Vol. 3. London: Rodwell and Martin, 1816.

Cicero. *Marcus Tullius Ciceroes three books of duties to Marcus his sonne.* Translated by Nicholas Grimalde. London: Richard Tottell, 1556. STC 5281.

Clarke, Danielle. "*Cymbeline* and Plutarch." *Notes and Queries* 42 (1995): 329–31.

Clubb, Louise George. "Intertextualities: Some Questions." In *The Italian World of English Renaissance Drama: Cultural Exchanges and Intertextuality,* edited by Michele Marrapodi and A. J. Hoenselaars, 179–89. Newark: University of Delaware Press and London: Associated University Presses, 1998.

Cohen, Walter. "The Undiscovered Country: Shakespeare and Mercantile Geography." In *Marxist Shakespeare,* edited by Jean E. Howard and Scott Cutler Shershow, 128–58. London: Routledge, 2001.

Colie, Rosalie L. *Shakespeare's Living Art.* Princeton, NJ: Princeton University Press, 1974.

Cormack, Bradin. "Marginal Waters: *Pericles* and the Idea of Jurisdiction." In *Literature, Mapping and the Politics of Space in Early Modern Britain,* edited by Andrew Gordon and Bernhard Klein, 155–80. Cambridge: Cambridge University Press, 2001.

Cormack, Lesley B. "Britannia Rules the Waves? Images of Empire in Elizabethan England." In *Literature, Mapping and the Politics of Space in Early Modern Britain,* edited by Andrew Gordon and Bernhard Klein, 45–68. Cambridge: Cambridge University Press, 2001.

Crişan, Ion Horaţiu. *Burebista and His Time.* Translated by Sanda Mihailescu. Bucharest: Bibliotheca Historica Romaniae, 1978.

Cuningham, William. *The Cosmographical Glasse, conteyning the Pleasant principles of Cosmographie, Geographie, Hydrographie, or Navigation.* London: John Day, 1559.

Dailey, Jeff. "Christian Underscoring in *Tamburlaine the Great, Part II.*" *Journal of Religion and Theatre* 4, no. 2 (2005): 146–59.

Daniell, David, ed. *Julius Caesar.* Arden edition. Walton-on-Thames, Surrey: Thomas Nelson, International Thomson Publishing, 1998.

Dávidházi, Péter. "Camel, Weasel, Whale: The Cloud-Scene in *Hamlet* as a Hungarian Parable." In *Shifting the Scene: Shakespeare in European* Culture, edited by Ladina Bezzola Lambert and Balz Engler, 95–110. Newark: University of Delaware Press, 2004.

Davis, Madison J., and Daniel Frankforter. *The Shakespeare Name Dictionary.* New York: Garland, 1995.

Dawson, Christopher. *The Making of Europe: An Introduction to the History of European Unity.* Washington, DC: The Catholic University of America Press, 2002.

Dekker, Thomas. *The Honest Whore.* In *The Chief Elizabethan Dramatists Excluding Shakespeare,* edited by William Allan Neilson. Boston and New York: Houghton Mifflin Company, 1911.

Delaney, Bill. "Shakespeare's *Julius Caesar.*" *Explicator* 60 (2001–2): 122–24.

Di Base, Carmine. "Ovid, Pettie, and the Mythic Foundation of *Cymbeline.*" *Cahiers Elisabéthains* 46 (1994): 59–70.

Dimmock, Matthew. *New Turkes: Dramatizing Islam and the Ottomans in Early Modern England.* Aldershot, England, and Burlington, VT: Ashgate, 2005.

Docherty, Thomas. *After Theory: Postmodern Theory.* Edinburgh: Edinburgh University Press, 1996.

Dorval, Patricia, ed. *Shakespeare et la France,* Société Française Shakespeare, Actes du Congrès de 2000. Paris: Société Française Shakespeare, 2001.

Eisaman Maus, Katharine. Introduction to *Titus Andronicus.* In *The Norton Shakespeare,* edited by Stephen Greenblatt, Walter Cohen, Jean E. Howard, and Katharine Eisaman Maus, 371–77. New York: Norton, 1997.

Evans, R. J. W. Review of "*Relaţiile politice ale Angliei cu Moldova, Ţara Românească şi*

Transilvania în secolele XVI–XVIII by L. Demeny and P. Cernovodeanu." *The English Historical Review* 91, no. 360 (July 1976): 640–41.

Falckenburgk, Jocob. *Britannia, siue de Apollonica humilitatis.* Londini: Richardi Graphei, 1578. Microfilm copy. STC 10674.

Farley-Hills, David. "Jonson, Shakespeare, and the Italian Theorists." *Journal of Anglo-Italian Studies* 6 (2001): 35–42.

Felperin, Howard. *Shakespearean Romance.* Princeton, NJ: Princeton University Press, 1972.

Field, Nathaniel. *A Woman Is a Weathercock.* In *The Tragedy of Nero and Other Plays,* edited by Herbert P. Horne, Havelock Ellis, Arthur Symons, and Wilson Verity. The Mermaid Series. London and New York: T. Fisher Unwin and Charles Scribner's Sons, 1904.

Fincham, Kenneth. "Abbot, George (1562–1633)." *Oxford Dictionary of National Biography,* edited by H. C. G. Matthew and Brian Harrison. Oxford: Oxford University Press, 2004. http://www.oxforddnb.com/view/article/4 (accessed September 20, 2008).

Fisher, Jasper. *Fuimus Troes, the True Trojans.* In *A Select Collection of Old Plays,* edited by Isaac Reed and Octavius Gilchrist. Vol. 7. London: Septimus Prowett, 1825.

Fletcher, John, and Philip Massinger. *The Knight of Malta.* In *The Dramatic Works of Ben Jonson, and Beaumont and Fletcher.* Edited by Peter Walley and George Collman. Vol. 3. London: John Stockdale, 1811.

Florio, John. *Florio's Second Fruites.* London: Thomas Orwin for Thomas Woodcock, 1591.

Foucault, Michel. "Of Other Spaces." *Diacritics* 16 (1986): 22–27.

———. "Space, Power, Knowledge." In *The Cultural Studies Reader,* edited by Simon During, 161–69. London: Routledge, 1993.

Frey, Charles. *Shakespeare's Vast Romance: A Study of* The Winter's Tale. Columbia: University of Missouri Press, 1980.

Frye, Northrop. *A Natural Perspective: The Development of Shakespearean Comedy and Romance.* New York: Columbia University Press, 1965.

Garber, Marjorie. *Shakespeare After All.* New York: Pantheon Books, 2004.

Geertz, Clifford. *Local Knowledge: Further Essays in Interpretive Anthropology.* New York: Basic Books, 1983.

The Geneva Bible. A facsimile of the 1560 edition. Madison: The University of Wisconsin Press, 1969.

Gilbert, Allan H. "Chapman's Fortune with Winged Hands." *Modern Language Notes* 52, no. 3 (March 1937): 190–92.

Gillies, John. "Introduction: Elizabethan Drama and the Cartographizations of Space." In *Playing the Globe: Genre and Geography in English Renaissance Drama,* edited by John Gillies and Virginia Mason Vaughan. Madison, NJ: Fairleigh Dickinson University Press and London: Associated University Presses, 1998.

———. *Shakespeare and the Geography of Difference.* Cambridge: Cambridge University Press, 1994.

Glapthorne, *Albertus Wallenstein.* In *The Old English Drama: A Selection of Plays from the Old English Dramatists.* Vol. 2. London: Hurst, Robinson & Co., 1825.

Goffman, Daniel. *The Ottoman Empire and Early Modern Europe.* Cambridge: Cambridge University Press, 2002.

Gordon, Andrew, and Bernhard Klein, eds. *Literature, Mapping, and the Politics of Space in Early Modern Britain.* Cambridge: Cambridge University Press, 2001.

Greenblatt, Stephen. *Marvelous Possessions: The Wonder of The New World.* Chicago: University of Chicago Press, 1991.

———. *Shakespearean Negotiations: The Circulation of Social Energy in Renaissance England.* Berkeley: University of California Press, 1988.

Greene, Robert. *The Comicall Historie of Alphonsus King of Aragon.* In *The Plays and Poems of Robert Greene.* Edited by J. Churton Collins. Vol. 1. Oxford: Clarendon Press, 1905.

———. *The Tragical Reign of Selimus* (1594). Gen. ed. W. W. Greg, ed. W. Bang. Malone Society Reprints. London: Charles Wittingham & Co, Chiswick Press, 1908.

Gurr, Andrew. "The Bear, the Statue, and Hysteria in *The Winter's Tale.*" *Shakespeare Quarterly* 34 (1983): 420–25.

Hagthorpe, John. *Englands Exchequer or a Discourse of the Sea and Navigation.* London, 1625. Amsterdam: Theatrum Orbis Terrarum, 1974.

Hakluyt, Richard. *The Second Volume of the Principal Navigations, Voyages, Traffiques, and Discoveries of the English Nation.* London: George Bishop, Ralph Newberie, and Robert Barker, 1599. STC 1262a.

———. *The Principal Navigations, Voyages, Trafiques and Discoveries of the English Nation.* London: Everyman, 1907.

Hall, Joseph. *Quo Vadis? A Just Censure of Travell.* Amsterdam: Theatrum Orbis Terrarum, 1975.

Halsall, Guy, ed. *Humour, History and Politics in Late Antiquity and the Early Middle Ages.* Cambridge: Cambridge University Press, 2002.

Hanna, Sara. "From Illyria to Elysium: Geographical Fantasy in *Twelfth Night.*" *Litteraria Pragensia* 12, no. 23 (2002): 21–45.

Hardison Londré, Felicia. "Elizabethan Views of the 'Other:' French, Spanish, and Russians in *Love's Labour's Lost.*" *Elizabethan Review* 3, no. 1 (1995): 3–20.

Harp, Richard L. "*The Winter's Tale:* An "Old Tale" Begetting Wonder." *Dalhousie Review* 58, no. 2 (1978): 295–308.

Hart, Jonathan. *Columbus, Shakespeare, and the Interpretation of the New World.* New York: Palgrave Macmillan, 2003.

Headlam Wells, Robin. *Shakespeare: Politics and the State.* London: Macmillan, 1986.

Helgerson, Richard. "The Folly of Maps and Modernity." In *Literature, Mapping, and the Politics of Space in Early Modern Britain,* edited by Andrew Gordon and Bernhard Klein, 241–62. Cambridge: Cambridge University Press, 2001.

Herodotus. *The Famous Hystory of Herodotus.* London: T. Marshe, 1584. STC 13224.

———. *The Histories.* Translated by Robin Waterfield. Introduction and Notes by Carolyn Dewald. Oxford's World Classics. Oxford: Oxford University Press, 1998.

Heylyn, Peter. *A Little Description of the Great World.* Oxford: Will. Turner, 1631. Microfilm copy. STC 13279.5.

Heywood, Thomas. *The Fair Maid of the West.* Part 1. In *The Dramatic Works of Thomas*

Heywood: With a Life of the Poet and Remarks on His Writings. Edited by J. Payne Collier, esq. Vol. 1. London: The Shakespeare Society, 1850.

———. *If You Know Not Me You Know Nobody. Part* 2. In Two *Historical Plays on the Life and Reign of Queen Elizabeth by Thomas Heywood.* Introduction and Notes by J. Payne Collier, esq. London: The Shakespeare Society, 1851.

Hoenselaars, A. J. "Italy Staged in English Renaissance Drama." In *Shakespeare's Italy: Functions of Italian Locations in English Renaissance Drama,* edited by Michele Marrapodi, A. J. Hoenselaars, Marcello Capuzzo, and L. Falzon Santucci, 30–48. Manchester: Manchester University Press, 1997.

———. "Mapping Shakespeare's Europe." In *Reclamations of Shakespeare,* edited by A. J. Hoenselaars. DQR Studies in Literature 15, 223–48. Amsterdam and Atlanta: Rodopi, 1994.

———. "Shakespeare, Foreigners, and National Ideologies." In *Shakespeare: Varied Perspectives,* edited by Vikram Chopra. New World Literature Series 90, 11–33. Delhi: B. R., 1996.

Holland, Peter. "Staging Europe in Shakespeare." In *Shifting the Scene: Shakespeare in European Culture,* edited by Ladina Bezzola Lambert and Balz Engler, 21–40. Newark: University of Delaware Press and London: Associated University Presses 2004.

Homer. *The Odyssey.* Translated by George Chapman. London: R. Field for Nathaniel Butler, 1615, STC 13637.

Hopton, Arthur. *Speculum Topographicum: or The Topographical Glasse.* Amsterdam: Theatrum Orbis Terrarum, 1974.

Howard, Claire. *English Travellers of the Renaissance.* New York: John Lane, 1914.

Howard, Jean E. "Introduction to *Cymbeline.*" In *The Norton Shakespeare,* edited by Stephen Greenblatt, Walter Cohen, Jean E. Howard, and Katharine Eisaman Maus, 2955–63. New York: Norton, 1997.

Hughes et al. *The Misfortunes of Arthur.* In *A Select Collection of Old English Plays: Originally Published by Robert Dodsley in 1744.* Edited by W. Carew Hazlitt. Vol. 4. London: Reeves and Turner, 1874.

Ide, Richard S. "Shakespeare and the Pirates." *Iowa State Journal of Research* 58 (1984): 311–18.

Iorga, Nicolae. *A History of Anglo-Romanian Relations.* Bucharest: Societatea anglo-română, 1931.

James, Heather. "Shakespeare's Learned Heroines in Ovid's Schoolroom." In *Shakespeare and the Classics,* edited by Charles Martindale and A. B. Taylor, 66–85. Cambridge and New York: Cambridge University Press, 2004.

Jonson, Ben. *Epicoene, or The Silent Woman.* Edited by Aurelia Henry. *Yale Studies in English* 31. Gen. ed. Albert S. Cook. New York: Henry Holt, 1906.

———. *Every Man in His Humour.* In *The Works of Ben Jonson.* Edited by W. Gifford, Introduction by Octavius Gilchrist. Vol. 1. London: W Bulmer & Co, 1816.

———. *Every Man Out of His Humour.* In *The Works of Ben Jonson.* Edited by W. Gifford. Vol. 2. London: W Bulmer & Co, 1816.

———. *The Masque of Queens Celebrated in the House of Fame.* London: N. Okes for R. Bonian and H. Wally, 1609. STC 14788.

———. *The Speeches at Prince Henry's Barriers.* In *The Works of Ben Jonson,* edited by Francis Cunningham and William Gifford. London. Bickers and Son, 1875.

———. *Volpone, or The Fox.* In *The Chief Elizabethan Dramatists Excluding Shakespeare.* Edited by William Allan Neilson. Boston and New York: Houghton Mifflin, 1911.

Jordan, Constance. *Shakespeare's Monarchies: Ruler and Subject in the Romances.* Ithaca, NY: Cornell University Press, 1997.

Kahn, Coppélia. *Roman Shakespeare: Warriors, Wounds and Women.* London: Routledge, 1997.

Kiefer, Frederick. *Writing on the Renaissance Stage: Written Words, Printed Pages, Metaphoric Books.* Newark: University of Delaware Press and London: Associated University Presses, 1996.

Kinney, Arthur F. "Imagining England: The Chorographical Glass." In *Soundings of Things Done: Essays in Early Modern Literature in Honor of S. K. Heiniger Jr.*, edited by Peter E. Medine and Joseph Wittreich, 181–214. Newark: University of Delaware Press and London: Associated University Presses, 1997.

Kujawinska-Courtney, Krystyna. "Shakespeare's Geography of the World." *Acta Universitatis Lodziensis* 66 (1980): 43–62.

Kyd, Thomas. *Cornelia.* In *A Select Collection of Old English Plays. Originally Published by Robert Dodsley in 1744.* Edited by W. Carew Hazlitt. Vol. 4. London: Reeves and Turner, 1874.

———. *Soliman and Perseda.* In *A Select Collection of Old English Plays: Originally Published by Robert Dodsley in 1744.* Edited by W. Carew Hazlitt. Vol. 5 London: Reeves and Turner, 1874.

Laroque, François. "Pagan Ritual, Christian Liturgy, and Folk Customs in *The Winter's Tale.*" *Cahiers Élisabéthains* 22 (1982): 25–33.

Leggatt, Alexander. *Shakespeare's Political Drama: The History Plays and the Roman Plays.* New York: Routledge, 1988.

Lithgow, William. *A Discourse of a Peregrination in Europe, Asia, and Africke.* London 1614. Amsterdam: Theatrum Orbis Terrarum, 1971.

Logan, Terence P., and Denzell S. Smith, eds. *The Predecessors of Shakespeare: A Survey and Bibliography of Recent Studies in English Renaissance Drama.* Lincoln: University of Nebraska Press, 1973.

Lowenstein, David, and Janel Mueller, eds. *The Cambridge History of Early Modern English Literature.* Cambridge: Cambridge University Press, 2002.

Lombardo, Agostino. "La Roma di Shakespeare," *Studi romani* 42 (1994): 5–15.

Maguin, Jean-Marie. "A Note on Shakespeare's Handling of Time and Space Data in *Antony and Cleopatra.*" *Cahiers Élisabéthains* 13 (1978): 61–67.

Malieckal, Bindu. "'Bondslaves and Pagans Shall Our Statesmen Be:' Moors, Turks, and Venetians in *Othello.*" *Shakespeare Yearbook* 10 (1999): 162–89.

Marcus, Leah S. *Puzzling Shakespeare: Local Readings and Its Discontents.* Berkeley: University of California Press, 1988.

Markley, Robert. "Riches, Power, Trade and Religion: The Far East and the English Imagination, 1600–1720." *Renaissance Studies* 17 (2003): 433–55.

Marlowe, Christopher. *The Jew of Malta.* In *A Select Collection of Old Plays.* Edited by Isaac Reed and Octavius Gilchrist. Vol. 8. London: Septimus Prowett, 1825.

———. *The Second Part of the Bloody Conquests of the Mighty Tamburlaine.* In *The Works of Christopher Marlowe,* edited by C. F. Tucker Brooke. Oxford: Clarendon Press, 1910.

———. *Tamburlaine, Part 1.* In *The Chief Elizabethan Dramatists Excluding Shakespeare.* Edited by William Allan Neilson. Boston and New York: Houghton Mifflin, 1911.

———. *The Two Tragicall Discourses of Mighty Tamburlaine, the Scythian Shepherd.* In *The Works of Christopher Marlowe.* Edited by C. F. Tucker Brooke. Oxford: Clarendon Press, 1910.

Marrapodi, Michele. " 'Of That Fatal Country': Sicily and the Rhetoric of Topography in *The Winter's Tale.*" In *Functions of Italian Locations in Renaissance Drama,* edited by Michele Marrapodi, A. J. Hoenselaars, Marcello Capuzzo, and L. Falzon Santucci, 213–28. Manchester: Manchester University Press, 1997.

Martindale, Charles, and Michelle Martindale. *Shakespeare and the Uses of Antiquity: An Introductory Essay.* London and New York: Routledge, 1990.

Massinger, Philip. *The City Madam.* In *Specimens of English Dramatic Poets who Lived about the Time of Shakespeare.* Edited by Charles Lamb. London: Taylor and Francis, 1854.

———. *The Picture.* In *A Select Collection of Old Plays.* Edited by R. Dodsley. Vol. 8. London: Pal Mall, 1744.

———. *The Renegado.* In *The Dramatic works of Massinger and Ford.* Introduction by Heartly Coleridge. London: Edward Moxon, 1840.

———. *The Roman Actor.* In *The Dramatic Works of Massinger and Ford.* Introduction by Heartly Coleridge. London: Edward Moxon, 1840.

Matar, Nabil. *Islam in Britain, 1558–1685.* Cambridge: Cambridge University Press, 1998.

———. *Turks, Moors, and Englishmen in the Age of Discovery.* New York: Columbia University Press, 1999.

Middleton, Thomas, and T. Dekkar. *The Roaring Girl or Moll Cutpurse.* In *A Select Collection of Old Plays.* Edited by Isaac Reed and Octavius Gilchrist. Vol. 6. London: Septimus Prowett, 1825.

McDonald, Russ. *The Bedford Companion to Shakespeare.* 2nd ed. Boston: Bedford/St. Martin's, 2001.

McEachern, Claire. "Literature and National Identity." In *The Cambridge History of Early Modern English Literature,* edited by David Loewenstein and Janel Mueller. Cambridge: Cambridge University Press, 2002.

McJannet, Linda. "Genre and Geography: The Eastern Mediterranean in *Pericles* and *The Comedy of Errors.*" In *Playing the Globe: Genre and Geography in English Renaissance Drama,* edited by John Gillies and Virginia Mason Vaughan, 86–106. Madison, NJ: Fairleigh Dickinson University Press and London: Associated University Presses, 1998.

Mela, Pomponius. *Pomponius Mela's Description of the World.* Ann Arbor: University of Michigan Press, 1998.

Milward, Peter. "The Religious Dimension of Shakespeare's Illyria." *Litteraria Pragensia* 12, no. 23 (2002): 59–65.

Miola, Robert S. "*Cymbeline:* Shakespeare's Valediction of Rome." In *Roman Images.* Selected Papers from the English Institute, edited by Annabel Patterson, 51–62. Baltimore and London: Johns Hopkins University Press, 1984.

———. "Reading the Classics." In *A Companion to Shakespeare,* edited by David Scott Kastan, 72–85. Blackwell Companions to Literature and Culture 3. Oxford: Blackwell, 1999.

———. "Shakespeare's Ancient Rome: Difference and Identity." In *Cambridge Companion to Shakespeare's History Plays,* edited by Michael Hattaway, 193–213. Cambridge Companions to Literature. Cambridge and New York: Cambridge University Press, 2002.

———. *Shakespeare's Reading.* Oxford: Oxford University Press, 2000.

———. *Shakespeare's Rome.* Cambridge: Cambridge University Press, 1983.

Mociornița, Maria. "Romanian-English Cultural Relations in the 16th and 17th Centuries." In *English Literature and Civilization: The Renaissance and the Restoration Period,* edited by Ioan Aurel Preda. Bucharest: Editura Didactica și Pedagogică, 1983.

Moryson, Fynes. *An Itinerary Containing His Ten Yeeres Travell through the Twelve Dominions of Germany, Bohmerland, Sweitzerland, Netherland, Denmarke, Poland, Italy, Turky, France, England, Scotland and Ireland.* Vol. 2. Glasgow: James MacLehose and Sons, 1907.

———. *An Itinerary written by F. Moryson.* Amsterdam: Theatrum Orbis Terrarum, 1973.

Mulryan, John. "Tradition and the Individual Talent: Shakespeare's and Jonson's Appropriation of the Classics." *Ben Jonson Journal* 10 (2003): 117–37.

Newes from diuers countries. London: Valentine Sims, 1597.

Nicolay, Nicholas. *The Navigations into Turkie.* London 1585. Amsterdam: Theatrum Orbis Terrarum, 1968.

Nicolet, Claude. *Space, Geography, and Politics in the Early Roman Empire.* Ann Arbor: The University of Michigan Press, 1991.

Nixon, Anthony. *The Three English Brothers.* London 1607. Amsterdam: Theatrum Orbis Terrarum, 1970.

Ornstein, Robert *Shakespeare's Comedies: From Roman Farce to Romantic Majesty.* Newark: University of Delaware Press, 1986.

Ortelius, Abraham. *His Epitome of the Theatre of the Worlde.* London: James Shawe, 1603. Microfilm copy, STC 18856.

———. *Ortelius his Epitome of the Theater of the Worlde: Now lately renewed and augmented by M. Coignet.* London: J. Norton, 1610. Microfilm copy, STC 18857.

———. *Theatrum Orbis Terrarum. The theatre of the whole world.* London: J. Norton, 1606. Microfilm copy, STC 18855.

Ovid, *The Fifteen Books of Ovid's Metamorphoses.* Translated by Arthur Golding. London: William Seres, 1567. STC 18956.

Pafford, J. H. P., ed. *The Winter's Tale.* Arden edition. 2nd ed. London: Routledge, 1991.

Palfrey, Simon. *Late Shakespeare: A New World of Words.* Oxford: Clarendon Press, 1997.

Palmer, Daryl W. "Jacobean Muscovites: Winter, Tyranny, and Knowledge in *The Winter's Tale.*" *Shakespeare Quarterly* 46 (Fall 1995): 323–39.

Palmer, Sir Thomas. *An Essay of the means how to make our travailles more profitable.* London 1606. Amsterdam: Theatrum Orbis Terrarum, 1972.

Parker, Patricia. "Barbers and Barbary: Early Modern Cultural Semantics." *Renaissance Drama* 33 (2004): 201–44.

Pearcy, Lee T. *The Mediated Muse: English Translations of Ovid 1560–1700.* Hamden, CT: Archon Books, 1984.

Peele, George or Robert Greene. *The Tragedy of Locrine.* Edited by Ronald B. McKerrow. London: The Malone Society Reprints, 1908.

Pliny. *The Historie of the World: Commonly Called, The Naturall Historie of C. Plinius Secundus.* Translated into English by Philemon Holland, Doctor in Physic. London: Adam Islip, 1601. STC 20029.

———. *Pliny's Natural History: A Selection from Philemon Holland's Translation.* Edited by J. Newsome. Oxford: Clarendon Press, 1964.

Plutarch. *The Lives of the Noble Grecians and Romanes, Compared together by that Grave Learned Philosopher and Historiographer Plutarke of Chaeronea.* Translated out of Greeke into French by JAMES AMIOT . . . and out of French into English, by Thomas North. London: Richard Field for Thomas Wight, 1595. STC 20067.5.

Poe, Marshall. *People Born to Slavery: Russia in Early Modern European Ethnography, 1476–1748.* Ithaca, NY: Cornell University Press, 2001.

Procházka, Martin. "Shakespeare's Illyria, Sicily, and Bohemia: Other Spaces, Other Times, or Other Economies?" *Litteraria Pragensia* 12, no. 23 (2002): 130–49.

Randall, Dale B. J. "'This Is the Chase': Or, the Further Pursuit of Shakespeare's Bear." *Shakespeare Jarbuch* 121 (1985): 89–95.

Reinhard Lupton, Julia. "*Othello* Circumcised: Shakespeare and the Pauline Discourse of Nations." *Representations* 57 (1997): 73–89.

Relihan, Constance C. "Liminal Geography: *Pericles* and the Politics of Place." *Philological Quarterly* 3 (1992): 281–99.

Rivers, Isabel. *Classical and Christian Ideas in English Renaissance Poetry.* A Students' Guide. 2nd ed. London: Routledge, 1994.

Roberts, Lewes. *The Marchants Mapp of Commerce.* London 1638. Amsterdam: Theatrum Orbis Terrarum, 1974.

Romer, F. E. Introduction to *Pomponius Mela's Description of the World.* Ann Arbor: University of Michigan Press, 1998.

Ronan, Clifford J. "An Ovidian 'Farthest Greece' in *Errors, Titus,* and *Pericles.*" *Discoveries: South-Central Renaissance Conference News and Notes* 19, no. 1 (2002): 3–4.

Rowley, William. *A Match at Midnight, a Pleasant Comedie.* In *A Select Collection of Old Plays.* Edited by Isaac Reed and Octavius Gilchrist. Vol. 7. London: Septimus Prowett, 1825.

Salustius, C. C. *The Conspiracie of Cateline.* London: Iaggard, 1608. STC 21625.

Sandys, George. *A Relation of the Journey begun An: Dom: 1610: Containing a description of the Turkish Empire.* Amsterdam: Theatrum Orbis Terrarum, 1973.

Schanzer, Ernest. "The Structural Pattern of *The Winter's Tale.*" *Review of English Literature* 52 (1964): 75.

Schoenbaum, S. *Shakespeare's Lives.* Oxford and New York: Oxford University Press, 1993.

Serpieri, Alessandro. "Contratti d'amore e di morte in *The Merchant of Venice.*" In The Merchant of Venice *dal testo alla scena.* Edited by Mariangela Tempera, 9–21. Bologna: Editrice CLUEB, 1994.

Serpieri, Alessandro, Ana Bernini, Aldo Celli, Serena Cenni, Claudia Corti, Keir Elam, Giovanna Mochi, Susan Payne, and Marcella Quadri. *Nel laboratorio di Shakespeare: Dalle fonti ai drammi.* Parma: Pratiche Editrice, 1988.

Shakespeare, William. *The Norton Shakespeare.* Edited by Stephen Greenblatt, Walter Cohen, Jean E. Howard, and Katharine Eisaman Maus. New York: Norton, 1997.

Sheen, Erica. "The Pannonians and the Dalmatians: Reading for a European History in *Cymbeline.*" In *Shakespeare in the New Europe,* edited by Michael Hattaway, Boika Sokolova, and Derek Roper, 310–20. Sheffield: Sheffield Academic Press, 1994.

Sherman, William H. "Stirrings and Searchings (1500–1720)." In *The Cambridge Companion to Travel Writing,* edited by Peter Hulme and Tim Youngs, 17–36. Cambridge: Cambridge University Press, 2002.

Shirley, James. *Honoria and Mammon.* In *The Dramatic Works and Poems of James Shirley.* Edited by William Gifford and Alexander Dyce. Vol. 6. London: John Murray, 1833.

———. *The Humorous Courtier.* In *The Dramatic Works and Poems of James Shirley.* Edited by William Gifford and Alexander Dyce. Vol. 4. London: John Murray, 1833.

———. *The Lady of Pleasure.* In *The Dramatic Works and Poems of James Shirley.* Edited by William Gifford and Alexander Dyce. Vol. 4. London: John Murray, 1833.

Simon, James R. "'Perplex'd Beyond Self-Explication': *Cymbeline* and Early Modern/Postmodern Europe." In *Shakespeare in the New Europe,* edited by Michael Hattaway, Boika Sokolova, and Derek Roper, 294–309. Sheffield: Sheffield Academic Press, 1994.

Slack, Paul. "Measuring the National Wealth in Seventeenth-Century England." *The Economic History Review* 57, no. 4 (2005): 607–35.

Smallwood, Robert. "'We Will Nothing Pay for Wearing Our Own Noses': Cosmopolitanism and Insularity in *Cymbeline.*" In *Shakespeare. Cosmopolitisme et insularité.* Actes du Congrès 1993, Societé Française Shakespeare, edited by M.T. Jones-Davies, 97–113. Paris: Belles Lettres, 1994.

Smith, Ian. "Barbarian Errors: Performing Race in Early Modern England," *Shakespeare Quarterly* 49 (1998): 168–86.

Soja, Edward. "History: Geography: Modernity." In *The Cultural Studies Reader,* edited by Simon During, 135–50. London: Routlege, 1993.

Sokolova, Boika. *Shakespeare's Romances as Interrogative Text: Their Alienation Strategies and Ideology.* Lewiston, NY: The Edwin Mellen Press, 1992.

Solinus, Caius Iulius. *The Excellent & Pleasante Worke Collectanea Rerum Memorabilium of Caius Julius Solinus. Translated from Latin (1587) by Arthur Golding.* Edited by Harry R. Warfel: Gainesville, FL: Scholars' Facsimiles Reprints, 1955.

de Sousa, Geraldo U. *Shakespeare's Cross-Cultural Encounters.* London: Macmillan, 1999.

Stephen, Henry. *A World of Wonders.* London, Imprinted for Iohn Norton, 1607.

Stokes, Francis Griffin. *Who's Who in Shakespeare.* London: Studio Editions, 1993.

Sugden, Edward H. *A Topographical Dictionary to the Works of Shakespeare and His Fellow Dramatists.* Manchester: Manchester University Press: 1925.

Summers, Joseph H. *Dreams of Love and Power: On Shakespeare's Plays.* Oxford: Clarendon Press, 1984.

Tannenhouse, Leonard. *Power on Display: The Politics of Shakespeare's Genres.* New York: Methuen, 1986.

Topsell, Edward. *The Historie of Serpents.* London 1608. Amsterdam: Theatrum Orbis Terrarum, 1973.

Tucker Brooke, C. F., ed. *The Shakespeare Apocrypha.* Oxford: Clarendon Press, 1908.

Turner, Henry S. *English Renaissance Stage: Geometry, Poetics, and the Practical Spatial Arts, 1580–1630.* Oxford and New York: Oxford University Press, 2006.

Uphaus, Robert W. *Beyond Tragedy: Structure and Experience in Shakespeare's Romances.* Lexington: University Press of Kentucky, 1981.

Velz, John W. "Portia and the Ovidian Grotesque." In *The Merchant of Venice: New Critical Essays.* Shakespeare Criticism 26. Edited by John W Mahon and Ellen Macleod Mahon, 179–86. New York and London: Routledge, 2002.

Vitkus, Daniel J., ed. Introduction to *Three Turk Plays from Early Modern England: Selimus, a Christian Turned Turk, and the Renegado.* New York: Columbia University Press, 2000.

———. "Adventuring Heroes in the Mediterranean: Mapping the Boundaries of Anglo-Islamic Exchange." *Journal of Medieval and Early Modern Studies* 37 (Winter 2007): 75–95.

———. *Turning Turk: English Theater and the Multicultural Mediterranean, 1570–1630.* Early Modern Cultural Studies. New York and Basingstoke: Palgrave Macmillan, 2003.

———. "Turning Turk in *Othello:* The Conversion and Damnation of the Moor." *Shakespeare Quarterly* 48 (1997): 145–76.

Wann, Louis. "The Oriental in Elizabethan Drama." *Modern Philology* 7 (January 1915): 423–47.

Warneke, Sara. "Educational Travelers: Popular Imagery and Public Criticism in Early Modern England." *Journal of Popular Culture* 28, no. 3 (1994): 71–94.

Webbe, Edward. *The rare and most wonderfull things which E. Webbe hath seene.* Amsterdam: Theatrum Orbis Terrarum, 1973.

Webster, John. *The Duchess of Malfi.* In *Elizabethan Drama.* Edited by Charles W. Eliot. Vol. 2. New York: P. F. Collier & Son, 1910.

———. *The Duchess of Malfi.* In *Six Plays by Contemporaries of Shakespeare.* Edited by C. B. Wheeler. London: H. Milford, Oxford University Press, 1915.

———. *The White Devil or Vittoria Corrombona.* In *Six Plays by Contemporaries of Shakespeare.* Edited by C. B. Wheeler. London: H. Milford, Oxford University Press, 1915.

Weimann, Robert. "Bifold Authority in Shakespeare's Theatre." In *Shakespeare in Performance,* edited by Robert Shaughnessy. New Casebook Series, 78–99. London: Macmillan, 2000.

Wells, Stanley, and Gary Taylor, eds. *William Shakespeare: The Complete Works*. Oxford: Clarendon Press, 1992.

West, Russell. *Spatial Representations and the Jacobean Stage: From Shakespeare to Webster*. New York: Palgrave Macmillan, 2002.

Wheater, Isabella. "Aristotelian Wealth and the Sea of Love: Shakespeare's Synthesis of Greek Philosophy and Roman Poetry in *The Merchant of Venice*." *Review of English Studies* 43 (1992): 467–87; *Review of English Studies* 44 (1993): 16–36.

Wickam, Glynne. "From Tragedy to Tragicomedy: *King Lear* as a Prologue." *Shakespeare Survey* 2 (1973): 33–48.

Wilders, John, ed. *Antony and Cleopatra*. Arden edition. Third series. London: Routledge, 1995.

Wittek, P. "The Turkish Documents in Hakluyt." *Bulletin of the Institute for Historical Research* 19 (1942–43): 121–38.

Wylson, Thomas, trans. *The three Orations of Demosthenes chiefe Orator among the Grecians, in favor of the Olynthians, a people in Thracia, now called Romania* . . . London: Henrie Denham, 1570. STC 6578.

Index